Hebrew Union College
and the Dead Sea Scrolls

Jason Kalman

Hebrew Union College–Jewish Institute of Religion
Cincinnati

ISBN 978-0-615-70346-6

On the cover: Ceramic Qumran Jar purchased by HUC-JIR President Nelson
Glueck, now in the Skirball Museum on the HUC-JIR Cincinnati campus.
Accession number: 1982 49.1A+B/A0869A+B. Photo courtesy of HUC-JIR.

Background image: Erez, Amit (Photographer). 2009 *Qumran settlement ruins,
Judean Desert, Israel* © iStockphoto.

Original layout and design by Jane Bobel Graphic Design.
Cover, revision, and typesetting by Michael Ball, Initiate Marketing Inc.

For Charlie

Table of Contents

Illustrations

Acknowledgments

This book could not have been completed without the support of The Jacob Rader Marcus Center of the American Jewish Archives in Cincinnati, Ohio. Most of my research for this study was carried out in the AJA in 2007–2008, and 2012. Established in 1947 to preserve the documentary heritage of American Jewry, the AJA is well known among historians of the American Jewish experience. However, it is too often overlooked as a resource for reconstructing the history of Jewish scholarship. As the depository for the official and private papers of the faculty and administration of the Hebrew Union College–Jewish Institute of Religion from its founding in 1875 along with those of generations of scholar-rabbis it is a remarkable resource for tracing the development of Jewish scholarship in North America and in Germany where many American students went for advanced degrees before World War II. The archivists, particularly the Senior Archivist for Research and Collections, Kevin Proffitt, were exceptionally helpful.

A significant portion of the content of this volume appeared previously under the title "Optimistic, Even with the Negatives: The Hebrew Union College–Jewish Institute of Religion and the Dead Sea Scrolls, 1948–1993," in *The American Jewish Archives Journal* 61 no. 1 (2009): 1–114. I wish to thank Professor Gary P. Zola, executive director of the AJA and editor of its journal, for granting permission to use this material.

I would like to take this opportunity to thank professors Martin Abegg, Michael Cook, Norman Golb, John Kampen, Stephen Kaufman, Michael A. Meyer, James Sanders, Marc Saperstein, Richard Sarason, and S. David Sperling for sharing their recollections of HUC-JIR and its faculty. Professor Sanders also offered significant feedback on the original manuscript which improved it both in content and form. Professors Ellis Rivkin and Ben Zion Wacholder have died since the original article appeared but I was very fortunate to spend time with them during its preparation and to hear their memories of the people and events described and explored here. Ben Zion Wacholder's family, Nina Wacholder and Robert Goldenberg, showed me tremendous hospitality and answered many questions during my visit in October 2008. I thank David Gilner, the director of libraries at HUC-JIR, for opening the library records to me. I also thank the president of HUC-JIR, Rabbi David Ellenson, for his reflections on his teacher, Harry M. Orlinsky, and for lifting restrictions and granting me access to private presidential files. During the week before the terrible accident which eventually took his life, Alfred Gottschalk, former HUC-JIR president and chancellor emeritus, kindly shared with me his memories of events involving HUC-JIR and the Dead Sea Scrolls and offered feedback on an early manuscript. Professors David H. Aaron, Matthew Collins, Jaqueline Du Toit, Richard Freund, Jonathan Sarna, Lawrence Schiffman, and Eileen Schuller offered constructive suggestions. My graduate assistant, Shane Cass, reviewed the manuscript and offered many helpful corrections. My colleagues at HUC-JIR have provided a fertile environment for me to grow and I am eternally grateful. I hope that this book does justice to a story in which many of them played roles. Funding for publication has been generously provided by the office of the dean of HUC-JIR's Cincinnati campus, Professor Jonathan Cohen. Where this book succeeds it is a result of their collective contribution; where it fails the responsibility is entirely my own.

Finally, I thank my wife, Dana, and my son, Charlie. None of this would be possible, meaningful, or fun without them.

Foreword

The story of Hebrew Union College–Jewish Institute of Religion and the Dead Sea Scrolls is one saga in the myriad accounts concerning the Dead Sea Scrolls, an additional layer in an incredibly complex narrative. Many major developments in the acquisition and study of the scrolls are accompanied by an HUC-JIR story; most frequently some pivotal HUC personality has a significant role in that advance. The story begins in 1948 and continues through the open access issues of the early 1990s until today.

The history that Jason Kalman has so thoroughly researched on the basis of unlimited access to all of the relevant files from the administration, faculty, and library of HUC-JIR, as well as interviews with major players in Canada, the United States, and Israel has multiple characters acting in different phases with conflicting objectives. He has compiled and written a history that brings all of the interacting strands into a coherent and compelling narrative about one institution that played a significant, but largely overlooked, role in the discovery, publication, and study of the Dead Sea Scrolls. On the one hand, his research stands as an illustration of the impact of the scrolls on the history of one educational institution and vice versa, and provides a model for examining other schools throughout Israel, Europe, and North America. On the other, Kalman's documentation and vivid story-telling recounts the role of a very particular institution which occupied a unique position and employed a remarkable set of characters. Although HUC-JIR is perceived as a peripheral player in the story of the Dead Sea Scrolls, Kalman makes clear the perception is unfounded.

The story begins with the recognition that had HUC president Nelson Glueck remained director of the American School of Oriental Research in Jerusalem for one more year, the three scrolls from St. Mark's monastery would have been brought to him for initial evaluation. Kalman carefully documents his role as interpreter and intermediary between the sometimes competing interests of Israel (Hebrew University and the State) and ASOR. As the most prominent person with feet planted firmly on all shores, Glueck could understand the competing claims, interpret them, and devise strategies to overcome obstacles. As an American Jew he also was in a position to speak to American interests with its Christian majority while having an identity that was both Jewish and Zionist and thereby able to speak to Israelis. Needless to say, he also was advancing the College-Institute itself as an academic center in Israel and the United

States. Shortly after the discovery of the scrolls he effected the merger of HUC and JIR. In Cincinnati he established the HUC graduate school which grants doctoral degrees and includes an interfaith fellows program. Well-known Dead Sea Scroll scholar James Sanders was an early graduate. Represented within the person of Glueck, we find the unique place that HUC-JIR held during those early years in the history of the scrolls, at the center of multiple conflicting interests while advancing its own case for being taken seriously as a center of academic study in Israel, Europe, and North America.

In the story of Professor Harry M. Orlinsky of HUC-JIR's New York campus we find another example of a "bridge" personality who was trusted for his integrity, scholarship, and commitment to Israel as evidenced by his close relationship with Yigael Yadin and the Israeli academic elite. He was likewise trusted by the American community of biblical scholars. The unique place of HUC-JIR and its faculty is appreciated only when these stories are brought together into one account.

This story of the scrolls played out, as is well known, for its first forty years with an initial prohibition against the involvement of Jewish scholars in the publication team of the biggest cache of materials, the fragments from the caves, primarily Cave 4. We then note the continuing failure to invite these same scholars to join the publication efforts even after 1967 when the scrolls had become the province of the state of Israel. Both American and Israeli Jewish scholars suffered under the same prohibitions. Ironically, the list of scholars possessing both the requisite expertise and interest but without access continued to grow and broaden to include more non-Jewish scholars, while with time the limitations appeared to become even more arbitrary. Ben Zion Wacholder of HUC-JIR's Cincinnati campus was an "outsider," not in the invited circles, even after the initial appointment of Jewish scholars to the team. He benefited, however, from crucial connections to Harvard professor John Strugnell, who headed the scrolls editorial team. Risking career, reputation, and relationships, Wacholder and Martin Abegg, his graduate student at the time, engaged in reconstruction work that made opening access to the unpublished scroll materials necessary. Incredible stories are recounted in this remarkable saga, which has not received adequate attention in the summaries and histories of the discoveries written up to this point.

Related in these pages is another story of equal importance for the history of the study of the scrolls. This is the account of the scrolls within the life of HUC-JIR, its faculty, and the Reform Jewish movement. On the whole, many Jewish scholars were critical of facile assumptions about the scrolls and their significance. Because in many cases they were aware of, and familiar with, Karaite and other sources from later periods in Jewish history some of the contents of the scrolls appeared "less unique" to them than to scholars trained primarily in "Christian-oriented" materials. This made them sensitive to alternative explanations for the origins and age of the scrolls. This can be identified already in some of the reactions to Johns Hopkins professor William F. Albright's quick identification of the first material he saw as products of the Second Temple era. Due to his reputation as dean of biblical archaeology and as a master epigrapher his conclusion carried significant weight and influence. For some scholars, however, the parallels to later Jewish literature meant that the scrolls could not be from the Second Temple period. For others the community described in the scrolls represented a minor divergent group outside of the main historical streams and events of first century Judaism. Names such as Norman Golb, Samuel Sandmel, and Ellis Rivkin, each one having a unique role in this internal history, also have their place in the story of the scrolls.

There have been remarkable changes in the study of the scrolls throughout the forty-five year period covered in this publication. The limited interaction between Jewish, Catholic, and Protestant scholars at the time of their discovery gave way to a much more comprehensive approach that characterizes the scholarly field today. Israeli, European, and North American scholars (and others around the world) all have contributed substantially to the study of the scrolls. In Kalman's story of the College-Institute, we see ties to many of these communities of scholars and to the wide spectrum of the viewpoints they represented. Kalman has brought the necessary, complex, and multifaceted role of this unique institution to our attention. The history of Qumran studies cannot be written without it.

John Kampen
Van Bogard Dunn Professor of Biblical Interpretation
Methodist Theological School in Ohio

Author's Note

Although my original history of HUC and the Dead Sea Scrolls was published in 2008, a number of factors inspired revisiting the topic and offering an updated and expanded version. First, the announcement in July 2008 that an Israel Antiquities Authority exhibit of the scrolls would be presented at the Cincinnati Museum Center brought inquiries from reporters and community members about rumors they had heard about "bootleg editions" of the Dead Sea Scrolls published by a faculty member at HUC-JIR's Cincinnati campus. Second, after the 2011 death of Ben Zion Wacholder, the professor responsible for these clandestine volumes, additional correspondence, manuscripts, and legal documents from his private collection were donated to the AJA. These added new dimensions and clarity to the history which needed to be shared. Third, feedback on my previous work brought with it new leads and suggestions which required follow through, and some corrections which needed to be made. Finally, changes in Dead Sea Scroll scholarship and several new publications clarified parts of the history of HUC's involvement with the scrolls which were still unclear.

Until relatively recently, Dead Sea Scroll scholars remained primarily concerned with deciphering the scrolls and explaining their content and historical significance. The story of where they came from, questions of acquisition and ownership, and the details of their study in the first decades after they were found, was frequently repeated based on the recollections of some of the early participants. Sharing the tale with the public had become the province of popular writers who sensationalized the story rather than academics trying to present an honest and thorough historical account. However, based on archival sources, several new studies have attempted to fill in gaps, to highlight significant actors who for various reasons had been ignored or forgotten, and in general to provide a fuller and more nuanced account of events and activities related to the scrolls. As well, some of these new volumes have tried to record the history of scrolls scholarship and how it has developed. Some seek to explain how the personalities involved, with all of their religious, political, national, and cultural biases, shaped the field. More and more scholars are now interested in how and why the scrolls are studied in the way that they are. Another area of interest is the question of how information about the scrolls is shared with and received by laypeople. Books on the scrolls sell rapidly in large numbers, related websites receive millions of hits, and museum exhibits attract visitors in the hundreds of thousands. Is the information shared reliable and what does it contribute to contemporary religion, culture, and discourse?

The story of HUC and the Dead Sea Scrolls has much to add to this discussion. Members of its administration and staff were influential in the original acquisition of the scrolls and arranging for their long-term security. Others were among the first group to study the newly discovered material. The College–Institute educated a number of students who went on to make significant contributions to scrolls scholarship including the editing of the first edition of several texts. Others helped open the circle of scholars who could access the previously restricted unpublished fragments. Many faculty members gave interviews to the media and gave lectures to the public about the scrolls and helped shape their popular reception. Finally, by training hundreds of rabbis, they shaped the place of the scrolls in the contemporary life of thousands of members of the Jewish community and beyond.

The narrative here has only been slightly revised from its original publication and corrections have been made. All of the notes have been rewritten and expanded to include and account for the newly available archival and secondary sources.

Jason Kalman
HUC-JIR, Cincinnati
University of the Free State, South Africa

Abbreviations

Alphabetized according to source

AAJR	American Academy of Jewish Research
AJA	American Jewish Archives, Cincinnati, Ohio
AOS	American Oriental Society
ASOR	American Schools of Oriental Research
BAR	*Biblical Archaeology Review*
BAS	Biblical Archaeology Society
BASOR	*Bulletin of the American Schools of Oriental Research*
CCAR	Central Conference of American Rabbis
DSD	*Dead Sea Discoveries*
DSS	Dead Sea Scrolls
DJD	*Discoveries in the Judaean Desert*
DHL	Doctor of Hebrew Letters
HUC	Hebrew Union College
HUC-JIR	Hebrew Union College – Jewish Institute of Religion
IAA	Israel Antiquities Authority
JIR	Jewish Institute of Religion
JQR	*Jewish Quarterly Review*
JBL	*Journal of Biblical Literature*
JJS	*Journal of Jewish Studies*
MS/MSS	Manuscript/Manuscripts
NABI	National Association of Biblical Instructors
SBL	Society of Biblical Literature
SBLE	Society of Biblical Literature and Exegesis
UTS	Union Theological Seminary
USD	United States Dollar

A number between 1 and 11 followed immediately by the letter Q is shorthand for indicating one of the eleven caves in which Dead Sea Scrolls were found. For example, 4Q indicates that a text was found in Qumran Cave 4.

Nelson Glueck and Yigael Yadin examine a photographic plate of the rolled Genesis Apocryphon Scroll, Cincinnati, 30 November 1956. The plate is published as illustration #1 in Nahman Avigad and Yigael Yadin's A Genesis Apocryphon: A Scroll From the Wilderness of Judaea *(Jerusalem: Magnes Press, 1956).*

(Courtesy American Jewish Archives)

Hebrew Union College and the Dead Sea Scrolls

I think the tide of events have [sic] *made our very interesting letters a part of history, perhaps a more important chapter of the history than we now realize.*[1]

Introduction

In 1969 Hebrew Union College–Jewish Institute of Religion president Nelson Glueck (1900–1971) solicited a $10,000 USD donation to help support Israeli efforts to make a security copy of the famed Dead Sea Scrolls, then housed in Jerusalem. The copy, consisting of more than one thousand photographic negatives, was secretly stored in the Klau Library on HUC-JIR's Cincinnati campus for more than twenty years. The inspiration to supply the funds resulted partly from Glueck's own involvement with the scrolls, going back to his tenure in mid-1948 with the American Schools of Oriental Research (ASOR); and also from his faculty's scholarly activities on the Cincinnati, New York, and Los Angeles campuses of HUC-JIR. The acquisition of the negatives set off a series of events that drew worldwide attention to the College more than twenty years after Glueck's death in 1971, when the public became aware that HUC-JIR had held the manuscripts in secret for more than two decades. The story of HUC-JIR and the scrolls during these five decades provides insight into the history of Jewish scholarship in the United States, particularly the relationship between Jewish academics, who worked primarily in seminaries and parochial Jewish academic institutions, and their non-Jewish colleagues, who held prominent positions in universities.[2] From the very beginning HUC-JIR's faculty and administration sought to participate in, and benefit from, the "greatest manuscript discovery of all time." Their efforts brought attention to the scrolls, and, in return, the scrolls brought attention to the institution.

The Discovery

In the winter of 1946–1947, nomadic Bedouin of the Ta'amireh tribe discovered a cave containing ancient scrolls in the cliffs that rise above the western shore of the Dead Sea.[3] Bedouin sold four of the scrolls to a Bethlehem antiquities dealer, Khalil Iskhander Shahin (Kando),[4] who in turn sold them to Mar Athanasius Yeshue Samuel, the metropolitan (archbishop) of the Syrian

Orthodox Church at St. Mark's Monastery in Jerusalem.[5] Three others were sold to Eleazar Lipa Sukenik,[6] a Hebrew University archaeologist, who purchased them through another Bethlehem antiquities dealer, Feidi al-Alami.[7] The Bedouin found perhaps the most significant cache in February 1952 in what became known as Cave 4.[8] In total, eleven caves were discovered, containing thousands of fragments from more than eight hundred Hebrew, Aramaic, and Greek manuscripts. After purchasing the first scrolls for the Hebrew University, Sukenik attempted to buy the remaining four scrolls in the possession of the metropolitan in February 1948. Simultaneously, ASOR and its officials were working to acquire the publication rights for the scrolls from the metropolitan, which his representative Father Boutros Sowmy had brought for examination to ASOR. The competing efforts of Sukenik and ASOR created the opportunity for Glueck to become involved in the events.

HUC's First Contact with the Scrolls

Glueck the Mediator: Hebrew University, ASOR, and the First Dead Sea Scrolls

From 1942 until 1947, the year he was appointed president of HUC, Nelson Glueck served as the director of ASOR in Jerusalem. Had he remained one more year, he likely would have been at the school when the first Dead Sea Scrolls were brought there on 19 February 1948.[9] Instead, the names Millar C. Burrows, who succeeded Glueck as director of the school, and John C. Trever, an annual fellow who had temporarily replaced Burrows while he was on hiatus in Baghdad, became intimately tied to the scrolls. Despite fate having directed him down a different path, Glueck, and the educational institution he administered, nevertheless became participants in the unfolding history of scroll research, and the general scroll story, from very early on. Although the scrolls never became a topic of Glueck's own research,[10] his actions from 1948 until just prior to his death in 1971 show a tremendous interest in supporting the efforts of scholars at HUC and elsewhere to study the scrolls. They also show his concern with helping Israel preserve the scrolls in its possession and with keeping the American public aware of the developments. Following the first announcements of the discoveries in April 1948, Glueck shared his excitement over the scrolls with Stephen S. Wise, president of the Jewish Institute of Religion. Wise reported to JIR's biblicist, Harry Orlinsky, that, "The excitement of President Glueck over the discovery of the Isaiah Texts, [when] we discussed it over the phone, was quite thrilling."[11] Along with his scholarly interest in the material, Glueck understood that HUC's institutional support of scroll study could serve to attract public attention and donor dollars and could raise the academic status of the institution. Finally, as a man who believed that the Bible still had much to teach his fellow Americans, he thought that the scrolls' popularity could encourage Bible study.

In the months before his death in New York City in October 1948, Judah Magnes, the chancellor and former president of Hebrew University, spent a significant amount of time with his long-time friend Glueck. Magnes's junior by two decades, Glueck followed a similar educational path. Both men were ordained at HUC—Magnes in 1900 and Glueck in 1923. Both earned their doctorates in Germany following their rabbinic ordinations—Magnes at the University of Heidelberg in 1902 in Semitic languages, Glueck at the University of Jena in 1926 in biblical studies.[12] Both men returned from Europe to join the faculty of HUC—Magnes as librarian and professor of Bible during 1903 and 1904 and Glueck as professor of Bible and biblical archaeology from 1928 until he assumed the presidency in 1947.[13] The two men became close friends during Glueck's first tenure as director of ASOR in Jerusalem in 1932–1933, succeeding his mentor, the doyen of biblical archaeology, William Foxwell Albright.[14] In a 1988 interview, Glueck's wife, Helen, noted that during those first years in Jerusalem, "Dr. and Mrs. Magnes were probably our best friends."[15] Further, it was Magnes who encouraged a very hesitant Glueck to accept the position of president of HUC when it was offered in 1947.[16]

Magnes was in the United States from April until October 1948 primarily to address the United Nations concerning the establishment of Israel as a bi-national state. He was to have returned to Israel in June, but he became ill and then died on 27 October 1948.[17] During the extended visit, Glueck and Magnes had the opportunity to discuss a program that would allow HUC's rabbinical students to begin their studies in Israel. Another topic of business was Magnes's appeal to Glueck to help negotiate a relationship between Hebrew University professor Eleazar Sukenik and ASOR with respect to the ownership of the scrolls and their publication rights.[18] Since Hebrew University owned some of the scrolls, it desperately wanted to buy the remainder and was concerned that ASOR's actions would prevent their purchase. Magnes only appealed to Glueck following his own attempt to negotiate with Millar Burrows, then the president of ASOR, directly.

Magnes's own relationship with ASOR went back to at least 1924, when he served as a Thayer fellow and traveled with the school to Baghdad where, inspired by Solomon Schechter's discovery in Old Cairo, he hoped to discover *genizot* (depositories for sacred texts unsuitable for ritual use).[19] With regard to the scrolls, he needed a third party whom all involved groups respected to help make the arrangements. Glueck was loyal to Magnes on the one hand and to ASOR on the other, and so he was a most appropriate candidate to act as mediator.

In late January 1948 Sukenik began to discuss buying the scrolls from a representative of Athanasius Yeshue Samuel, the Syrian metropolitan.[20] Samuel and his representative, Anton Kiraz, had heard of Sukenik's purchase of the first scrolls and hoped that he would be willing to pay an even higher price for the remainder of the cache. During the first week of February 1948, Sukenik met with Kiraz in the library of the YMCA building in Jerusalem. Although they did not agree on a price during that first discussion, Sukenik let the man know that he would be willing to buy the scrolls for the Hebrew University but first wanted to study them and to show them to Magnes, the university president. The scrolls were lent to Sukenik for a few days, during which he did in fact take them to Magnes with the hope that the meeting might encourage fundraising efforts to purchase them.[21] By 6 February the funds had not yet been secured, although assurances had been made, and the scrolls were returned to Kiraz at the YMCA. The men agreed to be in contact the following week to plan a meeting at the Yugoslav consulate between the archbishop and Magnes to negotiate the sale. No letter from the representative was forthcoming. As Sukenik wrote in his private diary:

> Eventually I received a letter informing me that they decided not to sell. They preferred to wait until the world was once again open to them, and they could find out the market price. I later discovered what happened. Some two weeks after I returned the scrolls one of the Syrian priests had gone to the American School of Oriental Research and had met some of its members. The Americans had managed to obtain permission to photograph and publish the scrolls, assuring the priest that they would be able to get a far higher price for the scrolls in the United States.[22]

Only in early June did Sukenik come to know of the activities at ASOR.[23] It is imaginable that the events surrounding the establishment of the State of Israel, along with the excitement of studying the previously purchased materials, had distracted the Hebrew University faculty from its pursuit. Correspondence between Magnes and Burrows suggests that ASOR was completely unaware that Hebrew University had been in discussion to buy the scrolls from St. Mark's Monastery; the archbishop had assured them that he had no immediate intention of selling and had planned to bring the scrolls to the United States for study. As Burrows noted:

> The news that Professor Sukenik is negotiating for the purchase of the manuscripts belonging to the Metropolitan of St. Mark's Convent is both surprising and puzzling. For one thing, I wonder how under present circumstances they are able to communicate. Beyond that, I am surprised that the Metropolitan would consider selling his manuscripts at this time. He definitely assured us that he had no intention of selling them, that he wanted us to publish them for him, and that, if he should consider selling them, he would make our right to publish them a condition of sale.[24]

Further, the agreement between ASOR and the archbishop was that even if the scrolls were sold, ASOR was to retain the publishing rights. Burrows suggested that if the Hebrew University purchased the material and excluded ASOR from the project it would be seen as a particularly unfortunate act:

> We have put a great deal of time and work and a considerable amount of money into the photographing and studying of these manuscripts. While we could have no way of compelling the Metropolitan to fulfill his agreement with us, we should certainly, to use the technical language of diplomacy, regard it as an unfriendly act on [Sukenik's] part, or on the part of the University, if we were done out of the privilege of publishing these three manuscripts. Perhaps some form of cooperation can be arranged. It would be highly desirable from all points of view, though it would be difficult under present conditions, and you and I know that Professor Sukenik is not especially good at teamwork.[25]

In response, Magnes recommended to Burrows that a committee of trustees including Sukenik, Umberto Cassuto, and David Werner Senator, the university rector, be established to facilitate Hebrew University's relationship with ASOR for the purpose of studying and publishing the scrolls.[26] This would have dealt with the issue of Sukenik's poor teamwork. Sukenik and Cassuto agreed to participate in the cooperative effort. More important, though, in the process of bringing the team together Magnes learned that Sukenik had communicated with an unnamed Syrian on 10 May 1948. This man claimed that the archbishop did not have sole ownership of the scrolls and could not unilaterally grant ASOR any rights.[27] The unnamed Syrian was again Anton Kiraz. Kiraz continued to assert his ownership of the scrolls well into the 1960s, and it was not until the 1980s that he and the archbishop reconciled their differences.[28] Burrows had been quite convinced by the archbishop that the scrolls were his personal property.[29] At the time, ASOR planned to publish a series of preliminary articles under the direction of William Albright in its *Bulletin*. ASOR hoped that, as a first form of cooperation, Sukenik and his Hebrew University colleagues might also publish material with them.[30] The discussion turned to the final publication of the material, which the men hoped could be published as a joint imprint of ASOR and the Hebrew University Press—perhaps the English edition to appear with one and the Hebrew with the other.[31] On 12 July 1948, Magnes wrote to Glueck with the hope that the HUC president might be able to offer guidance in how to proceed.[32] The Hebrew University was to forward copies of the correspondence between Magnes and Burrows to Glueck, but Glueck did not receive them and so did not respond to the issue. Magnes wrote again in September asking for advice.[33] The Hebrew University only sent copies of the correspondence on 22 October,[34] and they reached Glueck in early November, shortly after Magnes's death.[35] Perhaps in an attempt to honor his late friend, Glueck forwarded the correspondence to William Albright, then editor of the *ASOR Bulletin,* for input.[36] Albright's response echoed Burrows's previous critique of Sukenik:

I am more disgusted than I was before with the greed of Sukenik. He has plenty to do with the material already at his disposal, so why use questionable tactics to get all—or at least the Isaiah MS—under his control as well.... Sukenik's attitude is thoroughly indefensible.[37]

As late as October, Sukenik was still trying to get copies of John Trever's photographs and publication rights to the St. Mark's scrolls via Kiraz:

I have now a few requests to ask you:

1. Could I get the photographs made by the American School of Oriental Research which you promised me?

2. Could you confirm to me by writing what you have told me several times that we have the same rights of publication as the Americans. The Bishop [Samuel] insists that he is the sole proprietor of the manuscripts you have shown me....[38]

With Albright's position on the issue quite clear, Glueck could not have moved forward in attempting to negotiate a relationship between ASOR and the Hebrew University. Despite his inability to contribute to these matters, Glueck was certain that Magnes's efforts on behalf of the Hebrew University did not go unnoticed by ASOR's members. Glueck authored the obituary for Magnes that appeared in the *ASOR Bulletin* and noted: "[Magnes's] deep and excited interest in the Jerusalem Scrolls was characteristic of his abiding concern with everything that had to do with the Holy Land."[39] This point was in some ways one that Albright and Burrows did not acknowledge. Although to Sukenik's mind, publishing the scrolls could bring him academic stature, ASOR's move to publish the material and to encourage its sale in the United States challenged a more firmly held conviction, one held by Magnes as well: that the scrolls were Israel's national treasures. They tied the modern Israeli state to its ancient roots, as Sukenik noted in his personal journal when he learned that the archbishop preferred to hold out for an American buyer: "The Jewish people have lost a precious heritage."[40] Glueck appears to have understood this as well, but there was little he could do.

On 29 January 1949, the archbishop arrived in the United States carrying the scrolls with him to begin serving as the apostolic delegate to the United States and Canada. Because the earlier purchase that Magnes and Burrows discussed was never completed and Kiraz's claim of ownership never accepted, the materials were published by ASOR alone.[41] However, in 1955, following Sukenik's posthumous publication of the first scrolls in the Hebrew University's possession, Glueck looked back with appreciation on the efforts of Sukenik and Magnes:

In all of [the] effort to acquire as many of the scrolls as possible, Mr. Sukenik was assisted by the late Judah L. Magnes, the great first president of the Hebrew University. The entire world is indebted to them for the vision, skill and persistence they displayed.[42]

These events certainly gave Glueck a first-hand view of the scrolls, the attention they could draw, and an appreciation for their importance. During the remainder of his career he attempted to use them to gain publicity and to increase the academic stature of HUC-JIR.

The Seventy-Fifth Anniversary of HUC: Bringing the Scrolls Debate to Campus

In the period immediately following his inauguration, Glueck set to work improving the quality of HUC's rabbinic program and increasing the institution's academic stature. To the latter end, the College set out to establish a graduate school that would offer both Jewish and Christian students the opportunity to engage in doctoral studies. Additionally, Glueck attempted to have HUC, as an institution, support the work of national and international academic organizations. Hosting these organizations' annual meetings could draw the attention of the academic world and of the public, and in 1948, at the recommendation of his predecessor Julian Morgenstern,[43] Glueck invited five organizations—the Society of Biblical Literature, the National Association of Biblical Instructors, the American Oriental Society, the American Academy of Jewish Research, and ASOR—to hold their annual meetings at the College in Cincinnati to help celebrate the seventy-fifth anniversary of its founding. Only the AAJR refused the invitation, noting the expense of bringing most of its members from the New York area to Cincinnati.[44]

The text of the invitation to SBL suggests Glueck's motives more generally:

> Your acceptance of this invitation will give added significance to our celebration and we, in turn, will be happy to signalize our high regard for the Society of Biblical Literature and its imposing contributions to biblical scholarship."[45]

In truth, the invitation was more about having the academic societies acknowledge HUC rather than the other way around, but it was also an opportunity for the College to show off its library, along with the recently established American Jewish Archives, as was noted in a later press release:

> The meetings are the first of a whole series of national gatherings to take place at the College during its seventy-fifth anniversary year. As part of the year-long diamond jubilee observance, many scholarly, religious and cultural organizations are scheduled to convene at the College, thus giving hundreds of leaders—Jewish and non-Jewish—an opportunity to make or renew acquaintance with the College and its role today.[46]

From 28 to 30 December 1949, SBL held its annual meeting in conjunction with NABI (27 to 28 December) and ASOR (28 December).[47] In advance of the meetings, HUC issued three press releases. The first highlighted NABI's meeting and its discussions of contemporary issues in the teaching of religion.[48] The second provided an overview of NABI's sessions to be held as part of its meeting and announced a roundtable discussion open to the public as part of the SBL's meeting on the topic, *The Jewish Messiah and the Pauline Christ*.[49] The third release announced only the roundtable discussion.[50] The releases drew the media's attention to the activities at the Cincinnati campus, but in the days following only one topic excited the national press: the debate over the authenticity of the Dead Sea Scrolls.[51]

During the part of the gathering set aside for ASOR, the president, Carl Kraeling, announced that the scrolls belonging to St. Mark's, including the Isaiah and the Habakkuk texts, would be published imminently.[52] The joint meetings with SBL included seven presentations on the scrolls. Harry Orlinsky of the Jewish Institute of Religion (which merged with HUC the following month) spoke on the problematic use of the St. Mark's Isaiah Scroll in exploring the textual development of the book of Isaiah, while Robert Gordis of the Jewish Theological Seminary offered an opposing interpretation, that the scroll was suggestive of early Masoretic activity. John Trever, of the International Council on Religious Education, spoke about the fourth scroll from St. Mark's, which he related to the "Lost Apocryphal Book of Lamech." Ovid R. Sellers of McCormick Theological Seminary discussed the explorations of the Dead Sea Scroll cave. Isaiah Sonne of HUC Cincinnati's faculty spoke on gnostic and anti-Christian polemics he found evident in the scrolls and suggested that they were produced by a Jewish-gnostic sect of the second century of the Common Era. Solomon Zeitlin of Dropsie College challenged the usefulness of archaeology for establishing the date of the scrolls, since their provenance was already murky because of their discovery by Bedouin and not archaeologists. Finally, Ernest R. Lacheman of Wellesley College spoke on the methodological difficulty of dating the scrolls by their relation to ancient texts, including the Nash Papyrus.[53] The papers were somewhat unbalanced, given the debates rising in the wake of the scrolls' discovery. Sonne, Gordis, and Trever came out in favor of dating the scrolls to antiquity, while Zeitlin and Lacheman maintained medieval dates. Debates raged in both the public media and academic journals over the manuscripts' antiquity and authenticity[54] from the time the discovery was announced in April 1948.[55] As a result of the conference in Cincinnati, the public's attention was again drawn to this issue, and HUC received as much publicity as it could have hoped for.[56] On 29 December the *New York Times* reported that Sellers announced the previous day that the scrolls discovered in the clay pots near the Dead Sea dated from the first or second centuries BCE.[57]

On 30 December the *New York Times* reported on the scroll sessions that had taken place the day before:

> Disagreement among Bible scholars on the age of Old Testament manuscripts found in 1947 in the Dead Sea area arose anew here [yesterday] at a meeting of the Society of Biblical Literature and [E]xegesis. The meeting is being held at Hebrew Union College.[58]

According to the report, Lacheman suggested the scrolls dated to between the fourth and eighth centuries, Zeitlin placed them between the sixth and ninth centuries, Sonne maintained a second century date, and Orlinsky to between the fourth and eighth centuries. This last point, however, was in error. In contrast to the others at the conference, Orlinsky refused to take a clear position on the date of the material. Although the *Times* reporter was certain to note, "Drs. Orlinski [*sic*] and Sonne are of the Hebrew Union College,"[59] the error in reporting meant that the following month the College received coverage once again, when Orlinsky responded to the *Times* article:

> This statement constitutes fiction pure and simple! What I did say was essentially this: The St. Mark's Isaiah Scroll comes from a manuscript which was copied from memory. The text of St. Mark's agrees overwhelmingly with the traditional Hebrew text of Isaiah. Where the text of St. Mark's deviates from the traditional text, it is not merely because of the carelessness of the scribe but even more because of the faulty memory of the person responsible for its coming into being … Some scholars have been premature in attributing to the text of St. Mark's an importance equal to the traditional text. In my judgment, the Hebrew text of St. Mark's is of negligible value so far as reconstructing the original Hebrew text of Isaiah is concerned. The argument of date is not involved in this study.[60]

The AOS met at HUC in Cincinnati from 4 to 6 April 1950. Orlinsky returned and gave a similar paper to the one he presented at the SBL meeting, "The Orthography and Grammar of the St. Mark's Isaiah Scroll."[61] Burrows of Yale University presented the only other paper on the scrolls. In "The Dead Sea Discipline Scroll," Burrows provided "a brief sketch of the contents of this document and a few observations concerning its literary and historical relationships, with special reference to the Damascus Covenanter's Document."[62] This conference did not receive the attention of the previous year's meeting, but collectively they indicate the activity of HUC-JIR and its faculty in supporting Dead Sea Scrolls scholarship in its earliest stages. Additionally, the academics who visited the College during these two conferences proved particularly helpful to the library staff, who had compiled prior to 22 December 1949 a bibliography of material relating to the scrolls. The staff was able to distribute the bibliography to those visiting scholars with the hope that they would help fill lacunae.[63] Given the explosion in scroll scholarship, no attempt was made to continue the project following the conference.

Dead Sea Scroll Scholarship at HUC-JIR

During the fifty years following the discovery of the Dead Sea Scrolls, numerous members of the HUC-JIR permanent faculty and visiting scholars contributed to the study and teaching of them. The roster of visiting scholars who studied the scrolls includes, among others, Frank Moore Cross (director of archaeology, Jerusalem School, 1963–1964), Zeev Falk (visiting professor of liturgy and rabbinics, Jerusalem School, 1979–1980), Isaac Rabinowitz (visiting lecturer in Aramaic, New York School, 1954–1956), Lawrence Schiffman (lecturer on Bible, New York School, 1979–1981), Shemaryahu Talmon (visiting professor of Bible, Jerusalem School, 1968–1975), and Yigael Yadin, who served as chair of the Jerusalem School Committee from 1973 until 1975.[64] In Cincinnati, courses were offered in the 1950s and 1960s first by Isaiah Sonne, followed by Norman Golb, and then by Ben Zion Wacholder, who continued to offer them until the early 1990s. Samuel Sandmel and Ellis Rivkin, as teachers of Judaism in antiquity, made their boldest statement on the scrolls by excluding them from their scholarship and teaching.

On the New York campus, Harry Orlinsky offered the most significant scholarly contributions to scroll scholarship and teaching and was an active participant in acquiring the scrolls for the State of Israel. The scrolls likewise captured the attention of ethnomusicologist Eric Werner, who, in 1957, garnered attention for the College with a conference paper suggesting that the Isaiah Scroll included primitive musical notation similar to that used in the Byzantine period.[65]

The faculty roster of HUC-JIR in Los Angeles included Samson H. Levey, who offered electives on the scrolls in 1961 and 1975 while he served as professor of rabbinics and Jewish thought (1958–1981). The course catalogue only describes what was offered, not which courses had enrollment. Levey's papers do not include syllabi or student rosters for the courses, but a syllabus for a course that he taught with Loren Fisher at the Southern California School of Theology in the spring of 1959 may provide some insight to his organization of the intended courses at HUC-JIR . In this vein, the course was organized around four issues: (1) the discovery of the documents; (2) the organization of the Qumran community, its doctrines and beliefs, and the identification of the Qumran sect; (3) The Dead Sea Scrolls and the Old Testament, the Inter-Testamental Literature, and the New Testament; and (4) Messianism in the Dead Sea Scrolls.[66] Levey also published articles on the scrolls during this same period, although he continued to focus on his primary area of research, the Aramaic Bible translations (Targumim).[67]

As is clear from the roster of visiting scholars, Dead Sea Scroll scholarship on the Jerusalem campus was largely shaped by academics from outside HUC-JIR. However, Michael Klein, who served as lecturer in Aramaic and rabbinics (1973–1981), professor of biblical and targumic literature (1982–1988), and dean of the Jerusalem campus (1988–2000), played a significant role in the College's activities regarding the scrolls in the period before the editorial monopoly was broken.

The overview here provides a discussion of those faculty who explicitly and extensively contributed to scroll scholarship and teaching and those who deliberately (often boisterously) avoided it. Numerous scholars on all the campuses have, at various times, included discussion of the scrolls in their classes and publications; it is simply not possible to include them all.

HUC-JIR in the First Decade Following the Discovery of the Scrolls

*Isaiah Sonne,
Cincinnati, 1946*

(Courtesy American
Jewish Archives)

As is evident from the discussion of the conference participation, Sonne and Orlinsky involved themselves in the study of the scrolls from the time they first appeared. However, their excitement about the discoveries must be seen against a backdrop that includes Ellis Rivkin and Samuel Sandmel. Rivkin was mentored at Dropsie College by Zeitlin after completing his doctorate at Johns Hopkins. Until his death he continued to deny the antiquity of the scrolls. Sandmel, who accepted their antiquity, simply and utterly denied their importance.

Isaiah Sonne (1887–1960)

Sonne, a Galician scholar who specialized in the history of Italian Jewry and Hebrew literature and bibliography, came to HUC in Cincinnati in 1940 as a part of HUC's refugee scholars project.[68] He was appointed librarian and lecturer. From the collection of international newspaper articles he preserved in Hebrew, English, and German, it is clear that he followed news of the scrolls' discovery from their earliest appearance in the press.[69] Additionally, Sonne was the first scholar at HUC-JIR to offer an official course on the Dead Sea Scrolls. According to the HUC-JIR course catalogue for 1952–1953, in the spring semester Sonne offered "History 12. Seminar. The Dead Sea Scrolls: An analytical study of these newly discovered documents, especially the sectarian scrolls, to determine their date as well as their historical purport." At the time, only a single graduate student, James Sanders, attended the class. Sanders would later make his own major contributions to Dead Sea Scroll research, particularly as the editor of the Psalms Scroll from Qumran Cave 11.[70] That only one graduate student attended the course indicated a pattern that developed over the next several decades at the College, in which positive appreciation of the scrolls was nourished in the graduate school but largely dismissed in the rabbinical program. With regard to his experience in that first class, Sanders reports:

> I was the only student in the class! Yet, Sonne stood each meeting and lectured as though he was addressing a full room of students. I thoroughly enjoyed the readings he had me do, in the Cave One mss of course, and learned a great deal.… I had had courses on the Scrolls both at Vanderbilt University with J. Philip Hyatt and in Paris at the École des Hautes Études with André Dupont-Sommer, but since I was alone in Sonne's class I learned far more than in the earlier ones.[71]

Sonne's earliest public comment on the scrolls was his appearance at the April 1949 meeting of the Midwest Region of the SBL on the HUC campus in Cincinnati.[72] In the paper, "The Newly Discovered Isaiah Scroll," he argued that the section divisions in the Isaiah Scroll from St. Mark's suggested that the manuscript was likely used for the sabbatical reading of the prophets and that the "best historical setting for the Isaiah Scroll would seem to be the second and third centuries A.D."[73] This dating of the scrolls was consistent with his previous conclusions, which he had reached based on the Gnostic and anti-Christian tendencies found in the available scrolls, particularly the Thanksgiving Psalms. One month before the annual meetings, Nelson Glueck invited John Trever, then of the Council for Religious Education in Chicago, who had photographed the first scrolls for ASOR, to visit the Cincinnati campus to meet with faculty and students and to share his research.[74] Primarily he discussed the discovery of the scrolls and how they came to ASOR for examination.[75] The visit had a tremendous impact on Sonne, which resulted in a correspondence between the two scholars. According to Sonne, he derived further inspiration for his work on the scrolls "from Dr. Trever's interesting lecture on the scrolls last month in the College. On this occasion I had the opportunity for the first time to see photographs of the two Daniel fragments."[76] The two scholars most certainly impressed each other.

In late February Trever met with the archbishop Athanasius Samuel at Duke University, where his scrolls were on display. The archbishop had with him two Torah scrolls that he wished to sell. Trever recognized that they were modern scrolls, but he hoped that Sonne might be able to guide him in negotiating the purchase, particularly with respect to the value of these types of documents.[77] Although Trever assured Sonne that he would take the information to the archbishop and see if arrangements could be made for Sonne to examine the Torah scrolls for the College, nothing came of the efforts.[78] Simultaneously, the men discussed Zeitlin's challenge to the scrolls' authenticity. These communications led Trever to forward Sonne's reconstruction of the opening lines of the Manuscript of Discipline to Millar Burrows, who was publishing the document for the second volume of scrolls to appear from ASOR.[79] Although no response from Burrows is preserved, the two continued to share their work on occasion. In 1951 Sonne published an expanded version of his 1949 SBL talk on Gnosticism in the scrolls.[80] It was the first of close to twenty-five articles published in the *Hebrew Union College Annual* over the next half century, both by its faculty and by outsiders.[81] Upon receiving a copy from Sonne, Burrows offered an appreciative reply:

> As you may know, I have been inclined to discount the idea of Gnosticism in the Dead Sea Scrolls. As I indicated in my article in *Oudtestamentische Studien* (1950), the references to knowledge and the like are just what one might expect during the period of the transition from wisdom literature to the rabbinic literature. You have brought out a number of facts, however, which may necessitate a revision of my position.[82]

A number of additional letters suggest that Sonne continued to send Burrows copies of works in progress. In his "Remarks on 'Manual of Discipline,' Col. VI, 6–7"[83] Sonne included a paragraph thanking Burrows for bringing various interpretations of a particular passage to his attention.[84] In fact, Burrows recommended to Sonne that he publish the article.[85] Sonne had similarly positive correspondence with W.D. Davies of Duke University,[86] Arthur Jeffery of Columbia University,[87] and Franz Rosenthal, then at the University of Pennsylvania.[88] Rosenthal and Sonne agreed that the discovery and ongoing debate over the scrolls was a "lifesaver for our stagnant Biblical studies."[89]

However, not all of Sonne's communications were quite as positive. His friend Abraham Halkin wrote in his obituary for Sonne, "When the battle ensued over the dating of the Dead Sea Scrolls he took a middle position claiming that both sides exaggerated and their views must be examined painstakingly."[90] From his earliest conference presentations through his articles, Sonne challenged William Albright, Sukenik, Trever, and others who dated the scrolls by relying on paleography and archaeological grounds. He also attacked Zeitlin for his late dating of the scrolls by the incorrect use of rabbinic and medieval sources. His attack is encapsulated well in a single paragraph from an early article:

> None of the scholars who have been most outspoken, one way or the other, bases his opinion in a searching study of what the documents contain. Prof. Albright and Prof. H. L. Ginsberg, championing their antiquity, and Prof. Zeitlin, battling for the opposite view, blandly declare that they can determine the age of the scrolls without such scrutiny. Prof. Albright maintains that <<after an hour's study of the script with a lens,>> he could establish, by means of the key [Hebrew] letters ... the antiquity of the scrolls <<without a shade of doubt.>> Despite emphasis on <<positive, inner evidence,>> Zeitlin's approach is not much different. Zeitlin substitutes, for the key letters ... certain detached terms and idioms. Relying on isolated expressions and odd

bits of phraseology offered by Sukenik, Zeitlin claims to have fathomed the age of the scrolls with certainty.[91]

Although Trever and others of that group did not respond directly to Sonne, at least one other figure of similar thinking did. In the same article, Sonne, in a blanket statement, dismissed the work of all paleographers on the scrolls, asserting that they were driven by their particular theories rather than by the evidence.[92] Solomon Birnbaum, a paleographer at the School of Oriental and African Studies of the University of London, wrote to Sonne in response to the article. Noting that he had specialized in Hebrew paleographical research for more than twenty-five years, he stated that he was neither a biblicist nor a historian and had no "theories about the happenings or spiritual developments in any century BCE nor about the fashioning of the biblical text." Further, with respect to the fact that some pet theory drove his research, he demanded of Sonne: "I should be grateful if you would explain to me how this applies in my case."[93]

It was, however, the dispute with Zeitlin that became most vocal. Sonne attacked Zeitlin from the beginning in both his private correspondence and in print. At the SBL conference in 1949, with Zeitlin in attendance, Sonne noted, "We shall now touch upon Prof. Zeitlin's alleged 'positive, inner evidence.' It consists of a few isolated expressions and idioms picked up at random, and stated that they bear the stamp of the Middle Ages."[94] Sonne's "Final Verdict on the Scrolls"[95] is a seven-page attack on Zeitlin in which he concluded, "Our analysis has shown a) that the very premises of Zeitlin's rabbinic demonstration are lacking sound foundation; b) that his critical method in using the rabbinic material leaves much to be desired."[96] Sonne's boldest statements about Zeitlin were reserved for his private correspondence. When he submitted the "Final Verdict" to the *Journal of Biblical Literature* Sonne highlighted the need for his article in an accompanying letter to the editor:

> [E]nclosed please receive an article on the Dead Sea Scrolls. It is, as you will see, a reply to Prof. Zeitlin's last outburst on this subject. I consider his article as an insult to the intelligence of the American scholars which should not be left unanswered. (I trust that you will consider this statement as confidential.)[97]

To a certain degree, the disagreement between Sonne and the paleographers, including Albright, remained civil because the latter did not respond in any significant way to his challenges. By contrast, the matter between Zeitlin and Sonne appears to have become largely personal, with each scholar responding in print to the other's ad hominem barbs. So, for example, Zeitlin devoted the better part of his "The Hebrew Scrolls and the Status of Biblical Literature" to attacking Burrows and Sonne.[98] Of Sonne he noted critically:

He is reputed to be neither an archaeologist, nor a biblical scholar, nor a student of the Second Jewish Commonwealth; he certainly is not a rabbinical scholar. When the polemic about the Hebrew Scrolls became widespread Sonne entered the fray…Although he is not well equipped to engage in the discussion, he could not avoid the temptation of taking part in it.[99]

The critique did not stop Sonne from speaking or writing, and Zeitlin took him to task again in response to his work on the Bar Kochba letters.[100] Sonne's article was based on a public lecture, where Zeitlin was again in attendance and in which he commented publicly:

Unfortunately, his bias against the caves seems to have led to oversight by Zeitlin. Indeed, while he was gathering examples from all corners of the world … he overlooked examples from the very place and the only period we are dealing with.[101]

In the body of his response, Zeitlin repeated his criticism of Sonne:

Dr. Sonne is a scholar in his field of medieval Hebrew Bibliography. He knows of all the first editions, and the dates of the printing of every Hebrew book; but he could not resist the temptation to take part in the controversy about the Hebrew Scrolls although he is not equipped for it.[102]

In the footnote attached, he added that the publication of Sonne's article did "not do justice to him and [was] not a credit to the Academy for Jewish Research."[103] In perhaps his sharpest comment, in response to Sonne's "Hymn Against Heretics," Zeitlin offered, "I want to make clear to my Christian colleagues that not every Jew, even though he may bear the title rabbi or doctor, is a rabbinic scholar."[104]

The public dispute brought neither man honor. Sonne's approach with regard to the scrolls, however, was indicative of his approach generally. He was a particularly harsh critic and polemicist, as Halkin noted after Sonne's passing in 1960:

Owing to personal and external factors, he never knew the pleasures of peace and repose. This insecurity resulted in a degree of uncharitableness, in an extremely critical viewpoint, and an aimless drifting in the fields of culture and scholarship.[105]

Harry M. Orlinsky (1908–1992)

When Harry Orlinsky died in 1992, the *New York Times* published an obituary as was appropriate for the long-time professor of Bible at the New York campus

Harry M. Orlinsky, New York, Undated
(Courtesy American Jewish Archives)

of HUC-JIR. Among his important accomplishments, the obituary included the following:

> The Israeli Government recruited Dr. Orlinsky in 1954 to authenticate four Dead Sea Scrolls being offered for sale. He poured over them in a Manhattan bank vault, using a pseudonym to mask the Israeli connection, and called an unlisted number to give the code word to indicate that the scrolls were the genuine article.[106]

While the account is factually correct, it does not nearly do justice to the actual story, nor does it capture the broader contribution Orlinsky made to the study and teaching of the scrolls in the decades following their discovery. The story of Orlinsky and the scrolls is really the story of an independent thinker and student pushed and pulled by the influence of two teachers who absolutely disagreed. Orlinsky earned his doctorate in 1935 at Dropsie College.[107] During his graduate work, Orlinsky came under the influence of Solomon Zeitlin, who had begun teaching at Dropsie in 1925.[108] After completing his dissertation, Orlinsky received a postdoctoral fellowship under the tutelage of William Albright. Orlinsky began teaching at Baltimore Hebrew College while also attending Albright's seminars at Johns Hopkins. It was Albright who recommended Orlinsky to Stephen S. Wise of the Jewish Institute of Religion, who stole him away from Baltimore Hebrew College in 1943.[109] When Orlinsky received the rank of full professor of Bible at JIR in fall 1945, he listed those he had to thank for helping him reach the milestone: "my father and mother who really helped to develop in me an admiration for honesty and learning,… [Theophile James] Meek at Toronto, [Ephraim Avigdor] Speiser and [Solomon] Zeitlin in Philadelphia, and yourself [William F. Albright] in Jerusalem and Baltimore."[110]

By the time the scrolls were discovered, Orlinsky was already an active member of the Society of Biblical Literature, the American Oriental Society, and the American Schools of Oriental Research. Given these connections—his relationship to Zeitlin and Albright and his own scholarly interest in the history of the biblical text—the discovery of an ancient scroll of Isaiah caught his early attention. The St. Mark's Isaiah Scroll became his major concern; the other scrolls did not catch his fancy in quite the same way.[111] Here he should be contrasted with Sonne, whose interest was primarily in the sectarian material. It was Orlinsky's goal, though, not only to provide a sober evaluation of the scrolls in scholarly contexts but also to act as an intermediary who could bring an honest presentation of the material to his students and the public.[112]

Orlinsky's earliest discussion of the scrolls was presented in a paper at the annual meeting of the AOS at Yale in 1949: "The Recently Discovered Isaiah Scroll—Is It a Hoax?"[113] Given the title, Orlinsky was likely responding to Zeitlin's first article dismissing the antiquity and significance of the discovery:

"A Commentary on the Book of Habakkuk: Important Discovery or Hoax?" published in *Jewish Quarterly Review*.[114] The theme was the same as that presented in his paper the following December at the conference at HUC in Cincinnati.[115] The talk laid out the position Orlinsky maintained through the mid-1950s: that the scroll might be as old as Albright suggested, or it might stem from a later period (though not as late as Zeitlin argued); but whatever the date, the scroll had little value for reconstructing the biblical text as it appeared in antiquity. Orlinsky's conclusions, when published, made clear that the issue for him was not the date of the scrolls but their value for understanding the relationship of the masoretic text of the Hebrew Bible to other early versions. The text in the St. Mark's Isaiah Scroll differs from the text of Isaiah preserved in the Hebrew Bible as it has been received. The question, for Orlinsky and others, was whether the St. Mark's scroll more accurately and reliably reflected the "original" text of Isaiah than that in contemporary Bibles. Orlinsky concluded that it did not. Here his "ifs" are very important to note:

> If the St. Mark's Isaiah Scroll should turn out to be a document of the Second Jewish Commonwealth, then its chief value will consist of the fact that it helps to demonstrate the reliability of the masoretic text of the Hebrew Bible.... If the St. Mark's Isaiah Scroll should turn out to belong to the Mishnaic period, or later, then its value will be even less [than other known versions]....The unreliable character of St. Mark's [Isaiah scroll] is inductively determined.... Under no circumstances is the Hebrew text of St. Mark's to be given any independent value.[116]

The first conference at Yale made Orlinsky a prominent player in the debate over the scrolls. The second conference helped him secure his place, but more significantly it was his introduction to HUC's faculty and facilities in Cincinnati. Even before Glueck's inauguration as HUC president, discussions had been underway to merge HUC and JIR, where Orlinsky was a member of the faculty. By late 1949 the negotiations were nearing conclusion, and the merger was completed in January 1950.[117] The SBL conference provided Orlinsky the first opportunity to get to know his new colleagues in Cincinnati and for them to get to know him, although it is likely that many knew him already from interaction at academic conferences and the like. Of the conference, Orlinsky noted in writing to Glueck, "It was the first time that I had the chance to be at the College and to meet so many of its faculty. The grounds, buildings, etc., are indeed a pleasure to behold."[118] That Orlinsky commented on the greatness of the grounds and not his interaction with the faculty may leave his feelings about it an open question. Certainly a relationship between Orlinsky and Sonne was begun, but not an entirely positive one. Orlinsky published his first article on the Isaiah Scroll in June 1950 based largely on his talk in Cincinnati.[119] In concluding the paper, he notes Tovia Wechsler's suggestion that the Isaiah Scroll was in fact a scroll used for the *haftarot* (supplemental scriptural readings) as part of the Sabbath liturgy.[120] Sonne took offense that Orlinsky had cited the conclusion in Wechsler's name despite the fact that Orlinsky and Sonne had discussed the latter's April 1949 conference paper, where he made the same argument.[121] Orlinsky replied courteously that:

> I did not cite you to this effect for the simple enough reason that I do not make it a practice to cite any one from word of mouth. Mr. Wechsler's statement was in print, and so I cited it. Of course this should not prevent you in any way from claiming priority in the matter, since you read a paper to this effect in April 1949, as you write.[122]

Sonne was not particularly pleased, but he responded: "I know that this issue is not particularly important, and is not worthy, but I thought that since we are brothers, it is in good spirit to clarify the issue and to establish the truth of the matter."[123] Although it appears they remained cordial to each other, behind the scenes they made clear that any issues between them were never quite resolved.[124] For the most part, though, Orlinsky's dealings with Cincinnati faculty were in matters of curriculum development and administration; it was rare for him to have direct contact with Sonne in the years that followed.

Orlinsky in this period was an insider of the Albright circle who demanded a hearing for Zeitlin's questions even while he disagreed with some of his conclusions.[125] Following the appearance of Zeitlin's second attack on the early dating of the scrolls, Albright wrote to Orlinsky:

> I wish [Zeitlin] hadn't taken the flyer into paleography, since I had no conception how ignorant of this field he turns out to be. This article will cook his scholarly goose for good, in so far as discussions of this type of material are concerned. I am sorry, since I like him personally and we have always got along well together.... [N]othing will induce Zeitlin to change his mind.[126]

At least in the early years, Orlinsky was not entirely convinced of the paleographic and archaeological evidence for the early dating of the scrolls. More troublesome, though, was that he was convinced of the importance of Zeitlin's critique, and no one in Albright's camp was taking it seriously:

> I have not yet seen as yet Zeitlin's second article.... However, I must say this, that it simply will not do for scholars to continue to ignore his arguments from the contents, or to dismiss them with such adjectives as "extreme." I have in mind [John] Trever's note in the latest BASOR,[127] and [Ovid] Sellers' uncalled for reference to Zeitlin in the latest News-Letter of the Schools [of Oriental Research]. Ernest Wright is at least honest enough to admit that he does not control the material at all. Surely those among our mutual friends who keep on pooh-poohing Zeitlin's arguments and do have some control over the rabbinic material, ought either to respond in a scholarly vein in

print, or else admit they do not know enough about the material to write on it publicly. Anyone can give oral opinions.[128]

It was likely for this reason that Orlinsky, a biblicist, restricted his publications to the biblical scrolls and generally did not make broader comments about the sectarian materials. However, regarding the history of the biblical text, Orlinsky's views must be understood in connection to his studies with Zeitlin. In writing an appreciation of his teacher two decades later, Orlinsky asserted that it was only through the "methodology practiced by Dr. Zeitlin that the authors and transmitters of the biblical text can receive their just due and appreciation in history."[129] Equally, though, Orlinsky wanted Albright's input. As early as the preceding February, several months before his "debut" at the AOS meeting at Yale, Orlinsky had turned to Albright with his concerns about the Isaiah Scrolls:

> While I have not yet completed my study, I have become increasingly convinced that its history is far from being what Burrows, Sukenik, H.L.Ginsberg, and others have claimed it to be;... as soon as I get my manuscript in shape, I should like very much to meet with you and talk over the problems involved in the correct evaluation of the Isaiah Scroll, before I proceed to publish. You know how highly I regard your scholarly competence and your personal integrity.[130]

Because his publications dealt almost entirely with the Isaiah Scroll, his correspondence provides the only access to his thought on the sectarian material.[131] Here he set himself apart from Zeitlin, who was convinced of the Karaitic origins. Following being told that scholars were at work trying to prove this connection, Orlinsky commented:

> I do not see how this is possible. I have read a number of Karaitic commentaries on biblical books, and many Karaitic documents, including polemics. I reread them recently with the scrolls in mind. I am not able to see any connection between the new Scrolls and anything Karaitic.... Of course, here and there in the Habakkuk commentary there is something which sort of calls to mind something Karaitic, but I do not recall anything substantial and even approximately conclusive.[132]

Despite airing this view to Albright, not even a full month later, Orlinsky told Ellis Rivkin at HUC-JIR in Cincinnati that he was convinced of a Karaite period dating for the sectarian scrolls:

> So far, as I see it, neither the B.C. group nor the A.D. group has demonstrated its position; that is why I have refused to commit myself to any special date.
>
> However the situation has changed, in my eyes, as a result of Dr. Pinchos Rudolph Weis' [*sic*] article in the current *JQR*.[133] Rowley of Manchester has

been writing me for some weeks now about the forthcoming article by Weis, and how he himself (Rowley) has begun to give up a B.C. date in favor of a 7th century A.D.[134] date. I read Weis' article very carefully last week, and I now feel that unless and until Weis' arguments are refuted, it is hardly possible to adhere to a date prior to the Karaite period.[135]

Despite this explicit statement, Orlinsky generally refused to take a public position on the antiquity or lateness of the scrolls and absolutely refused to accept the idea that the Isaiah Scroll had any value for establishing the biblical text in antiquity.[136] In taking this position, he made a radical break with Albright, who was convinced, already in late 1949, that:

> The only possible attitude for a serious scholar to take now is that the new Isaiah scroll is authentic and pre-Christian (though not necessarily from before cir. 100 in date), and that it will therefore be basic to any future treatment of the material [regarding the history of Hebrew and the biblical text].[137]

The statement was a warning to Orlinsky, who was preparing his paper for the SBL meeting in Cincinnati. But it was a warning Orlinsky could not heed. His conference papers and early publications made his position clear, and he continued to argue the point in his correspondence. Despite the disagreement between the two men, Albright largely kept it out of the public eye, and it remained a dialogue among friends.[138] Within that dialogue, though, Albright continued to warn Orlinsky that his position would damage his reputation: "You are going to be out on a limb in the scrolls business before long," he warned him, "even though it will be much shorter than Zeitlin's…. For the life of me I have never been able to see how you could argue the archaeological evidence away as you have."[139] This comment is particularly important, as it really draws the contrast between the position of Albright's circle and that of Zeitlin's. For Albright, the archaeological and paleographical conclusions demonstrated that the scrolls were ancient. The objective was then to figure out what the content of the scrolls could teach about the time from whence they derived. For Zeitlin, the only issue was the content of the scrolls. The texts were atypical for the material of Jewish antiquity and showed an affinity with later materials. The archaeological and paleographic evidence was unreliable and, therefore, only the content question was worth asking. As Burke Long has noted, Orlinsky:

> [w]as increasingly at odds with the Albrighteans because of his reluctance to agree with Albright's assessment of the significance of the newly discovered Dead Sea Scrolls for sorting out variants in the Hebrew text of the Bible. This particular scholarly debate involved not only Albright's science of typology, which was widely accepted, especially among his students, but ideological conflict as well. Orlinsky doubted the "scientific" value of Albright's classifying scribal handwriting characteristics as datable "types."[140]

In 1953 Orlinsky was still suggesting to Albright that Zeitlin's ongoing critiques were valuable, even more valuable than those studies being published on Albright's editorial watch in the *Bulletin of the American Schools of Oriental Research*.[141] By late 1953 Orlinsky was still not settled on a date of composition for the scrolls:

> As I said at last April's meeting of the AOS, I am not aware of a single conclusive argument in favor of a B.C. date for any of the scrolls and fragments discussed, and neither can I point to a single conclusive argument against a mishnaic date. Scholars have too freely *insisted* on a B.C. date, when they could not *prove* it in any impartial court of competent judges. I myself simply cannot decide on the basis of the evidence to date, on the date of composition.[142]

Even while Albright told Orlinsky of new discoveries being studied by his student Frank Moore Cross, which moved the date back to the first century BCE,[143] Orlinsky remained skeptical and suggested that Cross was naïve in his conclusions.[144] This was not the first time Orlinsky had leveled a critique of a close Albright colleague or student. Previously he had suggested to Albright that Trever was a dishonest scholar of little integrity and even drafted an article trying to prove it.[145] In both cases, Albright defended his colleagues against Orlinsky's charge.[146] By the mid-1950s charges of this type, along with Orlinsky's refusal to accept Albright's dating of the scrolls, created some tension between them,[147] as became clear when HUC-JIR began to plan an international conference on the scrolls in late 1955 (see below). The real issue between the men by this period remained the dating. According to Orlinsky, he had managed to convince Albright that the textual variants in the Isaiah Scroll were not nearly as important as he had previously made out:

> After my paper in Washington on the Isaiah Scroll, Albright admitted that over 90% of the St. Mark's variants were worthless, and that I ought not to continue to try to prove what was now obvious, namely, that the text of St. Mark's had little value for the critic of the masoretic text of Isaiah. When I asked him to mention the name of at least one scholar in addition to myself who had written derogatorily of the Isaiah Scroll text since its discovery, he was unable to reply. The fact is, of course, that everyone had written only favorably of this newly-discovered text, and that it is only now, when they are being confronted with my detailed word-by-word analysis of these variants, that they are beginning to realize their utter worthlessness. I was also pleasantly surprised when Father Skehan of Catholic University, at the request of Albright ... got up to comment on my paper, and said that he did not agree with Albright that some 90% of the Scroll's variants were worthless, but that he was inclined to agree with me, that they were 100% worthless.[148]

Despite Orlinsky's view that the scrolls could not be accurately dated and that the Isaiah Scroll had little value for the study of the biblical text, he never gave up on the artifacts being worthy of study and preservation. He was the first to bring the scrolls to the attention of JIR students when he published, in 1949, a short Hebrew article on the discovery in *Reshith*, the JIR student journal.[149] Even then, he was sure to highlight the difficulty in dating the manuscripts.[150] Orlinsky only offered the Dead Sea Scrolls as an elective beginning in the 1961–1963 course catalogue: "Bible E39: A detailed study of the text and theology of the Dead Sea Scroll of Isaiah (Q Isa. 1)." However, through the 1950s, beginning in the 1952–1953 school year, he offered a course on the textual criticism of Isaiah chapters 40-66. These same chapters were the focus of his scholarly publications on the St. Mark's Scroll in this period. Beginning in 1958–1959, he offered a course on the history of the Masoretic text, "Bible E.33-Masoretic Text and Masorah: Origin and character." In the summer of 1959, at the invitation of Cyrus Gordon, Orlinsky taught a course on the scrolls in the Brandeis Summer School: The Dead Sea Scrolls and their Relevance for Old Testament Studies. According to the course description,

> After a survey of the entire subject, this course will focus on the textual criticism of the Hebrew Bible in light of the Dead Sea Scrolls. Among the topics analyzed will be: the origin and character of the Masorah, Kethib-Qere, variant readings in the ancient versions and in rabbinic literature, and the vocalization.[151]

Orlinsky's course on the scrolls continued to be offered at HUC-JIR until the early 1970s, when it was replaced with "Bible elective 114: The Jewish Apocryphal literature (and the DSS)." Between 1968 and 1970, Orlinsky also offered a course on the scrolls for alumni of the College, a sort of continuing rabbinic education program: "Bible A-201 –The book of (Second) Isaiah: A refresher course, dealing primarily with the theological and literary aspects of the book, and also with the Dead Sea Scrolls of Isaiah." Despite his regular teaching of the scrolls, he urged his students to avoid involving themselves in the debates. When a JIR graduate sent him a draft of an article titled, "The Suffering Servant and the Dead Sea Scrolls," he offered, "I know that the last mentioned [the Scrolls] is all the rage right now, but genuine and worthwhile scholarship cannot depend upon and derive from the obscure and unclear, sensational as it may be to some, or many, at the moment."[152] In this his comments reflected Zeitlin and would resonate in the writings of Ellis Rivkin and Samuel Sandmel as well.

Between publishing and teaching, Orlinsky was an active participant in the world of the Dead Sea Scrolls. In 1954, however, he became an actor in the purchase and acquisition of them.[153] On 1 July 1954, while leaving his house for a vacation with his wife to Toronto, Orlinsky received a phone call from

Yigael Yadin. Yadin was calling from the office of the Israeli Consul-General, Avraham Harman, in New York, and he needed Orlinsky's immediate help. On 1 June it had been brought to Yadin's attention that the four scrolls from St. Mark's were for sale in the United States. A classified advertisement in the *Wall Street Journal* listed a post office box and, knowing that the metropolitan would not sell the scrolls to an Israeli, had a third party contact the seller. Now they needed an unknown individual to examine the scrolls first-hand to ensure their authenticity. Yadin knew Orlinsky for various reasons, and they had become friendly through Orlinsky's efforts to found the American Friends of the Israel Exploration Society in 1951. Since Orlinsky had published serious studies of the Isaiah Scroll from St. Mark's, he was a perfect candidate for the job. Taking on the pseudonym Mr. Green, Orlinsky went to New York's Waldorf-Astoria Hotel, where there was a branch of the Chemical Bank and Trust Co. He was taken to the vault, where he examined the scrolls. First he examined the Isaiah text, then Pesher Habakkuk, and finally, the Manual of Discipline (Rule of the Community). A fourth scroll, identified then as the Lamech scroll and published later as the Genesis Apocryphon, was in the vault but in too poor condition to be unrolled. Orlinsky would later report to Yadin,

> I made a detailed inspection of the scrolls and compared them with the official reproduction published by the American Schools of Oriental Research, New Haven, edited by Professor Millar Burrows.[154] I am satisfied that the scrolls … are the authentic 4 DSS referred to and reproduced in the a/m work by Professor Burrows and that they are complete.[155]

In early 1956 Orlinsky explained what he did somewhat more explicitly to a Toronto journalist. Particularly noteworthy is that he carried out his job of examining and handling the physical manuscripts without dealing with the issue of dating the material:

> I had nothing to do with "authenticating" the Scrolls for—and purchased by—the Israel Government. What I was asked to do, and what I did, was to examine the Scrolls very carefully to make sure what the archbishop of the St. Marks Convent was offering for sale, was exactly what the Israel Government was ready to purchase; in other words, to make sure that no kind of substitute was being introduced. The matter of the authenticity of the Scrolls was never really doubted by anyone; it is the matter of date and authorship, and such other scholarly problems that have constituted the several and important points of difference among scholars.[156]

Following the examination, Orlinsky left the hotel and called an unlisted number for the consulate from the pay phone using the code-word *le-hayim* to indicate that the scrolls were authentic. Upon returning to the consulate by taxi, he signed a legal statement Harman and Yadin had prepared that swore to the authenticity of the scrolls he had viewed.[157] Orlinsky was sworn to secrecy until the scrolls were safely returned to Israel. On 13 February 1955 Israel announced the $250,000 purchase of the St. Mark's Scrolls.[158] Orlinsky's name was kept out of the press, and his correspondence shows that he kept the story quiet, even from Albright, who he knew was communicating with Yadin.[159] The first public news of his participation came in a November 1955 interview he gave to *American Judaism*, a magazine of the Union of American Hebrew Congregations. The interview describes all the difficulties with dating the material, why Orlinsky refused to offer a date for the composition, and the relative worthlessness of the Isaiah Scroll.[160] Of particular interest, though, is this comment from the article: "A legitimate question that a layman might ask at this point is, 'Are the Scrolls worth the reputed quarter of a million dollars that the Israeli Government paid?' In discounting the value of the scrolls to the field of Bible scholarship, Dr. Orlinsky emphasized, he does not discount their museum value."[161]

For all of Orlinsky's arguments about the scholarly aspect of the scrolls, whether from 200 BCE or 200 CE, they were Israel's national treasures, and he made the necessary effort to help acquire them. In 1957 Yadin gave a full accounting, which included discussion of Orlinsky's participation.[162] Orlinsky did not provide a full account of his own until "The Dead Sea Scrolls and Mr. Green" in 1974.[163] However, through his years of teaching, he continued to regale his students with the story of his adventure;[164] his participation in the events was always important to him. In 1985 he was invited to a New York conference in honor of the late Yigael Yadin, where he recalled the tale before an appreciative group of Dead Sea Scroll scholars.[165] Even three decades later, in his correspondence with Harman, they continued to discuss the story. Harman wrote to Orlinsky: "I often think of the stirring days when we were in conspiracy in rescuing the Dead Sea Scrolls."[166] When Orlinsky died in 1992, *Biblical Archaeology Review* memorialized him with a reprinting of his "Dead Sea Scrolls and Mr. Green" under the headline: "The Bible Scholar Who Became an Undercover Agent."[167]

Orlinsky never made scroll scholarship his primary academic endeavor, and by the early 1960s his period of active scroll scholarship and publication ended. His interest in the scrolls had been largely shaped by his interest in the history of the biblical text and the book of Isaiah. Having studied the scrolls thoroughly, it was time for other projects; however, his interest in the scrolls did not disappear. In 1990 Orlinsky participated in two events where he once again took the opportunity to challenge the status quo on the scrolls. On 25 March 1990, Orlinsky coordinated the first "Harry M. Orlinsky Symposium" at HUC-JIR in New York. The subject of the conference was "The Essenes and the Dead Sea Scrolls: 40 Years after Qumran," and the guest lecturers were John Strugnell and Harry Orlinsky.[168] In June and July he gave the closing remarks in a session devoted to surveying the previous forty years of Qumran scholarship. As he noted in the session, after forty years he was still disappointed that the Essene hypothesis connecting the settlement of Qumran with the ancient sect still held sway despite the limited evidence.[169] He asserted that he did not find the theory convincing in the fifties, and no new evidence had been brought forward to further support it.[170] Commenting to Wacholder, he had little kind to say about the growing group of Dead Sea Scroll scholars: "A lot of people who hardly know the data at the source have been orating a lot publicly about the cave(s) and scrolls and Qumran; very few of them could deal with the topic of the Symposium."[171] Even with his final public comments, Orlinsky challenged the establishment.

*Samuel Sandmel,
Cincinnati, February 1956*

(Courtesy American
Jewish Archives)

Samuel Sandmel (1911–1979)

Samuel Sandmel was ordained by HUC in 1937 before he went on to Yale University, where he earned his doctorate in 1949 under the guidance of Erwin R. Goodenough.[172] Following three years of service as professor of Jewish literature and thought at Vanderbilt University, Sandmel returned to HUC-JIR as professor of Bible and Hellenistic Literature and eventually was named provost of the College, 1957–1966. Sandmel's major contribution was as a Jewish scholar of the New Testament. In contrast to the general consensus among scholars of his period, Sandmel preferred to read the Gospels against the background of diasporic Judaism influenced by Hellenism rather than in a Palestinian Jewish context.[173] As a result of this approach, he also directed much attention to the writings of Josephus and Philo. Christian scriptures along with the works of these two ancient writers became the major focus of his teaching as well. However, in the 1955–1956 course catalogue, Sandmel was scheduled to replace Sonne, who had retired and been promoted to professor emeritus. In this regard "History 12 – The Dead Sea Scrolls" became Sandmel's. Although the course is described as "Reading, translation, and scrutiny of selected sections and lectures on the significance of the documents," the course description is immediately followed by an interesting note: "will not be offered in 1955–56." In the 1956–1957 course catalogue the course is listed as a graduate elective, and Sandmel's name is absent. Evidence suggests that although it appeared in the catalogue, the course was not offered.[174]

Sandmel's choice not to teach a course on the scrolls would have been consistent with his view of them at the time, and he maintained this position well into the 1970s: The Dead Sea Scrolls, although dating from antiquity,[175] have little to tell us about early Judaism or early Christianity. He made this point especially clear in early February 1956 while addressing a gathering of clergy of different faiths at Temple Emanu-El in Montreal, Canada.[176] Concerning the importance of the scrolls, Sandmel declared that they "change nothing, clarify nothing, and add relatively little to our knowledge of Christianity and Judaism."[177] His comments were genuinely intended to challenge the exaggerated claims Edmund Wilson had made about the scrolls and Christianity, not to dismiss them in their entirety.[178] In May 1955 Wilson had brought the scrolls to worldwide attention with a long article in the *New Yorker*,[179] which soon after became a bestselling book.[180] Lawrence Schiffman has argued that Wilson's interpretation of the scrolls in his article and subsequent books, "because of his substantial reputation, influenced all subsequent development of the depiction of the scrolls in the popular media."[181] Sandmel's comments caused a flurry of interest and they, along with numerous responses, were carried in newspapers throughout the United States and Canada.[182] It was not just Wilson who might have concerned Sandmel. During the same week, on 5 February 1956, the *New York Times* carried a report that John Allegro, a member of the scroll editorial team, argued that Qumran's Teacher of Righteousness had likely been persecuted and crucified in Christlike fashion at the hands of gentiles incited by a wicked Jewish priest and that Paul's teachings descended from traditions already evidenced among the Dead Sea sectarians.[183] Sandmel's comments were particularly disturbing to the faculty of McGill University who attended the talk, because the university had in the weeks preceding the lecture purchased several hundred fragments of Qumran material from Cave 4.[184]

The ten-page text of that evening's talk, "The Dead Sea Scrolls and the New Testament," is Sandmel's only preserved discussion solely on the Dead Sea Scrolls.[185] While he continued to discuss the scrolls in other works, these treatments were cursory. As is evident from the media coverage, Wilson was most clearly the target of his attack, although Sandmel seems to have been disturbed by having to respond to him:

> Had Mr. Wilson's article not become a book on the best seller list, the best treatment of it would have been to ignore it.… Certainly in the area of scholarship Mr. Wilson is undeserving of attention, for he is not important enough to merit focusing on. But the misconceptions which have emerged from his article are worth noting, even if their author is not.[186]

Despite the polemical aspect of the talk, Sandmel did reach a significant conclusion:

> The issues which need to be raised are these: If these scrolls are important, for what are they important? Do they shed new light on the question of

Christian origins? Do they throw any direct light on Christianity? Do they tell us anything about Jesus? Is the information significant in quality? Is it fresh and novel information which they supply, or is the information confined primarily to confirming what we already know or confined to adding a scattering of new details to knowledge we have already possessed?

Now if the quantity of information which the scrolls supply is relatively small, or if the significance of the quality of the information is relatively low, then the scrolls have little importance beyond being a discovery good and useful in a limited way. Only if the scrolls abundantly illumine great areas previously totally dark do they merit being greeted with extravagant enthusiasm.

Let it be clear that in my judgment, the scrolls are a striking discovery; but they have been accorded a fantastic welcome entirely out of proportion to their significance. They contribute a might [*sic*] to our understanding of sectarian movements in the period of Jewish history usually called the second temple.

Respecting Christianity, they offer a small and uncertain measure of information, which is limited to background information. They tell us not one word or one syllable about Christianity itself. They provide not one single point of departure for any need to reconsider in their light the origins of Christianity.

In quantity they cannot begin to vie with what we already possessed in rabbinic literature, the pseudepigrapha, Josephus, Philo and the Hellenistic-Jewish fragments. In quality the information they yield is so appallingly vague that scarcely any two scholars solve the questions of allusions and the historical data in the same way.

The Dead Sea Scrolls give us at most a drop for the bucket which was already half-full. They change nothing, they clarify nothing, they add precious little.[187]

Although the response to the comments was rather overblown, the press perceived Sandmel's statements, and his critique of Wilson in particular, as part of a general clergy backlash against a presumed attack on Christianity. From this perspective, the clergy were bothered by the presentation of Christianity as little more than the unoriginal repackaging of ideas already formulated by the community that produced the Dead Sea Scrolls. In reviewing Wilson's book, *The Scrolls From the Dead Sea*, literary critic Stanley Edgar Hyman noted:

As the implications of the Dead Sea scrolls began to emerge, we have been favored with a mounting chorus of warnings from clergy. J. Carter Swain told the First Presbyterian Church of Jamaica, Queens, in December, 1955, that the scrolls 'will not radically alter our picture of Christian origins, because the essential features of Jesus' ministry are too well known and established for that.' John Sutherland Bonnell welcomed the discoveries in a sermon at his Fifth Avenue Presbyterian Church in January, assuring Christians that they need not fear, since 'the place of Jesus Christ in history is unchallengeable.' After Allegro's broadcast, an unnamed English Catholic spokesman was quoted as saying 'any stick now seems big enough to use against Christianity,' and another, or perhaps the same one, called the broadcasts 'atheist in spirit.' *The New York Times* carried comments by Catholic, Protestant, and Jewish clergymen under the heading 'Dead Sea Scrolls Held Overvalued.' The priest, John J. Dougherty of the Immaculate Conception Seminary of Darlington, New Jersey, attacked Wilson and Dupont-Sommer[188] in *America* as 'mischief' but 'nothing new'; the rabbi, Samuel Sandmel of Hebrew Union College, warned against Wilson, remarking 'seldom have so many readers been led astray by one man'; and the minister, the same Bonnell, confined himself to urging Allegro to slow down.[189]

Sandmel was not attempting to explicitly defend Christianity from an atheist attack; he was a rabbi who specialized in the New Testament and certainly did not identify personally with its teachings. In recounting Sandmel's public statements as reported in the *New York Times*, John Haverstick of the *Saturday Review* suggested that Sandmel, whom he identified only anonymously as "a Conservative Jew," was among religious conservatives attempting to defend their theological positions against Wilson and others:

> To many eager religious liberals the Dupont-Sommer thesis [upon which Wilson relied heavily] has seemed to indicate that Jesus was not unique and, therefore, not divine. To conservatives it has seemed that the French devil's advocate was trying to shoot Christianity full of holes.… [S]aid a Conservative Jew: 'seldom have so many readers been led astray by one man.' [190]

Sandmel wrote an extensive letter to Norman Cousins, the *Saturday Review* editor, although it was abbreviated somewhat when it was published. The letter suggests Sandmel's motivations in making the bold statements in Montreal:

> I chance to be a Reform Jew, and what theological position I hold is in absolutely no way dependent on the Dead Sea Scrolls or on contentions about their bearing on New Testament writings.… There are a good many of us who study the scrolls out of a historical, not a theological interest. I claim to be one such.… In short, I deny the special relationship claimed for the Dead Sea Scrolls and Christianity not because it offends any theology, but because the claims are [an] affront to sober, prudent scholarship.[191]

Sandmel did on other occasions argue for the uniqueness of Christianity. In his 1961 presidential address before the annual meeting of the SBL, Sandmel attacked what he called "parallelomania"—the assumption that parallels between two bodies of material, e.g., the New Testament and the Dead Sea

Scrolls, necessarily indicated an influence.[192] In response, he commented on the attempts to find Pauline Christianity in the pre-Pauline Dead Sea Scrolls:

> Abstractly, it is conceivable that Paul had nothing of his own to say, and that his achievement was that he was only an eclectic. But this seems to me to break down at two points. First, no rabbinic parallels have been found to that which in Paul is Pauline; and secondly, it took Dupont-Sommer's emendations of the Qumran Scrolls to have them contain pre-Pauline Paulinism. I for one am prepared to believe that Paul was a person of an originality which went beyond the mere echoing of his predecessors or contemporaries. I am prepared to believe that Paul represents more than a hodgepodge of sources.[193]

As with his comments in Montreal, the *New York Times* covered Sandmel's SBL address under the headline "Scrolls Doubted as Link to Jesus."[194] The report accurately portrays the presidential address, and the reporter went to Wilson for a response to Sandmel's continued attack on his work. Refusing to be drawn into a battle, Wilson responded simply that:

> Biblical scholars almost without exception are committed to one point of view or to another: to show how different the Gospels are from the scrolls or how much alike they are.... I'm hoping to bring the whole thing up to date ... and deal with all these questions that have been raised.[195]

In general, Wilson's demurral was helpful. Although Sandmel continued to attack those who made too much of the parallels between the scrolls and the New Testament, after 1961 he moved away from attacking Wilson by name.

In 1956, it might be argued, Sandmel was simply being cautious about the scrolls; only limited quantities of the cave material had been published, and yet extensive and far-reaching claims were being made. This was especially true regarding the relationship between the scrolls and the New Testament, the latter being Sandmel's academic specialty. In accord with his own evaluation of the material, Sandmel concluded that the attention paid to the scrolls was little more than scholarly faddishness. Further, the scrolls simply distracted scholars from more informative sources for the reconstruction of early Judaism and Christianity. In 1958 Sandmel reviewed volumes four, five, and six of Erwin Goodenough's *Jewish Symbols in the Greco-Roman Period*.[196] He was certain that these, like the first three volumes, would not receive the attention they deserved because scholars were distracted by the scrolls, which, by comparison, were less significant:

> The six volumes have appeared at almost the same time that the Dead Sea scrolls changed from a novelty into a fad, so that the large work of Goodenough's may for the time being remain a casualty of the widespread preoccupation with the scrolls. There is no doubt in my mind that had Goodenough's materials emerged from a cave instead of being assembled from

the finest libraries in the world, researchers in the field would recognize that the scrolls, which have their own importance, cannot begin to vie in overall significance with the materials Goodenough has assembled. But the frenzy over the scrolls is bound to pass away, and when it does, Goodenough's work will receive the careful attention which it deserves.[197]

This perception that Goodenough's work was being lost in the fuss around the Dead Sea Scrolls may have gone back to Sandmel's days as a doctoral student under Goodenough's direction at Yale. Sandmel, who graduated in 1949, was at the school precisely during the years that Millar Burrows and the scrolls were at the center of attention and that Goodenough was at work on the first volumes of *Jewish Symbols*.[198] However, by the late 1960s, Sandmel was convinced that the lack of a methodological introduction to Goodenough's work was a greater handicap than its release amid the scroll fad.[199] Despite this Sandmel did not change his view that the wide-ranging interest in the scrolls was scholarly trendiness.

The fad[200] did not disappear quickly, and in 1966 Sandmel still hoped that "perhaps the fad aspect of the Scrolls has by now … passed away."[201] In article after article and volume after volume, Sandmel continued to challenge the use of the scrolls in discussing early Judaism and Christianity.[202] Although he indicated that in the earliest years the prospect of what the scrolls might reveal excited him, what they actually revealed was very little: "With the passing of months and of years, we have come to a better perspective on the scrolls. In light of that perspective perhaps many here [at the 1961 SBL meeting] will agree with me that the scrolls reflect the greatest exaggeration in the history of biblical scholarship."[203] The difficulty is that Sandmel never reevaluated his position. Although more of the ancient material was published, and many more critical "sober" articles and books were written, his critical perspective meant that he never used the scrolls in his own scholarship except as a target for denigration.

In part, this was an issue of Sandmel's distaste for the method of making claims based on textual parallels in dealing with the relationship between Qumran and Christianity. Regarding the scrolls' significance for early Judaism, Sandmel took a position, which he maintained into the 1970s, of consciously ignoring the material. In reviewing the 1970 reprint of Sandmel's 1958 volume *The Genius of Paul: A Study in History*,[204] Wayne Rollins noted, "The light that the Dead Sea Scrolls casts on our understanding of first century Judaism is consciously but nevertheless completely ignored."[205] In truth, Sandmel ignored the scrolls' contribution in 1958 and a decade later as well. In reviewing Sandmel's 1969 volume, *The First Christian Century in Judaism and Christianity: Certainties and Uncertainties*, Raymond Brown suggested that Sandmel made insufficient use of the scrolls for reconstructing first-century Judaism:

Although I agree with his cautions … on the misuse of the Dead Sea Scrolls in judging Palestinian Judaism, I would like to challenge him on whether he is using them sufficiently. After all, although sectarian and perhaps not broadly representative, they are contemporary with the first century in a way that the rabbinic documents and the available translations of the most important apocrypha are not.[206]

In the volume Sandmel's discussion of the scrolls is somewhat less provocative than in his earlier statements. In part, this was the result of what he termed "an armistice" in the "battle of the Dead Sea Scrolls" and the opportunity for a more calm evaluation of the material.[207] Although Brown recognized that Sandmel's lack of interest in the scrolls stemmed in part from his concern with Diaspora Judaism, Sandmel, from early on, was simply never convinced that the available scrolls could provide as much information as other previously known sources. While Sandmel acknowledged that "an understanding of the first Christian century is incomplete without the Scrolls,"[208] he actually estimated the number of surviving pages of Qumran sectarian material (thirty-five to forty-five pages, according to his count) and argued that they could not compare in importance with the hundreds of pages of the pseudepigraphal and rabbinic literature.[209] His disregard for the scrolls in the 1970s was just as apparent as in the previous decades. In some ways he was fighting the same old battles—granted, with a different tone—when he did discuss them. In an October 1973 lecture he gave at the Southern Baptist Seminary, he devoted significant time to taking William Albright to task for an argument about Hellenization that he made in the 1950s.[210]

Ellis Rivkin, Cincinnati, Founders' Day, 1956

(Courtesy American Jewish Archives)

In light of his maintained position, there is little doubt about why Sandmel never offered a course on the scrolls and concentrated on teaching and writing about the New Testament, Josephus, and Philo.[211]

Ellis Rivkin (1918–2010)

Ellis Rivkin came to HUC as a professor of history in the fall of 1949. He had earned his doctorate at The Johns Hopkins University in 1946 with a dissertation on the Venetian rabbi and polemicist Leon da Modena (1571–1648).[212] After receiving his degree he was awarded a two-year Cyrus Adler fellowship at Dropsie College in Philadelphia, which was extended for a third year while he continued to work on Modena.[213] With his arrival at HUC, his duties included teaching the introductory surveys of Jewish history, including the history of the Jews in antiquity.

Rivkin's role in the story of the scrolls and HUC-JIR might easily be overlooked. While Sandmel repeatedly challenged their significance in print over many years, Rivkin dismissed them for various reasons and purposefully ignored them in his publications. In and of itself, that he chose not to study the scrolls did not have a major impact in scholarly circles. However, among his rabbinic students it had particular force. A recent informal survey by the author of HUC-JIR alumni on two Internet list-servs, "HUCalum" and "RavKav," suggests that some pulpit rabbis continue to maintain that the scrolls are medieval documents as Rivkin taught them. A 1991 rabbinic thesis written under Rivkin's supervision concludes: "Concerning Zeitlin's dating of the Scrolls as medieval, I suspect that he may be correct...[The] Scrolls are, as Rivkin contends, opaque and atypical—hence not utilizable as a source for **any** period."[214]

The scrolls piqued Rivkin's interest from the beginning, and his correspondence with his mentor Harry Orlinsky[215] shows that he discussed the matters primarily with Solomon Zeitlin and Orlinsky himself, but also with John Trever and William Albright. Rivkin committed to a late date for the scrolls from early on. Zeitlin's attacks on Trever and the others involved in bringing news of the scrolls to the American public left a clear impression. Following Trever's 1949 visit to HUC (described above), Rivkin wrote to Orlinsky:

> Last night Dr. Trevor [sic] of the scrolls spoke to the faculty and students. His account of how the scrolls came into his hands certainly sounds fishy to me. He indicated that the original story was a fabrication and the events that had actually occurred were far different and far more complex than I had originally believed. Also his mention of the profound interest displayed by the Syrian monks in financial returns as well as the subsequent rifling of the cave and the destruction of the jars makes me more than ever suspicious of the whole business.[216]

> Could the manuscripts have been lying in the library of the convent for a long time and the Bedouin story invented to make the finds more palatable? For the life of me I cannot see how even the Isaiah scrolls can be dated positively on the basis of our present knowledge of the Second Commonwealth paleography. Zeitlin's evidence on the Commentary and on the Sectarian documents seems to me very well founded and noone [sic] has answered him yet. They merely refute his position by referring to the Isaiah scrolls and they ignore his other evidence.[217]

Rivkin continued to correspond with Orlinsky about these matters through the late 1950s, often calling on "Zeitlin's evidence" to support his view of the scrolls.[218] Orlinsky, although sympathetic to Zeitlin's arguments, warned Rivkin about accepting Zeitlin's evidence too quickly: "I agree in general with you when you write that 'Zeitlin's evidence is much more reliable than that of his opponents.' But the trouble has been in my judgment, that 'more reliable' is not enough; either one side demonstrates his date, or he doesn't."[219] Although not entirely uncritical of Zeitlin, Rivkin came to adhere to his position far more closely than Orlinsky could ever bring himself to do.

Rivkin, like his mentor Zeitlin, maintained throughout his career that the scrolls are of medieval origin,[220] and, whether ancient or medieval, methodological concerns prevent their use as historical sources. In evaluating Zeitlin's challenge to the scrolls' antiquity and the scholarly world's response, Rivkin noted that Zeitlin recognized certain linguistic features and word usage as unique to Karaite material from a later period. Rivkin noted in 1965 that scholars accepted that these features were similar to those of Karaite texts, but they would not accept the late date. Instead, they theorized about how these terms might have passed from the ancient sect to the medieval one. According to Rivkin, Zeitlin,

> refused to budge from his methodological stronghold, however determinedly besieged by scholars great in number and towering in reputation. Though these latter show little or no respect for Zeitlin's methodological principle, and though they make light of his erudition, they have quietly taken over the linguistic discovery that Zeitlin was the first to make.[221]

Rivkin never explicitly states in his evaluation that he agrees that the scrolls are medieval, but he most certainly adopted Zeitlin's methodology. Like Zeitlin, Rivkin dismisses all archaeological and paleographic material. As with Sandmel's concerns, this may have been legitimate in the first years following the discoveries, but archaeologists' additional exposure of similar materials in other caves certainly suggests that this conclusion might have needed to be reevaluated in later decades.

Rivkin is not uncritical of Zeitlin, but his criticism is largely an issue of presentation rather than method. He argues that Zeitlin failed to separate his methodological questions from the conclusions he reached. Thus, Zeitlin's challenge to the archaeological and paleographic grounds for dating the material was legitimate and should have been thoroughly treated. It garnered no direct response, however, because the rest of the scholarly world was attacking Zeitlin's answer that the material was medieval rather than exploring the ramifications of his critique of their method. From Rivkin's perspective, Zeitlin's presentation of his findings and his criticism of others, along with his obsessive need to demonstrate the lateness of the scrolls, distracted his readership from the real issues.[222] The real issue for Rivkin was that the scrolls simply were not a reliable historical source, not because they could not be adequately dated but because even if they could, they would provide no clear information:

[W]hat scholars are confronted with when they study the Dead Sea Scrolls are not only opaque sources which do not clearly and unambiguously reveal their provenance, but opaque sources which unlike other opaque sources from the intertestamental period have no attestation to their existence before 1947.... They have no manuscript history and they are not cited by other early writers. This renders them opaque in a qualitatively different way from the opaqueness which characterizes so many of the pseudepigraphic writings.[223]

According to Rivkin, since the scrolls are opaque, and likely medieval, they can add nothing to the study of ancient Jewish history. So, in his 1978 work exploring the nature of the community of Pharisees at the beginning of the Common Era, Rivkin makes no mention of the scrolls. Reviewer Shaye Cohen noted this omission, along with its implications:

On the basis of [the first century historian Josephus Flavius' *Antiquities*] 13:297, Rivkin contends that the Pharisees were the only Jews to accept a Two-Fold Law, but such a contention is ludicrous. After the Torah was canonized and its text established, an oral law was inevitable, for how else could one live by a code which was elliptic, obscure, and self-contradictory? *Jubilees* and the Dead Sea Scrolls (resolutely ignored by Rivkin) attest unequivocally to a non-pharisaic (anti-pharisaic?) oral law and exegesis.[224]

Rivkin has marked a certain amount of success in carrying on Zeitlin's concerns about the scrolls. Those who have examined his project on the Pharisees, which resulted from decades of research and writing, have largely discussed methodological issues. While medieval provenance would have been enough to exclude the scrolls from a work on the Pharisees, those responding to the volume had methodological concerns about the texts. Like Cohen, Robert Seltzer and Jack Bemporad noted difficulties raised by the absence of Dead Sea Scroll discussion in Rivkin's work:

We also have considerable data about late Second Temple apocalypticism. There may have been apocalyptic Pharisees, but belief in the imminent coming of God's Kingdom has not been shown to have been an essential attribute of Pharisaism. It was a belief of Jesus and his circle. Jesus and his disciples, as well as John the Baptist and his circle, may have had some traits in common with the Essenes (ritual immersion, a reputation for healing, sharing of property). Some of the Dead Sea Scrolls flesh out our knowledge of apocalyptic sects, but Rivkin's suspicions about the Scrolls bars data derived from them from incorporation into the foundational definition.[225]

According to Lloyd Bailey, suspicion alone did not account for their exclusion.[226] To avoid errors that may have been introduced into the discussion by texts where, for example, the term *haverim* is assumed to be synonymous with "Pharisees," Rivkin included in his work only those texts where the latter term appeared explicitly. Therefore, suggests Bailey, the Apocrypha, Pseudepigrapha, and Dead Sea Scrolls were excluded. Further, he notes:

> Several reviewers, failing notice of this methodological consideration, have criticized Rivkin for neglecting the last three sources. In theory, the excluded sources might contain relevant information, but their use would introduce an unnecessary possibility of error.[227]

From a methodological perspective this was precisely Rivkin's concern:

> [If] unknown writings [such as the scrolls] show themselves to be atypical and opaque, they must be sealed off from the known, lest in their desperation to know more of a period of which so little is known, scholars allow the unknown to contaminate the known and compound thereby our woeful ignorance.[228]

Possibility of error or not, Rivkin's acceptance of the scrolls' medieval dating was enough to keep them from the discussion of the Pharisees.[229]

The scrolls' discovery and the first debates over their authenticity took place while Rivkin was still with Zeitlin at Dropsie as a postdoctoral fellow and continued on the HUC campus with the Society of Biblical Literature, American Schools of Oriental Research, and American Oriental Society meetings in 1949 and 1950. According to Rivkin's recollection, his views did not bring him into direct conflict with his colleagues. His relationship with Sonne was amicable but not particularly friendly. He and Sandmel agreed on the difficulty of using the scrolls to reconstruct history, but they disagreed on the dating.[230] Their relationship was somewhat troublesome, in part because Rivkin was becoming more generalist while Sandmel encouraged specialization; but also because they disagreed on a number of specific issues about the reconstruction of the Jewish past.[231]

Despite their disagreements, their complementary attacks on the scrolls acted as a one-two punch regarding the inclusion of the material in the rabbinical school curriculum. Both men agreed that to study the scrolls in a Second Temple context was to explain one unknown with another.[232] Neither Sandmel nor Rivkin ever included Qumran materials among the texts for study in their courses. In Rivkin's own words, he "never used any of the scrolls in his classes as historical sources, only those sources that could be certified and ascertained as coming from the Inter-Testamental period."[233] Between them, during the three decades following Sonne's retirement in 1956, they taught almost all of the core courses on Hellenistic literature and Second Temple history and many of the electives. Therefore, the rabbinic students in Cincinnati during that period were exposed to the scrolls only through Sandmel or Rivkin's dismissive assessments of the material.

Changing the Tone: Nelson Glueck and the Tenth Anniversary of the Discovery of the Dead Sea Scrolls

Nelson Glueck was certainly not a scrolls scholar but, as a populariser extraordinaire of biblical archaeology, he immediately recognized their value. By 1956, when Sandmel made his very public comments about the limited value of the scrolls, the press had devoted many pages to them. For reference, it is worthwhile to note that between 1894 and 1991—the year access to the scrolls was provided to all scholars—only nine SBL meetings received coverage in substantial articles in the *New York Times*, despite the conferences being held almost solely in New York. Three of these—the meetings of 1894, 1895, and 1910—took place before the discovery of the scrolls.[234] Of the remaining six meetings appearing in newspaper articles—1949, 1955, 1956, 1958, 1961, 1991—all but the article covering the 1958 meeting discuss the scrolls.[235] The 1949 conference was the one held in Cincinnati and is discussed above. The 1961 meeting was where Sandmel attacked scrolls scholarship in his "Parallelomania" presidential address. The 1958 article, which does not discuss the scrolls, highlights that Harry Orlinsky of HUC spoke at an important session.[236] In general, SBL and the Dead Sea Scrolls focused a significant amount of attention on HUC-JIR. But just what kind of attention was it? Sonne had been critical of scholarship on the scrolls but not their antiquity. Orlinsky was hesitant about dating the material at all. Sandmel agreed they were old but declared them valueless. Rivkin, who did not appear in the press, challenged the scrolls back on campus. Just what Glueck, the College president, thought of this situation is worthy of exploration.

As noted, Glueck had participated in discussions concerning the scrolls in 1948 with Judah Magnes and William Albright. Further, he was a loyal student of Albright; already in his late sixties he wrote to his mentor, "You are and continue to be the most important single influence in my life. I am, and will always remain, endlessly grateful to you."[237] Given his close relationship to Albright, who immediately had dated the scrolls to antiquity, along with his close relations with John Trever, Millar Burrows, and others through ASOR and SBL, it seems unlikely that Glueck would have taken an opposing stance on the scrolls, despite the debate among HUC-JIR faculty. Additionally, through specific actions, he demonstrated his concern for the scrolls and their importance and simultaneously challenged his faculty's views. First, in 1955 and 1958, he reviewed books on the Dead Sea Scrolls in a very public forum, the *New York Times*. In 1956 and 1957 he unsuccessfully attempted to bring Orlinsky, Sandmel, and Sonne together to organize an international conference in Cincinnati in honor of the tenth anniversary of the scrolls' discovery. Finally, in 1958, he hired Albright's student, Norman Golb, who had already published on the scrolls, as a Cincinnati faculty member. His clearest act, the acquisition of a set of negatives of the scrolls in 1969, remained largely secret until the 1990s and is discussed in greater detail below.

In May 1955 Edmund Wilson boosted public awareness and interest in the scrolls in an unprecedented way. As is clear from Sandmel's response, a more balanced view of the scrolls was needed. In November 1955 Glueck suggested in a *New York Times* review that more balanced scholarship could be found. The review, "New Light on the Dim Past," discusses Burrows's *The Dead Sea Scrolls* and Eleazar Sukenik's posthumous *The Dead Sea Scrolls of the Hebrew University*.[238] That Glueck chose to discuss the books of the two men between whom he had been asked to mediate years before is somewhat ironic. In the case of Burrows, whose second book Glueck also reviewed in the *New York Times*, these published statements suggest Glueck's loyalty to a friend as well to Burrows's interpretation of the material. In the first review Glueck attempted to increase public interest in the book—but even more so in the scrolls, by pushing the adventure story aspect of the discovery and the early scholarship. Glueck described the story as one of

> [c]hance discovery, rich rewards, high intrigue, intemperate accusations and flaming defense, ingenious hypotheses and illuminating facts, carbon 14 tests and laboratory examinations of leather and linen and ink, religious pride and prejudice.[239]

For Glueck, archaeology was a dangerous adventure, and he knew this aspect would appeal to the public. Toward the end of the review he notes that Sukenik risked life and limb to cross the border in Jerusalem to acquire the scrolls:

> At the literal risk of his life, during the days and weeks of hectic negotiating with Syrian monks and Arab merchants ... Sukenik managed to secure three of [the scrolls] ... for the Hebrew University.... In the midst of [the] modern Jewish War of Liberation, when it was worth a man's life to attempt to cross certain lines or be in certain areas in Jerusalem, this brave scholar ignored shot and shell to obtain these scrolls.

> The drain on his energies and heart may well have contributed to his early death a few years thereafter.[240]

In many ways, this depiction of archaeology and scroll adventures foreshadowed Glueck's own adventures as an archaeologist in the Negev, as reported in *Time Magazine* in 1963. Noting that Glueck sometimes got shot at while searching the desert for sites, the journalist asked Glueck why he kept returning. Glueck replied, "There is something there ... not just things to find, but the threads of history to tie up. That is the great reward of my kind of exploring.... What the explorer is after ... is more important than his life."[241]

Regarding the scrolls specifically, Glueck's *New York Times* review high-lighted a number of issues: that the scrolls provide insight into the lives and philosophies of Jewish groups in the first centuries before and during the Common Era; that the group appears similar to the Essenes but that no conclusive evidence allows for identifying the Qumranites with them; and that the previous attempts to demonstrate a close relationship between the documents and early Christianity were no more than exaggerations. The most substantial portion of the review is Glueck's treatment of the history of the biblical text. In discussing the Isaiah Scroll he noted, "This and thousands of fragments of the Old Testament were found being nine centuries earlier than the previously, earliest known Hebrew manuscripts of the Bible.… They furnish invaluable evidence of the fidelity of the later Masoretic text."[242]

In formulating his comment in this way, Glueck managed to avoid dealing with Orlinsky's challenge to the importance of the particular scroll, but he was still able to come to a satisfying conclusion. The statement makes clear Glueck's commitment to the antiquity of the scrolls generally. Further, Glueck was an archaeologist who believed his findings confirmed the historicity of the biblical narratives, as he later claimed:

> As a matter of fact, however, it may be stated categorically that no archaeological discovery has ever controverted a biblical reference. Scores of archaeological findings have been made which confirm in clear outline or in exact detail historical statements in the Bible.[243]

Given this mindset, Glueck must have very much appreciated that not only could the biblical tales be confirmed but that the written source he used to trace his way through the desert could, thanks to the scrolls, be demonstrated to be ancient as well.

In 1958, with the appearance of Burrows's second volume on the scrolls, Glueck had an additional opportunity to make his views on them known. However, in contrast to the first review, in which he dealt with the details of the scrolls, in the second review Glueck spoke to the significance of their discovery. Noting that some interpreters suggested that it was through his literary talents that Wilson had been able to arouse interest in the scrolls, Glueck suggested an alternative reading of the circumstances:

> This reviewer wonders if it may not also be said that the times were propitious for Wilson's type of article. Could it not be that the Dead Sea Scrolls, so amazingly exhumed from their long forgotten cave-burials and suddenly transported over the space of some twenty centuries to the attention of the world, were hailed unconsciously by myriads as a symbol of luminescent hope in an age of otherwise unrelieved darkness?[244]

There can be little doubt that in the wake of World War II and the Korean War, the destructive forces that were so apparent in the period weighed heavily on Glueck. His biographers, Jonathan Brown and Laurence Kutler, have noted of the period that:

> When the Korean War broke out in June 1950 and American troops began fighting and dying there, Glueck saw the conflict as a prelude to the apocalypse. He had been thoroughly frightened by President Truman's authorization of the development of the hydrogen bomb.[245]

Although this may be somewhat overstated, all evidence suggests that Glueck believed that a return to religion could give hope to the masses in what were certainly dark times. An interview he gave in the period leading up to his inauguration as HUC president is clear on this matter. The *New York Times* reported:

> [Glueck] rejoices when in his explorations he makes discoveries that confirm statements in the Bible.
>
> For he sees in religion the only salvation for the world in these confused days.… "Never before," he said, "have leaders of the spirit been needed so much as at present. And they are needed at once, for we have been more effective in our methods of destruction than in those of creation.… We even hear talk of an impending war. To combat the dangers that surround us we must turn to the moral law.… They who struggle toward God shall prevail."[246]

That Glueck felt this spiritual lift of the scrolls before he wrote the article is difficult to demonstrate, but it seems most plausible. Likewise, it might be concluded that he may have perceived the challenges leveled by some of his faculty as undermining this position.

HUC-JIR Organizes an International Conference on the Dead Sea Scrolls

Perhaps in an effort to bring some of his faculty around or, at least, to benefit from the publicity the scrolls attracted, Glueck turned to Orlinsky to help organize an international conference on the scrolls to be held in 1957 at HUC-JIR. To attract a large and distinguished group of participants, the organizing committee chair had to be well connected in the world of biblical studies and have knowledge of the scrolls. Both Sandmel and Orlinsky were well connected with the Society of Biblical Literature, but given Orlinsky's close relationship with William Albright and Sandmel's disinterest in the scrolls, the former was the only real candidate for the job. He began by assembling a list of potential conference participants and seeking members for an organizing committee. Within the College, Sonne, Julius Lewy, Sheldon Blank, and Sandmel were asked to participate.[247] Sonne ultimately declined for personal reasons.[248] In light of these "personal reasons," it is worthwhile noting that even before Sonne was asked to participate, a press release had been issued indicating that

Orlinsky, Sandmel, Blank, and Lewy were participating.[249] The conference, Glueck stated, was being held because:

> The scrolls and fragments have supplied answers to some old problems. But they have posed many more questions than they have clarified. Specialists disagree on the date of composition, the identity of the Jewish group or groups who composed them, the precise historic circumstances which brought them into being, and their pertinence and relevance to what we already know about the history of the Jewish people before and after the destruction of the Second Temple. The year 1957, which will mark a decade since the discovery of the scrolls, will provide an opportune time to reach something of a consensus of opinion, and assess with greater confidence the significance of these documents.[250]

Given the ongoing debates of the period, this statement was quite neutral—which was absolutely necessary if the conference was to succeed.

In late January Orlinsky compiled a list of 150 potential participants for the committee to vet.[251] Although not officially participating, Sonne suggested some additional names, including Geza Vermes and Alexander Scheiber.[252] Orlinsky began by writing unofficially to scholars around the world to see if there was interest in participating in the program. While the responses were generally positive, indicating that HUC-JIR should move forward, a reply from Ben Zion Dinur of the Hebrew University indicated a potential problem.[253] Dinur, alerted to the news by Joseph Aviram of the Israel Exploration Society, to whom Orlinsky had written informally, was at the time coordinating the Second World Congress of Jewish Studies, to be held in Jerusalem in late July and early August 1957. This congress was to include sessions commemorating the tenth anniversary of the discovery of the scrolls.[254] Dinur was particularly concerned that a conference the following month at HUC-JIR might discourage participants from attending the congress in Jerusalem.[255] Dinur had been at work since 1953 on organizing the meeting, and 1957 marked a decade since the first congress.[256] Glueck and Orlinsky agreed to try to push off the conference to the third week of September so as to avoid any direct conflict, but they insisted on moving forward and looking for joint sponsorship.[257] Among the potential partners was the Israel Exploration Society.[258] In April, Albright agreed to join the steering committee, although he was concerned that changing the conference date would create a conflict with the Congress of Orientalists, which was to meet in Munich in the late summer of 1957.[259] With Albright onboard, the committee turned to finding additional members.

Exploring the makeup of the organizing committee provides a relatively clear window on the discussion of scroll research at HUC-JIR during that period. Orlinsky suggested that Roland de Vaux, Millar Burrows, Henry H. Rowley, James Muilenberg, Patrick Skehan, Yigael Yadin, and Benjamin

Mazar be included on the team, along with the members of the HUC-JIR faculty and Albright.[260] The list excluded Frank Moore Cross, John Trever, and David Noel Freedman—young scroll scholars closely tied to Albright but for whom Orlinsky had limited scholarly respect. Glueck wanted Albright heavily involved in the project and suggested to Orlinsky that Albright be consulted on the membership of the committee before invitations be sent out.[261] Orlinsky replied that he was not averse to having Albright vet the list but that he should not be asked to recommend additional members: "I should not care to ask him to submit additional names because we may well become loaded with young second raters."[262] Glueck did not wait for Orlinsky's reply and by the end of April had already written to and received a reply from Albright. The issue in the committee's makeup stemmed in large part from the fact that Orlinsky and Sandmel were both highly skeptical of the work on the scrolls, and Blank and Lewy were not active participants in the field. By contrast, Glueck aligned himself with Albright and his students on scroll matters. Orlinsky's preference to keep Albright students out of the organizing created a rift between Orlinsky and Glueck. Glueck, in fact, was concerned that Orlinsky's direction could negatively affect the quality of the symposium, as he noted to Albright:

> I have decided to take this whole thing into my own hands to see to it that it doesn't get off track and comports with the highest possible standards. Should we add the name of Frank Cross and/or the name of [William] Brownlee?[263]

Albright hoped that in formulating the committee correctly, with outside members outnumbering inside members (HUC-JIR faculty), Glueck would be able to get what he wanted without having to assert his authority over his faculty directly.[264] According to Albright, Orlinsky coordinating the conference was troubling:

> I talked at some length with Harry Orlinsky … and he is now worried chiefly (so he says) about how he is going to avert an open break with Zeitlin. He has apparently come over at least two-thirds of the way, and is just not going to admit changing his mind. Luckily for us, he has been publicly somewhat neutral of late, so he can shift without any too obvious change. It might be well to drop a private hint to the scholars whom you invite about this change in Orlinsky's attitude, since one or more may otherwise decline or abstain from participation just because they don't want to find themselves in an embarrassing situation. (For instance, I had no intention of having anything to do with the Symposium, because the announced membership of the committee appeared to be stacked against the age and authenticity of the Scrolls; I have now changed my mind.)[265]

Glueck took these issues to Orlinsky but, rather than opening up the committee to the additional members, it resulted in a break between the two men; Orlinsky tendered his resignation:

> It is clear that you [Glueck] feel that my presence on the Committee constitutes something of an obstacle to achieving the maximum success that we hope it will be. Accordingly, I should like to resign from the Committee.[266]

Glueck, however, rejected the resignation and persuaded Orlinsky to stay on.[267]

While the back-and-forth correspondence is useful for gaining insight into the debate over the scrolls at HUC-JIR, it did not produce an international conference. Dinur was not particularly pleased with HUC-JIR's decision to move ahead with the symposium and continued, behind the scenes, to push to have the conference further delayed or cancelled.[268] To shore up its position, HUC-JIR turned to the Union Theological Seminary (UTS) in New York City as a cosponsor with the intention that faculty member Muilenberg would agree to join the organizing committee. The idea was for a three-day international conference, ideally alternating between the two institutions' campuses.[269] It seems that Glueck hoped that a joint conference in New York could attract greater participation than if held in Cincinnati. UTS responded positively but, because of Dinur's continued pushing, a date conflict with the Congress of Orientalists,[270] and the inability of certain invitees to attend, Glueck gave up, and the conference was cancelled.[271]

A core group of scholars including Albright, Solomon Zeitlin, Edward Yechezkel Kutscher, and Patrick Skehan eventually met in Philadelphia on 20 May 1957 to celebrate the tenth anniversary of the scrolls' discovery and the first jubilee of Dropsie College.[272] Orlinsky gave the opening address, acknowledging that it had been hoped that the conference at HUC-JIR could have taken place and providing details of some of the planning. The address also provides a wonderful window on Orlinsky's sense of humor. In opening the conference he remarked:

> The Dead Sea Scrolls, as you all know, are so called because they are not dead, they do not come from the sea, and not every one of the documents is a scroll. Otherwise the title is correct…

> The year 1957 marking a decade since the discovery of the Scrolls, provides an opportune time to assess with greater confidence the significance of these documents and perhaps to reach a greater consensus of opinion. It is not secret at all that the Hebrew Union College–Jewish Institute of Religion had planned an international symposium on the Dead Sea Scrolls, to be held in the New York School in September of this year. Competent scholars the world over were to be invited, and panel discussions held in such specific and significant

areas as archaeology, linguistics, biblical textual criticism, rabbinic analysis, palaeography, messianism, and the "teacher of Righteousness."[273] For various reasons, this grand symposium had to be cancelled.…

> This afternoon's Symposium [at Dropsie College] is the first in the world in which the Scrolls will be discussed from A to Z, beginning with Prof. Albright and ending with Prof. Zeitlin.[274]

The conference could have brought HUC-JIR tremendous attention, but it was not to be.[275] At the very least, the effort to bring it about highlights Glueck's interest in the scrolls and his attempt to put the College at the forefront of their scholarship.

In truth, since Jewish scholars were kept from the editorial team for the documents found in Cave 4, the faculty could not have access to the material and so was not involved directly in editing and studying the manuscripts. As early as 1956 or 1957 Sandmel had concerns about access to the unpublished materials:

> Certain people working in the Scrolls, however, have been able to inform me that John [the Baptist] when a youth belonged to the Essenes; one scholar even suggested that the Essenes may have adopted John when he was a boy. Now this may be only speculation—or it may be based, as we have occasionally [been] assured in the past, on Scrolls materials which some have seen but which have not been published yet!"[276]

The conference could have generated an opportunity for a Jewish institution and its scholars to participate in the process of studying the material, despite the issue of access.

Norman Golb
Cincinnati,
May 1962

(©*The American Israelite*, reprinted with permission)

Norman Golb (b. 1928)

At the same time as the conference plans were coming undone, Glueck made a move to hire a replacement for Isaiah Sonne. In his place he hired Norman Golb, who taught at the College in Cincinnati from 1958 until 1963, when he took up an appointment at the University of Chicago, where he continues to teach. According to Golb the two men met in Israel in 1956 while Golb was a Warburg fellow at the Hebrew University of Jerusalem.[277] Golb earned his doctorate with Albright at Johns Hopkins in 1954 with a dissertation titled, "The Cairo Damascus Covenant and Karaite Literature." During 1957–1958 he served as visiting lecturer in Hebrew and Semitic studies at the University of Wisconsin. During that time he published his first academic articles on the scrolls. The first, "Literary and Doctrinal Aspects of the Damascus Covenant in the Light of Karaite Literature,"[278] explored the relationship between specific documents among the Dead Sea Scrolls and some medieval Jewish writings. The second, "The Dietary Laws of the Damascus Covenant in Relation to Those of the Karaites," examined similar issues.[279] In contrast to Zeitlin and others who suggested that the similarities between the scrolls and the medieval sources demonstrated the lateness of the scrolls, Golb concluded, "The presence among the Qumran finds of fragments of the Covenant [extant in a medieval copy] bears witness to its antiquity."[280]

In February 1958 Glueck hired Golb,[281] a student of the scrolls who was committed to their significance and antiquity, to teach on the same campus as Ellis Rivkin and Samuel Sandmel. When Golb arrived in 1958 he recognized that the teaching of the scrolls remained a lacuna in the curriculum. The material had not been taught since Sonne's departure. Golb approached Sandmel, the provost, for permission to teach a course on the scrolls.[282] Permission was granted, and the course appears in the course catalogue as an elective for the years 1958–1959 and 1959–1960:[283]

Apocryphal Literature E2 – Dr Golb –

The Hebrew Texts of the Dead Sea Scrolls. The significance of the Scrolls for the development of Judaism.

Golb recalled that Sandmel was invited to one of the lectures and gave a long diatribe describing the scrolls as valueless.[284] Despite Sandmel's lack of enthusiasm for the scrolls, the course appeared again in the catalogues for 1961–1962 and 1962–1963.

Glueck's enthusiasm for Golb is demonstrable in two ways. First, in 1959, Golb applied to the American Philosophical Society for a grant that would allow him to study in England during the summer of 1959 to continue his work on his project, "The Qumran Covenanters and the Karaites: Studies in Their Relationship."[285] Glueck himself wrote the reference letter to the society noting:

We [HUC-JIR] could not be more satisfied with him than we are. In every way he has fulfilled and is fulfilling the hopes that we had and have for him.… There is no question in my mind but that in his chosen field of work, he will make continuing important contributions.[286]

While the content of the letter might be written off as simply containing the standard platitudes, given that Golb was teaching and researching the Dead Sea Scrolls, Glueck's statement that he was fulfilling the hopes that the institution had for him may have been something more.[287] Between 1958 and 1963, Golb went on to give no fewer than four academic conference presentations and to publish two articles on the scrolls.[288] He also traveled to speak at Reform congregations to share his findings with the community. In 1961 he spoke in the same forum in Montreal, where five years previously Sandmel declared the scrolls inconsequential for reconstructing early Jewish and Christian history. In contrast to Sandmel, Golb noted:

> I would say that for the students of Jewish history the scrolls from Wadi Qumran have considerable value indeed…. They show that medieval sectarianism, while arising in response to the changing social and religious climate of medieval Iraq and Iran, at the same time incorporated within its midst the surviving remnants of a once-active sectarian movement which in Talmudic times had almost faded entirely away…. With regard to the history of religion in general: we may say that these discoveries are of considerable importance for our knowledge of many aspects of religious life in late Hellenistic Palestine.[289]

The contrast between Golb and his faculty colleagues regarding the issue of the scrolls was quite sharp. Golb suggests that after giving his 1959 SBL paper on the Damscus Document, his reception from Rivkin, Sandmel, and Jacob Rader Marcus was less than positive, although Sheldon Blank, who had attended the meeting, was quite pleased with it. The relationship with Rivkin was damaged further when Golb was appointed to substitute teach his history surveys, including ancient Jewish history, while he was on leave with a Guggenheim fellowship in 1962.[290] Whether Glueck had any influence on Golb's choice to teach Rivkin's courses is impossible to say. As provost, Sandmel controlled course assignments. The only alternative instructor for this course on ancient Jewish history would have been Sandmel himself, and administrative affairs likely kept him too busy to take on more teaching. Given that he already disagreed with Rivkin on so many issues concerning ancient Jewish history, replacing him with another colleague with whom he disagreed likely was not a terrible concern; the core course needed to be taught. However, for a brief moment HUC-JIR had a scholar thoroughly engrossed in scroll scholarship who used the scrolls as reliable historical sources while teaching rabbinical students.[291]

The situation was not to last. In 1963 Rivkin returned to his regular teaching, and in mid-1963 Golb left for the University of Chicago. In his letter of resignation, Golb suggested to Glueck that he had considered the new offer "in view of the various circumstances prevailing at the time."[292] At least part of those circumstances, according to Golb, was the discontent of some of his colleagues with his choice of research interests.[293]

To replace Golb, Glueck moved Ben Zion Wacholder from the Los Angeles campus to Cincinnati as professor of Talmud and rabbinics. Although he published and offered courses on the scrolls as early as the 1960s, his major contributions to scroll research and teaching came in the late 1970s and 1980s. His efforts are taken up below. There can be no doubt, however, that from the time of Golb's departure onward, the rabbinical students at the Cincinnati campus had little positive contact with the scrolls, despite Glueck's best efforts.

Bringing the Scrolls to HUC-JIR

HUC-JIR Secures a Copy of the Scrolls

In 1965 the Shrine of the Book was built in West Jerusalem to house the "complete" Dead Sea Scrolls, which had been purchased by Eliezer Sukenik in 1948 and by his son, Yigael Yadin, with the help of Harry Orlinsky, in 1954.[294] In 1967, as noted, the Israelis captured the Palestine Archaeological Museum where the Cave 4 fragments were housed. In light of the war, the Israelis soon recognized that there was a need, for security purposes, to make copies of the scrolls and to house them in a safe locale. This required two things: the funds to make the copies and an institution to house them. In truth, some photographs and negatives of the scrolls were already available. The first complete scrolls discovered had been photographed by John Trever at the American School of Oriental Research in Jerusalem in 1948.[295] The three scrolls Sukenik acquired for the Hebrew University were unrolled and photographed by James and Helena Bieberkraut of the Hebrew University before the end of May 1949. Because three of the four scrolls Sukenik purchased had already been published, only the Genesis Apocryphon remained rolled and unphotographed. These efforts were likewise carried out by the Bieberkrauts in 1954.[296] The vast majority of the photographs of the materials from Caves 4 to 11, which were taken before the Six-Day War, were taken by Najib Albina of the Palestine Archaeological Museum.[297] To help fund the new activities, Avraham Harman, the president of the Hebrew University and a member of the board of trustees of the Shrine of the Book,[298] entered into an agreement with HUC-JIR through the office of president Nelson Glueck. In March 1969 Glueck visited Jerusalem for the meeting of the consortium that supported the College's Biblical Archaeology School in Jerusalem. Much of the visit was, however, devoted to honoring the American biblical scholar William Albright, who was Glueck's mentor. On 13 March 1969 Albright was honored with a dinner at the King David Hotel, where he was presented with a *festschrift* in celebration of his eightieth birthday.[299] This was followed by a celebration at the residence of Israeli President Zalman Shazar, who further honored Albright by naming him a *Yekir ha-Ir* (a "worthy" of the city)[300] on behalf of the city of Jerusalem.

On 19 March Harman and his wife threw a party for Albright at their residence. Glueck sat between Harman and Roland de Vaux and across from Yadin and Albright. It is unclear whether the conversation about the scrolls took place then, but given the company, the topic of the scrolls was almost certainly discussed. Of the dinner discussion, Glueck only notes:

Left to right: *G. Ernest Wright, Nelson Glueck, Zalman Shazar, William F. Albright, Jerusalem, 13 March 1969*

(Courtesy American Jewish Archives)

I utilized the opportunity to discuss with President Harman the possibility of getting 25 double rooms in the Hebrew University's new dormitory building program on Mt. Scopus for our HUC students.... There were several other matters we discussed, including the possibility of some interchange of credits between the Hebrew University and our Jerusalem School.[301]

In reporting on the meeting to HUC-JIR's board of governors, Glueck commented only that Harman had approached him while in Jerusalem:

> In Jerusalem, in March, the President of the Hebrew University came to me and said, 'We are considering making a number of institutions around the world depositories for copies of the negatives and prints of all Dead Sea Scrolls. We would like the Hebrew Union College to be our depository on this continent [North America]. The total cost of this will be X tens of thousands of dollars. If you accept this, I think your cost would be about $15,000.'
>
> I said, 'Well, that sounds too rich for my blood, maybe, how about ten, which I think maybe I could raise.'[302]

The board of trustees of the Shrine of the Book agreed upon the arrangement in mid-April.[303] Harman, who represented the board, suggested that a few sets of high-quality negatives would be produced of the Dead Sea Scrolls. One of these sets, along with one set of positive prints, would be turned over for care to HUC-JIR in Cincinnati with the restriction that they could not be used for any purpose. The agreement further stipulated that eventually the trustees would grant permission for the positives to be available for academic purposes to faculty and students on the Cincinnati and New York campuses and for public display in the College library. No publication of the texts or reproduction would be permitted. When the trustees would eventually decide that the material could be completely released, they would grant HUC-JIR a six-month head start in appreciation of its efforts in securing the negatives. Other institutions would then be granted access. It was also understood that HUC-JIR's position as sole holder of negatives might not remain a unique situation. (It would prove not to be in the 1980s and 1990s, when negatives were placed in the holdings of the Ancient Biblical Manuscript Center in Claremont, California; the Huntington Library in San Marino, California; and at the Oxford Center for Post-Graduate Hebrew Studies in England.) In exchange, HUC-JIR promised the sum of

$10,000 to make the work of duplicating the negatives, printing positives, and establishing an inventory of the material possible.[304]

By early May, with the agreement of HUC-JIR Cincinnati librarian, Herbert Zafren, the assistant to the president in New York, Fritz Bamberger, and the chair of the board of governors, S.L. Kopald Jr., the agreement was ratified.[305] Glueck made clear to Harman that it would take some time before the funds could be secured. Glueck sent a letter asking board member Philip D. Sang for the funds in late April.[306] The two met at Chicago's Standard Club during the week of 14 May and Sang, who, between at least 1966 and 1970, chaired HUC-JIR's committee on library and archives,[307] agreed to provide the $10,000.[308] Glueck immediately reported the news to Harman.[309]

Glueck's approach to Sang is particularly important in understanding the significance of this activity for Glueck and HUC-JIR. In describing the opportunity, Glueck called it "a great coup for our Hebrew Union College."[310] However, asking Sang for the money was an act of double-dipping, which may have proved damaging. Simultaneous to this request, the College was conducting a capital campaign for a new building on the Jerusalem campus. To that point, only $250,000 of the $400,000 budgeted for the project had been raised, and construction had already begun. Glueck approached Sang for $50,000 on top of the funds for the scrolls, which he did not receive.[311] Glueck's motivation for acquiring the negatives and prints was quite clear—the $10,000 would provide the College "with the privilege of showing the prints at our various schools before anybody else is permitted to."[312] But that was certainly not Glueck's only motivation. His enthusiasm stemmed at least in part from the scrolls being a great archaeological discovery. On top of acquiring the security copy of the scrolls, Glueck also purchased a large ceramic jar and lid from the site of Qumran.[313] As well, the $10,000 for Harman may have been a *quid pro quo*. Glueck needed residence rooms in the dormitory at Hebrew University for HUC-JIR students studying in Jerusalem, primarily through an American Friends of the Hebrew University program, and Harman needed the funds for the scrolls.[314] More likely than that, though, was Glueck's first-hand knowledge that the scrolls could never be entirely secure while they were in Jerusalem. A security copy was a necessity, as Glueck had seen when he was in Israel immediately following the Six Day War in 1967. Glueck had toured the Rockefeller Museum (formerly the Palestine Archaeological Museum), where the scrolls had been stored, studied, and exhibited when the Jordanians had controlled East Jerusalem. It was Glueck's first access to the Museum since 1947, and the destruction from the days of warring in the previous weeks made a significant impression on him:

> Later on in the afternoon, when we got back to Jerusalem, Moshe Dothan
> and Levi Yitzhak Rachmani of the Israel Archaeological Museum took us

through the heavily padlocked and strongly guarded Palestine or Rockefeller Archaeological Museum. It had gotten shot up pretty much, and in some places bullet shells were scattered about. They told us that during the last few days a half dozen unexploded shells had been removed. If they had not been duds, the museum would have been destroyed and the invaluable collections smashed to dust.... Some of the collections in the museum were partly shattered by bullets hitting display cases, but others stood comparatively intact.... The Dead Sea Scrolls material has not yet been checked. The writing tablets[315] of Qumran have been partly broken but can be repaired again.[316]

In light of his experience, he very much understood the need for the security copy of the scrolls. How could he not find the funds?

In mid-July 1969, Glueck was again in Israel and met with Harman to further discuss the housing issue for HUC-JIR students in Jerusalem. Harman promised fifty beds in the Hebrew University residences. The conversation then turned to the scrolls project and a new offer. Harman was very pleased that HUC-JIR was providing the $10,000. In light of HUC-JIR's support he hoped that Glueck might be able to help raise an additional $50,000 to sponsor a Hebrew University project to microfilm the manuscripts preserved in St. Catherine's Monastery in the Sinai.[317] Although Glueck was enthusiastic about the new project, the College could not risk its own fundraising, as Glueck wrote to the director of the Klau library:[318]

> If we stumble across someone who might donate to us $50,000 to be given to the Hebrew University for this purpose, the HUC would be the recipient of one complete positive copy of all the manuscripts microfilmed at St. Catherine's Monastery by the Hebrew University.
>
> It goes without saying that such a $50,000 gift would be one that might not otherwise be given to HUC for its most direct needs or would be one that someone would give in addition to whatever he gave to HUC.
>
> If such a sum were available, I am very anxious to cooperate with the Hebrew University and the President Avraham Harman on this project.[319]

Glueck was not quite as motivated about this project as he had been with the scrolls. Perhaps the financial strain was too great; perhaps the Sang donation for the scrolls at the expense of a contribution to the building fund had made Glueck somewhat more wary. In any case, the College does not appear to have raised the funds.

At the end of February 1970 Magen Broshi, curator of the Dead Sea Scrolls for the Israel Museum from 1964 until 1994, forwarded a copy of a negative to Glueck as an example of the quality of the work then underway. By that point, four hundred of the presumed one thousand negatives had been made.[320] The unnumbered negative on Kodak film measures 5 inches (128mm) tall and

7 inches (178mm) wide.[321] The text can be identified as a letter on papyrus from the administrators of Bet-Mašiko to Yešua' ben Galgula published as Wadi Murabba'at Papyrus No. 42 in 1960.[322]

By November the negatives had still not been received. Bamberger, who was responsible for "scholarly projects and public relations,"[323] pushed Glueck to follow up with Broshi. Bamberger hoped that, at the very least, some of the four hundred negatives could be sent so that the College could hold a public event and garner publicity.[324] Given the financial investment and the very limited access promised in return, the only real benefit that the College could hope for was the publicity for the school.

Bamberger was not the only one troubled that monies had been sent but that no goods had been received. The College librarians and Glueck were rather concerned and were curious as to the whereabouts of the negatives.[325] Two weeks later Broshi replied that the materials had mostly been photographed and that some 1,200 negatives were already copied. He offered to bring them personally to the College's representative in New York in January 1971.[326]

Broshi's letter of December 1970 raised a significant new issue. While the original agreement between Glueck and Harman satisfied the Israelis, another group had an interest in who would control and have access to a set of negatives. After the discovery of the Cave 4 cache in 1952, the Jordanian government, who at that time controlled the area where the scrolls were found, granted publication rights to scholars picked by G. Lankester Harding, the Jordanian director of antiquities, and de Vaux, of the École Biblique et Archéologique Française, who chaired the board of trustees of the Palestine Archaeological Museum (later the Rockefeller), where the fragments were housed.[327] As an act of goodwill after the capture of East Jerusalem and the museum, the Israeli authorities allowed these scholars to maintain their exclusive publication rights.[328] To maintain quiet from the members of this editorial team, a group of "worried unfriendly people,"[329] a formal restrictive agreement was to be required of HUC-JIR that would explicitly prohibit the use of the negatives (and presumably the positives that had not yet been made and would later prove an issue), "for study, reproduction or any other purpose,"[330] without the express written permission from the board of directors of the Shrine of the Book. The agreement raised particular concerns for Zafren, who could not understand why the College would pay "a rather large sum of money to have a negative made and then [would be] asked to become the custodian of materials that [could not] be used for any purpose—and this without time limit."[331] The College delayed its response to the agreement, first while it decided how to respond,[332] and then as a result of Glueck's death on 12 February 1971. His successor, Alfred Gottschalk, responded to the draft agreement in November 1971 with a modified version based on suggestions from Zafren.[333] In contrast to the draft Broshi forwarded, the College agreed to "not use or allow the use of the negatives for reproduction or for any purpose other than study without an explicit written authorization" from the board of the Shrine of the Book.[334]

By March 1972 no response was forthcoming from Broshi or any other representative of the board of trustees. Although no letter is preserved, Gottschalk's action after 6 March[335] encouraged Broshi to ship 1,348 negatives via El Al Israel Airlines on 24 March 1972.[336] A follow-up letter from Broshi indicates his certainty that the College would guard the scrolls but makes absolutely no mention of the specific details of the official agreement to which Gottschalk had responded.[337] Gottschalk and Zafren remained under the impression that the shipping of the negatives indicated the approval of the agreement's reformulation, allowing the material to be studied by HUC-JIR faculty and students.

When the negatives finally arrived, the College was greatly pleased to receive them but was concerned that neither the positives nor a complete inventory list had been included with the shipment. Since the goal of securing a set of prints in Cincinnati was to ensure that a complete set was preserved, the inventory list was absolutely necessary.[338] The assembly of an inventory list by Broshi and the Israelis was somewhat complicated by the fact that the members of the editorial team were not entirely cooperative. From 1960 on, most no longer lived in Jerusalem; and, since Israel's takeover in 1967, some, like Jozef T. Milik, refused to return to Jerusalem. The initial list for assembling the negatives was accomplished with the cooperation of de Vaux, the editor-in-chief, by asking each of the team members to turn over a list of photographs of their as-yet unpublished allocations. De Vaux's death on 10 September 1971 complicated the process of arranging and collating the lists. By contrast, the Israelis did not see the set of positives as a necessity and did not immediately make them.[339] An incomplete inventory list finally arrived in mid-June 1972.[340] Because the negatives were only identified by numbers, HUC-JIR's collection was worthless for study, as the individual negatives could not be identified. Further, the negatives could be damaged by use. The College continued to wait for the positives.

Gottschalk and Broshi were scheduled to meet in Jerusalem in the summer of 1972 to discuss the issue of the photographic positives, but it does not appear that the meeting took place.[341] By early the following year, the College was still concerned that the positives and the complete inventory list had not arrived, and it still had not been able to use the material for publicity purposes. After four years, no one but the parties directly involved knew of HUC-JIR's participation and cooperation in helping provide security for Israel's national treasures.

Releasing the Scrolls

The matter remained quiet until October 1975, when Michael Klein, the Targum specialist on the faculty of the Jerusalem campus, requested the opportunity to view several negatives in the HUC-JIR collection.[342] Because the acquisition of the negatives was never made public, it remains unclear how

Klein came to know of it; but it is most likely that he discovered it from his sources in Jerusalem.[343] The request opened the issue of how the original agreement should be understood.

Gottschalk understood his agreement to "not use or allow the use of the negatives for reproduction or for any purpose other than study without an explicit written authorization" from the board of the Shrine of the Book to mean that "a scholar who wishes to study the material has the right to do so and with that would undoubtedly go the right to publish the findings of his study, providing he gives proper credit in the footnote apparatus."[344] Zafren accepted that the material could be studied, and although he hoped that Gottschalk's interpretation was correct, thought that the publication of the results of the study would be unacceptable.[345] Both men agreed that Broshi should be consulted before granting permission for Klein to use the material. In fact, Zafren recommended to Klein that he approach Broshi for specific permission.[346] Zafren contacted Broshi in July 1976 for general clarification of the policy, as well as to remind him that the College was still due the positives and a complete inventory list going back to the original agreement between Glueck and Harman in 1969. Broshi's response to the inquiry for permission was one of surprise. In fact, he quoted back the words of the original draft agreement to Zafren indicating that the College "shall not use or allow the use of the negatives for study, reproduction or any other purpose."[347] It seems rather clear Broshi either never read closely or ignored Gottschalk's response of November 1971. Broshi's position was rather sensitive as he, and the Israeli authorities, had agreed to preserve the exclusive publication rights of the international editorial team that had been working on the material since its discovery in the early 1950s.[348] Zafren was convinced that the Israeli refusal to forward the promised inventory list and the positives was a way of ensuring that the materials could not be used at all, since using the negatives would risk seriously damaging them.[349] Broshi and Gottschalk agreed to meet to discuss the issues further during the summer of 1976.

Broshi, Gottschalk, and Klein met on 29 July 1976 at the HUC-JIR Jerusalem campus. The result of the conversations was that the negatives could not be used for any purpose but that the Shrine of the Book would help to the best of its ability to get access to the material for HUC-JIR's scholars. However, that access to the unpublished material would still require the permission of the individual editors assigned to publish it. According to Broshi, a new inventory list was being

Avraham Harman and Alfred Gottschalk, Cincinnati, Undated

(Courtesy American Jewish Archives)

compiled but, because of financial difficulties, the positives were expected to be delayed for several more years.[350] Broshi encouraged Klein to approach the editors, Patrick Skehan, Pierre Benoit, and Milik, directly for permission to access the fragments of 4Q Targum Leviticus, which interested him.[351]

Klein did contact Skehan and he replied, but the result was not positive for either scholar. In responding to Klein, Skehan wrote:

> Since I note that your letter included a carbon copy to Dr. Magen Broshi, I feel obliged to tell you in addition, that I should not under any circumstance grant through any Israeli functionary, any permission to dispense, for any purpose, or to any extent, of anything whatsoever that is lawfully housed in the Palestine Archaeological Museum.[352]

Klein did not get to see the texts; and Skehan's response had shades of anti-Israel bias and, as some suggested, antisemitism.[353]

From HUC-JIR's perspective, the matter was laid to rest until January 1980, when by coincidence two events took place. First, HUC-JIR professor Jacob Rader Marcus suggested to Zafren that the College library explore the possibility of acquiring a security copy of photographs of all the manuscripts in the Jewish National and University Library in Jerusalem.[354] This led to Zafren's suggestion to Gottschalk that they take up the issue of permission to use the negatives again with Broshi, since neither the complete inventory list nor the positives had been received.[355]

Almost simultaneously, James Sanders and Elizabeth Hay Bechtel of the Ancient Biblical Manuscript Center in California approached Harman at the Hebrew University for permission to store archival-quality copies of the negatives of the scrolls for security purposes.[356] The approach was made after consultation with Yadin and Benoit, the editor-in-chief following de Vaux's death, and was based on Sanders's assumption that he was helping to fulfill Yadin's desire to have a security copy of the scrolls stored away from Israel.[357] It is clear from his original request to Harman that Sanders did not know of the agreement with HUC-JIR or the negatives housed in Cincinnati. As a result of that meeting, Sanders learned that HUC-JIR had a copy of the negatives. Sanders turned to Avraham Biran, the director of the Nelson Glueck School of Biblical Archaeology of the Jerusalem Campus of HUC-JIR.[358] Biran directed Sanders to Gottschalk and Zafren, since the negatives were in Cincinnati. Zafren in particular was disturbed by what he thought was Sanders's "desire to 'relieve' [HUC-JIR] of the Dead Sea Scrolls material,"[359] but neither was opposed to an additional set of negatives being made, providing that no group would have access to the material for research purposes and publication before HUC-JIR. Zafren also suggested that it might be best if HUC-JIR provided the funds for the positives to be made.[360] At least then they would be assured of having a copy. The letters between Zafren and Sanders are quite cordial, and it should

be remembered that Sanders was the
first graduate student to complete a
doctorate at HUC-JIR in Cincinnati
in 1954, during Zafren's first years
following his appointment as librarian of the Cincinnati Klau Library
in 1950. Sanders's request created
no bad blood, and he spoke at the
College several times subsequently.[361]
In the end, however, new positives
were made from the negatives at the
Shrine of the Book between 1984
and 1986, and these were deposited
at the Ancient Biblical Manuscript
Center.[362] The communication from Sanders did raise some concerns for
HUC-JIR. It had been a decade since the original agreement was made. The
College still had not received the positive prints or the complete inventory list
that they had, in essence, paid for. Further, they still had not been able to use
the materials for publicity purposes. Finally, the deposition of another copy
of the negatives in the United States meant that the six-month head-start on
scholarship and exhibition promised to Glueck was at risk.[363]

*James A. Sanders, Nelson Glueck, and
G. Ernest Wright, New York, 7 June 1970*
(Courtesy American Jewish Archives)

Broshi and Zafren met in Jerusalem in late May 1980.[364] Although
Gottschalk had encouraged Zafren to use the meeting "to break this open and
free the issue,"[365] the meeting did not achieve this goal. The men agreed that a
new inventory list would be supplied and that inquiries would be made as to
the cost of producing prints from the negatives.[366] By the end of June Broshi
informed Zafren that Elisha Qimron[367] was at work on the new inventory lists,
with Bechtel supplying the funds for the project. It was expected that the cost
of producing the prints from 2,500 total negatives would amount to between
$1,850 for 13x18cm contacts and $3,700 for 18x24cm prints.[368] The College
did not want to supply the funds for images that could not be used, particularly
since the original $10,000 contribution was supposed to guarantee copies for
them. However, at least in their discussions, the College representatives hoped
that if they put forward the funds for positives, Broshi might be able to arrange
more access to the materials.[369] By that point, though, Gottschalk was becoming
more troubled by the restrictions and encouraged Zafren to approach Biran in
Jerusalem to work on the College's behalf to get more access.[370] Biran joined
HUC-JIR in 1974 after retiring from his position as director of the Department
of Antiquities of the State of Israel (since September 1989, the Israel Antiquities
Authority, or IAA), where he had served from 1961 until 1974. Prior to his
appointment to the Department of Antiquities he had served as the Israeli consul
in Los Angeles, the military governor of Jerusalem, and liaison between the

United Nations and the Israeli military. His relationship with Nelson Glueck went back to his participation in the latter's archaeological excavations in the 1930s.[371]

Although primarily an archaeologist concerned with Iron Age Israel, Biran had a special connection to the Dead Sea Scrolls. During the Six Day War of June 1967, Yadin served as the liaison between the Israeli Prime Minister, the military chief of staff, and the defense minister. On Thursday, 15 June, Yadin was informed that the Rockefeller Museum had been captured by Israeli troops from the Jordanian Arab Legion. He contacted Hebrew University professor Nahman Avigad and the director of the Department of Antiquities, Biran, to go to the museum and ensure that the scrolls were in safes to protect them during the continued mortar fire. Biran and Avigad, as Yadin notes, were the first Israeli scholars to have access to the Cave 4 material since its discovery fifteen years earlier.[372] Further, Biran was involved in establishing Israel's agreement with de Vaux and the editorial committee. Several weeks following the war, de Vaux met with antiquities director Biran and Yadin on behalf of the Shrine of the Book. They met at Biran's new office at the Rockefeller, where it had been moved from its previous location at the Israel Museum. Biran described the meeting as follows:

> De Vaux was worried that we would not honor the agreement they had with Jordan.... We assured him that we would. We felt that we had to honor the rights of scholars working on the material. It would be completely unfair for us to come and say: 'You can't work on something' after they had spent years on it.[373]

Despite the possibilities that Biran's history and connections offered, the College decided to wait until the inventory list had been received before involving him. If the Israelis decided not to send the list because of Biran's interference, the College would be left with $10,000 in unidentifiable negatives.[374] The desire to hold off in pushing for access may have also been influenced by direct contact from Sanders in late August. The possibility remains that HUC-JIR saw Sanders as an ally in getting the material released. Sanders informed Zafren that Broshi, Benoit, and others had agreed to allow new negatives to be made and stored at the Ancient Biblical Manuscript Center. Sanders turned to Zafren to get a better idea of the quantity of negatives in HUC-JIR's collection to delineate which materials still needed to be photographed.[375] The discussion preserved in the correspondence focuses on the issue of whether HUC-JIR's 1,347 negatives accounted for the whole collection.[376] It seems that Zafren, in particular, wanted to make sure that when access was granted, HUC-JIR would have copies of all the Qumran material. The discussion Sanders initiated encouraged Zafren to approach Broshi once again for a copy of the inventory list so that HUC-JIR might see if its collection was complete and to finally inform him that the College could not supply the funds to produce the positives.[377] A preliminary inventory list by Qimron was supplied in early January 1981. The final inventory, a total of three lists, was completed in July 1981[378] and turned over to Zafren during a visit to Jerusalem in mid-August.[379]

However, despite these moves forward, the issue of access to the material remained. In July 1982, Gottschalk approached Harman, with whom the original agreement had been made, to have him lift the restrictions. According to Gottschalk, Harman acceded to his request in a personal conversation. However, in August, Gottschalk was still waiting for written confirmation.[380] And so, the College waited. In fact, for the next nine years the College took no explicit action to release the material. In part there was no need to release it. With the exception of Klein in Jerusalem, who had already had his hand slapped by the editorial team, no HUC-JIR faculty members were calling for access to the material; and among outside scholars only Sanders, who had access to a copy at his own institution, knew the details of HUC-JIR's collection, since no publicity had ever been prepared.

In 1989 things changed. That June, Hershel Shanks, publisher of *Biblical Archaeology Review,* made the first bold challenge to the scrolls' editorial team in public.[381] His call was not entirely new, as he had raised the issue of the delayed scroll publication in print already five years earlier.[382] But the 1989 effort was the beginning of a crusade to get the material released to the public and to scholars outside the Dead Sea Scroll editorial team.[383] The public outcry, which resulted in response to Shanks's challenge, encouraged Gottschalk and Zafren to make another attempt to get permission to release their material to HUC-JIR's faculty and students. On 28 September 1989 Zafren (with Gottschalk's approval) wrote to Broshi that the College intended to give access to the negatives to the faculty and students for study purposes in line with oral arrangements made with Harman in 1982.[384] As well, by this point Ben Zion Wacholder, professor of Talmud and rabbinics at HUC-JIR, Cincinnati, claimed to have heard rumors that students in Jerusalem and California had been given access to the material and took this information to Zafren and Gottschalk.[385] Wacholder had good reason to want the scrolls released.

Wacholder joined the Cincinnati faculty in 1963 after six years as the librarian of the Los Angeles campus.[386] Although his academic background was in Greek historiography, his early serious interest in the scrolls is evidenced by his first publications on the topic in 1964 and 1966.[387] Over the next forty years he published more than a dozen articles and two books, the most recent in 2007.[388] The first evidence of Wacholder explicitly teaching about the scrolls at HUC-JIR, Cincinnati, appears in the 1964–1966 course catalogue, where he was scheduled to teach a Talmud elective (Talmud E-10) titled "The Qumran Texts and Early Halakhah." The course was offered for the next decade and a half. Beginning with Yadin's publication of the Temple Scroll in 1977,[389] Wacholder began teaching seminars on it[390] and offering more general introductory courses, which he continued to offer until his retirement.[391] His students, including Martin Abegg,[392] James Bowley,[393] and John Kampen,[394] have continued to make contributions to Dead Sea Scroll studies.[395]

In 1983 Wacholder published *The Dawn of Qumran*. The book argues that the scroll identified previously as the Temple Scroll should best be understood as a new Torah, superior to the Mosaic Torah, written by the Teacher of Righteousness, Zadok, for the community established at the end of days. At the time, the book was lauded for the theses it put forth. As James VanderKam suggested in his review of the book, "Wacholder's theses are extremely important.... It would come as no surprise if the book should prove to be one of the most important and widely discussed publications on the Dead Sea Scrolls."[396] With time, Wacholder's views have come to be seen as idiosyncratic, but the challenges he raised to the accepted convention in 1983 are still appreciated for their importance.[397] The issue here, though, is not to judge the quality of the argument but to set the context for the events that follow.[398]

In his earliest efforts, Wacholder notes that his conclusions were provisional.[399] He was well aware that the limited body of Qumran material available made substantial conclusions difficult for those who were not privy to the content of the unpublished scrolls. The acknowledgements in *The Dawn of Qumran* indicate Wacholder's appreciation to John Strugnell, who shared "his notes on the hitherto unpublished fragments of the sectarian Torah."[400] Wacholder, like most other scholars, was forced to rely on the kindness of the editors to see Qumran materials even thirty years after their discovery, and the situation was not soon to change.

In May 1985 Wacholder attended a New York University conference on the Dead Sea Scrolls in memory of Yadin.[401] The activities at the conference inspired Shanks, among others, to question the lock that the editorial team had on the scrolls. Strugnell, who at that time was still editor-in-chief, gave a paper and shared photos of his text.[402] Wacholder was

The New York University Conference on the Dead Sea Scrolls in Memory of Yigael Yadin, New York, May 1985.
Left to right, standing: *Elisha Qimron, Daniel R. Schwartz, Hartmut Stegemann, John J. Collins, Johann Maier, Lawrence Schiffman.* Left to right, seated: *Joseph M. Baumgarten, Harry M. Orlinsky, Ben Zion Wacholder, John Strugnell, Carol A. Newsom*

(Courtesy American Jewish Archives)

impressed with the new texts, but the level of aggrava-
tion that he and other scholars must have felt at having
to wait for bits and pieces of new scrolls information
can only be imagined.[403] Recounting another incident,
Shanks reported that later in the conference Strugnell
described the progress that was being made on publishing the material:

> Strugnell's report on publication progress was followed,
> as were other sessions, by an opportunity for questions. A
> question was posed to Strugnell by Ben Zion Wacholder
> who recently completed an important book-length
> study, entitled *The Dawn of Qumran*, on the Temple
> Scroll and fragments of it already published. Wacholder,
> a white-haired concentration camp survivor, is almost

Ben Zion Wacholder,
Cincinnati, Undated

(Courtesy American
Jewish Archives)

totally blind (he can tell time by holding his watch to within an inch of his
right eye), so he has perforce almost memorized the contents of the Temple
Scroll and its fragments. His interest in the subject is understandably keen.
He would love to "see"—have read to him, as is his customary method
of learning—a still unpublished fragment of the Temple Scroll. Docilely,
Wacholder asked Strugnell if he knew whether the unpublished fragment
of the Temple Scroll contained any portions of text that were not in the
published scroll and its fragments.[404] Strugnell replied that the unpublished
fragment did contain additional text, but that the new material probably
did not add anything especially significant; he then said, however, that the
unpublished fragment was approximately 25 years older than the published
texts of the Temple Scroll. Grateful, Wacholder thanked Strugnell for
the information. [405]

Describing the event in a later interview, Shanks described Wacholder and other
scholars on the outside like him:

> 'These guys are sitting around the table wide-eyed,' Shanks recalled, acidly
> mimicking the Eastern European accent of one prominent scholar, 'Vunderful
> … vunderful!' 'And they can't even see the material. Inside they're seething
> with anger.'[406]

Shanks's recollections are somewhat problematic because his reporting of these
stories deliberately served his propagandist agenda of pushing for the release
of the scrolls. That is, he needed to portray Wacholder as the sympathetic old
man. In fact, Wacholder would use a similar tactic in his sole description of
these events. In a 1991 interview, when asked why he pushed so hard to have
the scrolls released, Wacholder's response was consistent with Shanks's view:
He said, "I'm sick and tired of all this waiting" and worried "he would not live
to see many more texts" because of the slow publication process.[407]

Shanks's intuition about the general situation was accurate. The scholars were caught. If they wanted those who had access to share what they knew, they could not attack them for not releasing the material. Certainly it must have been a frustrating situation. The rumors Wacholder heard in 1989 of others selectively gaining access to the materials must have been all that much more frustrating, and that he saw them as an opportunity to have HUC-JIR open access to their negatives to him is certainly understandable.

But, Broshi denied the rumors. His response, which he claimed to have penned within a half hour of receiving Zafren's letter that suggested that the College would be breaking the contract, came with an implicit threat: "I am afraid that a decision like this will create a scandal, I do not see how you could defend yourself."[408]

Gottschalk and Zafren fundamentally agreed that the fact that the original negatives had been sent based on Gottschalk's agreement not to use the material for a purpose other than study gave them the unilateral right to release the material to their staff and students. What remained was the question of whether they should do so, as Zafren noted: "The bottom-line may be that we have a 'legal' basis to act unilaterally, but this won't resolve the question of whether we *want* to do what the Shrine of the Book asks us not to do."[409] They decided to approach Broshi for the rights to make the negatives of already published material available.[410] The motivation for releasing already published material is unclear. If it was already published, who needed to see the negatives? One may suppose that the negatives included some images of previously published scrolls that had not appeared and that, if part of the collection was made available, the rest might soon follow. In response to this approach to Broshi, the board of the Shrine of the Book had Harman reply to Gottschalk. The reply indicated that the board was only the trustee for the original seven scrolls acquired by Sukenik and Yadin and not any of the fragments.[411] The College could use negatives of the original scrolls. By contrast, permission to use images of the fragments would require permission of Amir Drori, the director of the Division of Antiquities of the Israel Ministry of Education and Culture.[412] Harman copied Drori on the letter; Drori concurred with Harman's assessment and emphasized that no use whatsoever could be made of the negatives of unpublished material without the permission of the IAA and the editor responsible for the fragments.[413] Harman's letter highlights an important issue. Part of the difficulty HUC-JIR and others faced in trying to have the scrolls released was that it was never clear who had control of any particular piece. The players were numerous: the IAA, the board of the Shrine of the Book, Broshi, and the editors individually and collectively.

During this same period a potential ally contacted HUC-JIR. At the end of December, Shanks contacted the College for an explanation of its agreement regarding the negatives in its collection. Shanks's particular interest was in whether there was a written agreement between the College and Israeli authorities.[414] As Shanks acknowledged in the letter, the news of HUC-JIR's having the negatives was never made public. Shanks's inquiry is even more interesting in light of the fact that he announced before a crowd of 325 people at the University of Cincinnati on 31 October, more than a month earlier, that HUC-JIR had copies of the scrolls for safekeeping, "[b]ut their scholars cannot look at them."[415] He certainly seemed to know the details of the agreement. Exactly who told whom what, or who leaked the information, remains unclear. However, Shanks had frequent contact with Wacholder at various conferences and with Michael Klein. His friendship with Klein went back to 1973 and was close enough that their families had traveled together.[416] Of this period Shanks notes, "Michael gave me greatly needed emotional support in the dark days of the fight to free the Dead Sea Scrolls, when most of Israel—the scholars, the archaeologists, the media and the courts—seemed to be against me."[417] Klein supported Shanks's efforts and had supplied him with the letter he had received from Skehan. Klein, in fact, suggested to Zafren that HUC-JIR support Shanks's efforts by pushing Broshi to let the College make the negatives available to the faculty and students. After Gottschalk informed Broshi that he intended to make the materials available for study, Broshi approached Klein. Concerning this meeting Klein reported:

> Finally, I told Broshi that I thought that your decision might even have the favorable effect of putting additional pressure on the assigned scholars who have been tarrying for decades and delaying the publication of important texts to which they have had exclusive access. I thought that this might help the campaign that Hershel Shanks has been waging in *BAR* for several years. I think this shocked Broshi and he begged me not to 'pour oil on the fire by communicating this to you.'[418]

However, Shanks was not the ally HUC-JIR wanted at that particular moment, although the relationship between Wacholder and Shanks later proved quite significant. Zafren's response to Shanks made clear that the College had no plans to release the material without Israeli approval. The letter is carefully worded. According to Zafren, the College agreed "not to allow any further reproduction or publication of the material in [HUC-JIR's] trust." He made no mention of allowing study access to the students and faculty, refusing to concede this point to the Israelis. Zafren highlighted that the Israeli interpretation of the agreement was that the negatives were a security copy, not to be used, and that the College "was honor-bound by a commitment made twenty years ago."[419] Highlighting the Israeli interpretation may have been Zafren telling Shanks that he disagreed, but nothing came of this interaction except to provide Shanks details he could use in his campaign.

The College's efforts to make photographs of the early published scrolls available continued. At least initially, the goal was to provide access for the faculty and students. However, Zafren in particular wanted to make the material available to scholars everywhere. On the one hand, the issue was simply doing what was right regarding the role of a library;[420] on the other, he did not want the College accused of engaging in unfair competition practices.[421] In an early draft of Gottschalk's letter to Harman, he responded that he was grateful that the board of the Shrine of the Book made the "scrolls open for study by our students and faculty,"[422] while the final letter was changed to read simply "open for study."[423] Further, the College requested that positive photographs of at least these scrolls be provided to HUC-JIR in line with the original letter of agreement between Harman and Glueck in 1969, just as the College continued to honor that agreement by not releasing the negatives in its care.[424] By May 1990, no response was received from Harman,[425] and the situation remained stagnant well into August 1991.[426] Although Shanks shared the news of HUC-JIR's collection of negatives in *Biblical Archaeology Review* in late 1989,[427] the College continued to keep the news of their negatives quiet. A synagogue lecturer approached Zafren for material about the negatives, and while he shared limited information he noted:

> We have never publicly announced that we have these materials nor have we ever publicly denied it. I suppose it is no longer a secret, and I trust that you will use your best judgment in introducing information into your discussion.... and, as you can see, no useful purpose would be served by announcing that we have unusable material.[428]

In any case, limiting the requests for access that the College would have to deny would only have proven an inconvenience. Shanks hoped that the publicity would promote a public backlash, that the team of editors, the IAA, and the institutions housing negatives, would all feel pressured to ensure that "outside scholars are given access to the unpublished documents for their own research."[429]

Taking Matters into Their Own Hands: A Professor, a Student, a Concordance, and a Personal Computer

In 1988 Ben Zion Wacholder approached John Strugnell, the editor-in-chief, for permission to photocopy the Dead Sea Scrolls concordance assembled in Jerusalem. It is reported that the two scholars were traveling together in a taxi to give papers at a conference at Haifa University to celebrate the fortieth anniversary of the scrolls when Wacholder raised the issue of the concordance.[430] The concordance had been compiled on 3 inch by 5 inch cards in the scrollery in Jerusalem in the late 1950s by Joseph Fitzmyer, Raymond Brown, Willard Oxtoby, and Javier Teixidor. The fact of its existence had largely been kept a secret until its limited publication for the editors' use in 1988.[431] In a mid-1986 interview that Shanks conducted with Avi Eitan, Israel's then-director of antiquities, Shanks could not get Eitan to confirm that the concordance existed. Only in reviewing the transcript of the interview did he finally confirm it.[432] In the interview, Shanks kept pushing Eitan to admit the importance of the concordance to scholars since they could not see the scrolls themselves, but he would not take up the issue. In any case, Strugnell granted the permission in a private letter to Wacholder and sent him a formal authorization to be used if Wacholder could find a party willing to copy the 2,500 pages of the concordance.[433] Wacholder's relationship with Strugnell was quite positive, and Strugnell had helped Wacholder by making his own notes about unpublished texts available to him when Wacholder was preparing *The Dawn of Qumran*.[434] The official release indicated that the copy was for "Prof. B.Z. Wacholder"[435] but includes no specific restrictions as to its use. Wacholder approached David Gilner, the librarian at HUC-JIR, Cincinnati, for aid in acquiring a copy.[436] Gilner agreed on condition that in exchange for covering the amount it would cost to copy and bind the volumes,[437] Wacholder should allow it to become library property rather than a personal copy. According to Gilner, Wacholder did not want to pay for the copy and agreed to the conditions.[438] Since there were no particular restrictions, ownership of the copy was not an issue. Gilner approached Baltimore Hebrew College professor Joseph Baumgarten, who granted permission for his college to copy the volumes.[439] However, the copying had to be delayed because he would be taking the copy for his personal use to Jerusalem between January and May 1990.[440] In March, a notice appeared in *BAR* about the availability of the concordance. According to the notice, a copy was deposited in the Harvard Divinity School library for in-library use. Baltimore Hebrew College likewise had a copy for in-library use (although the notice points out that at press time it was unavailable because it was in the possession of Baumgarten.)[441] Of particular interest is a statement in the notice that one of the reasons for avoiding broad availability of the concordance was possibly the concern of the editors that "an unauthorized person might reconstruct an unpublished text by using" it.[442] Perhaps the *BAR* editors meant for the statement to inspire efforts. In the meantime, Gilner asked the Harvard University Library to acquire a copy for Wacholder.[443] In April 1990 Harvard declined to copy the material because unbinding the five volumes and copying the material would be too complex.[444]

Meanwhile pressure was building on the editorial team to release more of their material. In response, Strugnell, the editor-in-chief, said in an interview with ABC's *Good Morning America* of those applying pressure: "It seems we've acquired a bunch of fleas who are in the business of annoying us." Responding, *BAR* published what journalist Neil Asher Silberman has called the "most famous and most outrageous of Hershel Shanks's *BAR* covers."[445] At the center of the cover Strugnell's face appears on a television screen with the quote below. Surrounding the image are large silhouettes of fleas with the names of the "annoying" scholars and various institutions identifying them. Wacholder's name is emblazoned on a flea in the lower right corner and is quoted inside as simply noting that, "Almost anybody who doesn't have access is frustrated."[446] An editorial note suggests that anyone else who "wants to be an acknowledged flea" should communicate with *BAR.* Two volumes later, among the identified fleas, was Stephen Kaufman, Wacholder's Cincinnati colleague.[447] Kaufman noted that the pressure tactics were working and that Wacholder had been granted permission to publish several fragments and photographs of previously unpublished Temple Scroll fragments.[448] On 5 March 1990, Wacholder received copies of five plates of the fragments of 11QT[b] and official permission from the IAA to publish them.[449] The article appeared in the *Hebrew Union College Annual* in 1991.[450] The problem with these fragments, however, was that they were from Cave 11. In contrast to the Cave 4 material, which the editorial team controlled tightly, permission to publish some Cave 11 material, including these particular fragments, had been granted to the Dutch Academy of Sciences in exchange for financial support in 1962.[451] It was the Dutch who owned the publication rights and not the editorial team who had granted Wacholder permission to publish the texts. However, all the photographic plates included in the article indicate that permission to reproduce them was granted by both the Dutch and the IAA who appear to have shared control of the images. Thus, Kaufman's assertion was correct regarding the Dutch but not the Cave 4 editorial team.

Returning to the issue of the concordance, because of Harvard's refusal to cooperate, Gilner approached Baumgarten again in May 1990.[452] The copies were completed in early August[453] and bound and sent in October.[454] The HUC-JIR library catalogued the volumes as reference works and stored them in the reserves cage for added security, with the intention of having open in-library use by November. The concordance drew no immediate publicity, and its primary user was Martin Abegg, Wacholder's research assistant and a graduate student working on a doctoral dissertation on the War Scroll.[455] He received permission to remove the material from the cage for more extended periods.[456]

At the 1990 Society of Biblical Literature meeting in New Orleans, Abegg offered a paper based on his dissertation research, "4Q491 (4QMilhama[a])—An 'Ensemble' of Manuscripts?"[457] The response to his paper was troubling, as he and Wacholder noted the following September: "As is common in Dead Sea research, the unknown contents of unpublished scroll manuscripts were used to challenge our ideas."[458]

Of the same meeting, Shanks noted that the status quo regarding Dead Sea Scroll research continued as before. Harvard students could establish names for themselves because their teachers, Strugnell and Frank Moore Cross, could, as members of the editorial team, grant them exclusive access. Meanwhile, senior scholars stood on the sidelines with bated breath, waiting for someone to share news of the unpublished manuscripts:

There is something demeaning about senior scholars having to ask Sidnie White, already a major Qumran scholar at age 31, if she would identify and spell certain Hebrew words in unpublished texts that she, through Cross and Strugnell, has access to. As this inquiry was taking place in one session, I looked over at the white-haired Ben-Zion Wacholder of Hebrew Union College, who was listening intently to absorb in his legendary capacious memory the facts young Sidnie White was generously divulging.[459]

Upon his return to Cincinnati, Abegg set to work examining the concordance, which had just recently been catalogued and made available. He hoped to garner more information about the texts that had been discussed in response to his paper. He was particularly interested in examining two texts related to the War Scroll, 4Q280 and 4Q285, which had appeared in preliminary studies by scroll editor Jozef Milik.[460] Looking for the texts in the concordance, Abegg realized that the entire text could be reconstructed because each word was provided in context. He started first with the War Scroll fragments, then a series of calendars (4QMishmarot haKohanim, 4Q320–330), and then, as a treat for his teacher, the texts of the Damascus Document, preserved in Cave 4 (4Q266–273).[461]

Initially Abegg reconstructed the texts by cutting and pasting the entries manually into a word processor on a Macintosh computer. Because the computer could only accept texts that were typed from left to right, the Hebrew words had to be entered in reverse, starting with the last letter first.[462] Eventually Abegg created a computer program that he called "Glue,"[463] which automatically placed the words in their correct position once entered.[464] He described the process of reconstruction in a September 1991 interview:

> My first attempt at reconstructing the manuscripts began by locating words in the Preliminary Concordance common to any text, such as prepositions, and then allowing the context to lead me through the work. For example, the preposition "in" might have revealed the phrase: "in the beginning" with the reference of Genesis 1:1. By then looking up the word "beginning," one would find the phrase: "the beginning God created," which when added to the first phrase would produce "in the beginning God created." In this fashion I was able to "cut and paste" a text on the computer screen. The quality of these texts gave us the impetus to tackle the concordance on a larger scale. After entering every entry with its corresponding reference into a data base, I programmed the computer to sort material by manuscript, fragment, column, and line number. I then wrote a program to recognize overlapping phrases in each line and to perform the "cut and paste" job that I had done manually.[465]

To reconstruct the unpublished corpus, Abegg entered 42,000 lines of Hebrew and 10,500 lines of Aramaic.[466] He approached Wacholder with the first fifty pages of reconstructed texts in early 1991. Wacholder wanted to publish, but

Scan of original halftone plate of Martin Abegg and Ben Zion Wacholder, Cincinnati, September 1991

(©*The American Israelite*, reprinted with permission)

Abegg was concerned that bootlegging the texts might cost him a career before he had even completed his doctorate. Wacholder understood his concerns well, as is apparent from an interview he and Abegg gave in September 1991:

> "He was taking a risk," Wacholder said of Abegg. "I am untouchable. I am old, I am tenured." But ultimately, Wacholder predicted, the work [would] be helpful to Abegg.

Abegg hoped Wacholder was right.

> "I certainly would like to work," he said.[467]

Colleagues, including Edward Cook[468] and Bruce Zuckerman, recommended to Abegg that he avoid publishing the material.[469] HUC-JIR professor Stephen Kaufman likewise counseled him against it.[470] Shanks encouraged him to publish the material to circumvent the editorial team that had hoarded the material for decades.[471] Ultimately, Abegg agreed to publish the material, even while completing his dissertation. More than a decade later, Abegg explained his reasoning in moving forward with a project that could have derailed his scholarly career before it started:

> The straw that broke the camel's back was Ben Zion [Wacholder] himself. Here was a man who was one of a very special generation who had been uprooted from Eastern Europe during World War II, who had spent their whole lives studying Jewish literature and law and knew it by heart, and yet had been kept away from this material all these years. For Ben Zion and others like him, I finally made the decision.[472]

The initial publication was to consist of five volumes of reconstructed texts, work primarily done by Abegg, and an English translation to be done primarily by Wacholder.[473]

Wacholder approached the Dutch publishing firm of E J. Brill in Leiden first.[474] Brill had a long history of publishing scroll-related volumes and text editions. Its series *Studies on the Texts of the Desert of Judah* began with the publication of the Manual of Discipline in 1957.[475] Wachholder's discussion with Brill was not fruitful, and he eventually sought another publisher. The reason for Brill's disinterest in the project is not clear. However, at the same

1990 SBL meeting where Abegg's paper had been challenged, Robert Eisenman, of California State University at Long Beach, met with Brill representatives to discuss publishing a facsimile edition of a collection of black and white photos of all the scroll fragments in his possession. The source of these photos remains anonymous. Brill agreed, in principle, to publish the volumes. Initially the volumes were scheduled to appear in March 1991, but the ongoing work of studying the photographs delayed their appearance. That same March, a Polish scholar, Zdzislaw Jan Kapera, was taken to task at the International Congress on the Dead Sea Scrolls in Madrid for providing an anonymous transcription of the unpublished text of 4QMMT to subscribers of his journal *Qumran Chronicle*. In the week before the congress, Kapera received a letter from Amir Drori, the director of the IAA, challenging the unauthorized distribution of the text. The very public challenge to Kapera at the conference, along with the news of the IAA's response, scared Brill and led to the cancellation of the contract with Eisenman.[476] Collectively, these issues may likewise have kept Brill from accepting Wacholder and Abegg's reconstructed texts for publication.

Wacholder turned to Shanks in the spring of 1991 to publish the material, and with the financial support of the Manfred and Anne Lehmann Foundation, the first volume appeared on 4 September 1991. *A Preliminary Edition of the Unpublished Dead Sea Scrolls: The Hebrew and Aramaic Texts from Cave Four, Fascicle 1*[477] included the texts that Abegg had prepared following the 1990 SBL meeting for his dissertation work and for Wacholder's research.[478]

The response to the publication was immediate. Members of the editorial team were less than pleased about having their own work undermined and their rights to produce first editions circumvented. They responded in three ways.

First they challenged the morality and legality of what Abegg and Wacholder had done. Cross called the texts pirated and said they would have no real effect on the pace of publication of the scrolls. "About the only good thing it should do," Cross said, "is to remove the paranoia surrounding the unpublished scrolls."[479] New York University professor Lawrence Schiffman was quoted as saying, "I don't know if what they've done is ethical. You're really publishing another person's work."[480] Finally, Strugnell of the Harvard Divinity School, who headed the official committee until he was forced to resign amid charges of incompetence and antisemitism in late 1990, said he had given the concordance to Wacholder only for his scholarly use. Concerning the texts he commented most bluntly: "What else would you call it but stealing?"[481] In general, the media noted, "critics charged that Dr. Wacholder violated an agreement by which he received the concordance from then-scrolls committee head John Strugnell."[482]

An examination of the authorization Strugnell gave Wacholder shows no restriction on its use: "To whom it may concern: If you are willing, for my part I authorize making one complete photographic or Xerox reproduction of your copy of our publication 'A Preliminary Concordance to the Hebrew and Aramaic Fragments from Qumran cave II-X' (5 vols., Gottingen 1988) for *Prof B Z Wacholder*."[483]

Given that copies were also available for in-library use at Harvard and Baltimore Hebrew College, the only real advantage Wacholder and Abegg had was the ability to use the concordance for longer time periods. That they chose to reconstruct the text with the concordance did not violate any agreement Wacholder had with Strugnell.

As a side note, this particular challenge did not die easily; it appeared again in a 1993 review of the second fascicle of Wacholder and Abegg's work. In May 1993 David Gilner responded to the suggestion in the previous volume of *BAR* that HUC-JIR had given access to the concordance without permission.

> Joseph Fitzmyer states that a copy of the preliminary concordance that he helped to prepare 'was deposited at Hebrew Union College (along with a few other institutions) for safekeeping.' This assertion is incorrect. The library purchased a copy of the work in 1990, catalogued it and made it available ... [With regard to the concordance and the negatives the] library kept in trust what it was given in trust, and made open that which had been openly acquired.[484]

Fitzmyer replied in that same volume that he never claimed safekeeping and that the *BAR*'s editors added it to his article.[485] The editors admitted that it was their change and apologized.[486] It is clear, though, that the College remained sensitive to the perception that it had behaved inappropriately.

Charging Abegg and Wacholder with impropriety gave way to a second type of challenge from the editorial team. Since the material was now available, the editors, at best, could only discourage people from purchasing and using it. Strugnell commented, "The concordance was not meant to produce a version of the scrolls. The reconstruction of the scrolls is about 20 percent wrong, and the people who will try to use it will never know what is right and what is wrong."[487] Eugene Ulrich of the University of Notre Dame "agreed that the volume was about '80 per cent accurate.' But he called it a 'pastiche' of material that contained very little that was new."[488] Further, he asked, "'How can you trust it?' The concordance was known to contain errors, as such reconstructions based on it would also prove problematic."[489] Interviewed on the *MacNeil-Lehrer News Hour* he stated, "The reliability of such a document is highly questionable."[490] Emanuel Tov, by then editor-in-chief, commented that in examining the texts he found many imprecisions.[491] James VanderKam wrote the whole thing off; he was quoted predicting that the edition would be outdated by 1997: "It seems to be just a last-ditch kind of ploy by some people who feel they don't have access to the scrolls."[492]

The team's final reaction came with the most serious threat. In response to the announcement of the publication, Emile Puech, a member of the editorial committee, told a *Chicago Tribune* reporter that they would sue.[493] Although Wacholder and Abegg's agreement with Shanks did not come with an offer of legal protection, Shanks had given them the name of a Washington, DC law firm that would agree to take their case pro bono if a legal challenge was raised to their text edition.[494] However, a trial never became an issue because news of another infringement of the editors' rights inspired by Wacholder and Abegg was soon to break.

Wacholder and Abegg mounted their own public defense to these challenges. First, they argued for the ethics of their actions. Wacholder was concerned that part of the reason for the monopoly was to keep Jewish scholars out. This he ascertained from Strugnell's comments about Judaism and the fact that, despite Israeli control, the core of non-Jewish editors had remained in place without interference since the capture of the materials. Based on his reconstructions, he told the *Jerusalem Post* that, in contrast to accusations that publication was being delayed because the scrolls contained material that might undermine the theological positions of rabbinic Judaism or Christianity, he found no evidence in the scrolls of anything that might undermine them.[495] Further, Abegg argued that the ability to reconstruct the scrolls from the concordance made in the 1960s suggested that preliminary editions of the scrolls could also have been made available then. The scrolls were already generally deciphered, or the concordance would not have been possible. What was unethical, Abegg asserted, was the unnecessary hoarding of the scrolls for so many decades.[496] Some of the scholars feared that erroneous material in the reconstructions would be used as the basis for numerous scholarly treatises and dissertations. Wacholder, however, played down those fears: "These scholars, with all their eminence and the best ability, have themselves introduced misconceptions.... They will have to eat their words, and these texts will show it."[497]

Wacholder and Abegg did not go undefended by outsiders either. No less than the editors of the *New York Times* took up their cause. In the days immediately following the announcement of the publication and the outcry from the editorial team they wrote:

> Some on the committee might be tempted to charge the Cincinnati scholars with piracy. On the contrary, Mr. Wacholder and Mr. Abegg are to be applauded for their work—and for sifting through layer upon layer of obfuscation. The committee with its obsessive secrecy and cloak and dagger scholarship, long ago exhausted its credibility with scholars and laymen alike.

> The two Cincinnatians seem to know what the scroll committee forgot: that the scrolls and what they say about the common roots of Christianity and Rabbinic Judaism belong to civilization, not to a few sequestered professors.[498]

Ziony Zevit of the University of Judaism in Los Angeles (now American Jewish University) responded positively to the publication, noting:

> For years we have been trying to open up access to the scrolls to qualified scholars ... but those who are in charge of deciphering and publishing them have made the scrolls available only to their students. Serious scholars have found themselves closed out.[499]

A prominent leader of the Reform movement, Rabbi Gunther Plaut, came out in their support as well:

> I have no idea whether Prof. Wacholder and Company have done a good job, but they have succeeded in breaking a scholarly stranglehold. The fragments should long ago have been photographed and surrendered to anyone who wanted to study them. Too much hangs on their understanding to continue scholarly hide-and-seek games.[500]

Commenting on the ethical issues he noted:

> 'Pirated version' implies that the scrolls belong to someone who has violated a copyright. No such thing; they belong to the world and its time that the veil of secrecy is torn away so that a lot of scholars may have a go at deciphering material.[501]

Reform Judaism, an official publication of the Union of American Hebrew Congregations (now Union of Reform Judaism) showed its support as well, publishing in 1992 a volume devoted to the scrolls that included an article by Wacholder and an interview with Abegg.[502] Even Schiffman, an official editor of Cave 4 materials who had challenged the ethics of bootlegging the scrolls, had to concede the value of Wacholder and Abegg's efforts: "'For my own research, this is very important,' said Schiffman.... 'When you get rid of the hoopla, they have put a lot into the arena that some scholars have been wanting for a long time.'"[503]

A thorough study of the first volume later proved it to be far more accurate than anyone had supposed previously. Hartmut Stegemann of Gottingen University examined the edition and concluded that it was "a trustworthy representation of about 98% of the textual evidence."[504] That it had gone into a second printing by the time the second volume of texts appeared in July 1992 proves its success.[505] The difficulty Abegg and Wacholder faced in the wake of the first volume was finding funding to support the work on the remaining volumes.

To help recoup costs and maintain the work of reconstructing the texts, a public plea was made for donations to "The Dead Sea Scroll Project, Institute for Mediterranean Studies," which Wacholder had established. Donors who contributed $500 or more received an inscribed copy of Volume 1.[506] *BAR* likewise ran the plea for funds to support the publication.[507] As a result, various individuals, companies, and nonprofit foundations came forward with help.[508] Apple Computer, which had received much publicity in the news coverage, provided two new computers and a printer for Wacholder and Abegg to use.[509]

The two men set to work. Over the next three years, two more volumes of texts and a concordance to the reconstruction appeared. However, publication did not go entirely smoothly. The publication of the first reconstructions changed the relationship between HUC-JIR and the Israeli authorities in the matter of the scroll negatives; but more important, it had begun to undermine the editorial team's control over the unpublished scroll material. Wacholder and Abegg's work continued as these changes unfolded.

Bringing the Monopoly to an End

In 1969, when Glueck formulated his deal with Harman, HUC-JIR was the sole North American institution with a set of security negatives; however, by 1991 things had changed significantly. As noted above, James Sanders approached HUC-JIR in 1979 about making duplicates of its negatives for the Ancient Biblical Manuscript Center in Claremont, California. Instead of making copies the Manuscript Center decided to produce a new set of negatives from the originals in Israel and from photographs of previously unrecorded materials. The photographer of the Huntington Library, Robert Schlosser, made diapositive photographs between 1984 and 1986 with Elizabeth Hay Bechtel's monies (she had previously helped acquire the publication rights for the Cave 11 Psalms scroll).[510] Prior to her death in 1987, Bechtel had, because of various disagreements, ended her relationship with Sanders and the Ancient Biblical Manuscript Center and had turned over a duplicate of the negatives for storage at the Huntington Library.[511] Finally, in May 1990, the Oxford Centre for Postgraduate Hebrew Studies came into possession of a set of negatives as the result of an agreement to help fund the official editorial project.[512] On 22 September 1991 the Huntington Library announced its plan to release its scrolls photographs.[513]

Abegg and Wacholder responded publicly to Huntington's decision to make their copy of the negatives public:

> What has delighted us most is that barely three weeks after the appearance of our "A Preliminary Edition of the Dead Sea Scrolls," the Huntington Library in San Marino, despite threats of lawsuits and heated criticisms from biblical scholars and Israeli authorities, decided to make available its cache of photographs of ancient texts.[514]

In California, reporters turned to Lewis Barth, Dean of HUC-JIR's Los Angeles campus, for a response to the announcement:

What the scrolls should provide ... is more information on the patterns of life among the Jews who lived in Qumran, of the sect known as the Essenes. During the first century, the time of John the Baptist and of Jesus, the Essenes were an important part of Jewish life in Israel. For Christians these scrolls provide more information on the background out of which Christianity developed. From a Jewish perspective this was a very important historical period because of the emergence of rabbinical Judaism. Until now we have been dependent for this information mainly on the writings of Josephus and on some of the already published scrolls.... Scholars will want this information not to confirm or deny what the past should have been but what the past actually was. ... In the world of scholarship, libraries tend to keep the original documents they are studying and make copies available to others for their research. In these matters each library sets up its own requirements and generally they require an acknowledgment of the source library if the material is published based on documents they have made available. When the Israelis originally obtained the scrolls such precautions were sensible until they could determine what they actually had. But the restrictions have long since outlived their usefulness.[515]

Several newspapers linked the actions of the Huntington Library to Wacholder and Abegg's publication. The *New York Times* came out in their support again:

The Dead Sea Scrolls, held captive for four decades by researchers, are now under welcome attack from guerrilla scholars. Earlier this month, a pair of biblical scholars published a computer-generated version of a scroll reproduced from an index called a concordance. Now the Huntington Library, in California, has surprised the world with its photographs of the scroll manuscripts. It is opening them to all scholars—a just and valuable act.[516]

The *Cincinnati Post* editorialized: "Anyone with even the mildest interest in mankind's religious heritage owes thanks to Wacholder and Abegg, and to the Huntington Library."[517] However, not everyone was pleased. The *Jerusalem Post* was not nearly as enthusiastic as the American newspapers had been:

Although applauded by the *New York Times* for "breaking the scrolls cartel," the moves raise serious ethical, moral and legal questions. In the first instance, the bootleg version of the scrolls—inaccurate versions, say Israeli scholars—undermines the work of scholars who have been laboring over these documents for years and are in the process of bringing them to publication.[518]

In response to Huntington's announcement, HUC-JIR held a press conference on 24 September 1991 to announce that it could not release its cache of negatives to the public. Gottschalk cited several reasons for not releasing them. First was that Glueck had promised to keep them secure. Second, unlike HUC-JIR and the other institutions, Huntington's copies were unauthorized and therefore could be released. Finally—and this issue was likely the most significant—HUC-JIR maintained major rabbinic and archaeological programs through its campus in Jerusalem. At the time it was in the midst of preparing to renovate its campus, and Israel had given the College a $500,000 construction grant.[519] Acting unilaterally to open Israel's national treasures to the public was politically unwise. Gottschalk was attempting to serve two masters. On the one hand, he did not want to upset the Israelis who, at least in Jerusalem, held the purse strings; on the other, public sentiment was against the College's helping the editorial team maintain its monopoly on scroll access. In the same release, Gottschalk made certain to highlight that the College was working to have the Israelis increase access to the materials. HUC-JIR was trying to get the authorities to allow a "more liberal reading" of its contract. HUC-JIR's president also suggested an alternative possibility: If all the institutions that had signed agreements with the authorities agreed that given the current circumstances there was no longer a good reason for the contracts, they could collectively open the material.[520] Presumably this could protect them from legal action; it would be difficult for the IAA to initiate legal proceedings against them all. As for Abegg and Wacholder, Gottschalk was enthusiastic in suggesting their actions had changed the status quo regarding control of the scrolls: "They blew the lid off."[521]

The following day, in response to the Huntington declaration and the public support for releasing the material, Emanuel Tov and Amir Drori invited an HUC-JIR representative to appear at a meeting in Jerusalem on 4 December 1991 to discuss the issue of access to the scrolls. Also invited were participants from the Ancient Biblical Manuscript Center, the Huntington Library, and the Qumran Centre at the Oxford Centre for Post-Graduate Hebrew Studies.[522]

The press picked up notice of the meeting, which suggested that the goal was to solve the problems with Huntington and the other libraries without legal action; the IAA preferred discussion, negotiation, and compromise.[523] Given the public outcry, Israel could not afford the bad press that a lawsuit would almost certainly bring. On 9 October 1991, Gottschalk indicated his willingness to attend.[524]

In late September, Zafren began formulating the College's response to the IAA. First, he noted that Harman's letter in 1989 was the first the College knew of the two different authorities controlling different collections of the scrolls. Harman's letter was a runaround, intended to confuse the situation and to make challenging it more difficult. Second, it was not clear that the College had, in fact, ever received negatives of the original seven scrolls. Zafren's examination of the negatives showed that 1QpHab, 1Qh (Thanksgiving), 3Q7, and much of 6Q8 of the Genesis Apocryphon were also not included. As far as Zafren was concerned, HUC-JIR had laid out funds for what Broshi claimed in his letter of 7 May 1972 was a complete set of the unpublished fragments. However in comparing the inventory lists to the negative numbers, it appeared that 151 negatives were in the collection but did not appear on the inventory list. Broshi later indicated that there were 2,500 negatives but HUC-JIR only received 1,378. At the very least, Zafren surmised, the College could request help identifying what it did or did not have in its collection, it could ask for a complete set for when the material was eventually released, and it could ask for positives of the available scrolls. Alternatively, since Harman insisted that the relationship was with the board of the Shrine of the Book for the seven scrolls, HUC-JIR could argue that there was, in fact, no agreement with the IAA for the other materials. Thus, they could do as they liked with them.[525] Ultimately, Zafren recommended that Gottschalk request a complete set of prints, even if they had to lay out the funds to do it. Asking that they be made in Israel would ensure that all the institutions ended up with the same collection of prints. Zafren had Gilner explore the cost for producing prints from the negatives in HUC-JIR's collection.[526] The price that Gilner estimated—between $6 and $10 per print—would prove prohibitive, given that the set would remain incomplete.[527]

The other institutions that held negatives also needed to decide how to respond to the IAA's invitation for the 4 December meeting in Jerusalem. William Moffett, director of the Huntington Library, contacted Wacholder to congratulate him on the preliminary edition and to indicate that it had inspired him to release his photographs. He also told Wacholder that he would send a complimentary facsimile of the manuscripts, compliments of the Huntington Library, and asked for cooperation with the other institutions in responding to the IAA.[528] The press did not explicitly make the connection between the preliminary edition and Moffett's actions, although a single article noted that this connection was generally accepted among scholars: "Many scholars believe that Wacholder's work provided the impetus for the Huntington Library to open its photographic collection of the scrolls."[529]

David Patterson of Oxford contacted Gottschalk directly. From Oxford's perspective, there was hope that the restrictions might be lifted, as they did not wish to encourage the exclusive rights of editors who had kept the material from other scholars for a long period. They were concerned, however, for young students at work on unpublished materials who might have their work derailed if the ban on access was lifted.[530]

Ultimately, Gottschalk did not want to release the material unilaterally; he wanted the Israelis to grant him permission. He emphasized to Patterson that he had worked for ten years, with no effect, to have the scrolls released. As far as he was concerned, "The only ones who have a copyright on the Dead Sea Scrolls ... are the authors and editors of the original scrolls, and they are not around to give advice at this time."[531] Moffett also contacted Gottschalk to discuss the possibility of formulating a coordinated response to Tov and Drori.[532] Moffett had likewise contacted James Sanders and scheduled a meeting for the two men at the Huntington Library on 1 November 1991.[533]

In responding to Moffett, Gottschalk indicated admiration for the Huntington Library's release of the material but highlighted the fact that unlike HUC-JIR, the library was not bound by an official agreement. Again he pointed out that he had correspondence that spanned more than a decade trying to release the scrolls.[534] Gottschalk's suggestion that his hands were tied in this regard but that he had tried to have the Israelis change the rules again indicates Gottschalk's sense of the public outcry. When Shanks announced that HUC-JIR held scroll negatives, he essentially directed public attention, and perhaps scorn, in the direction of the College. To help protect HUC-JIR's reputation, Gottschalk wanted to write an op-ed piece for the *New York Times* that would highlight that HUC-JIR could not release its negatives but that for more than five years the institution had worked, despite the constant Israeli refusal, to have them released.[535] Although no op-ed piece appeared, Gottschalk's intention was consistent with his other correspondence and statements to the press. The College must have been pulled in two directions. On the one hand it had to keep the promises it made, on the other, it could have been a hero to the anti-monopoly movement. The College was torn, and the efforts to get the scrolls released within the system were the best it could do.

In contrast to Oxford and HUC-JIR, the Huntington Library could afford to be more adversarial in dealing with the authorities. Both schools relied on cooperation from the Israelis in scholarly matters, but they also held rights to various manuscripts. They could not afford to set the precedent of undermining scholarly publishing rights if they wanted their own preserved. The Huntington Library, in communicating with Gottschalk and Patterson, indicated that it had still not decided whether to participate in the meeting but that it wanted to assure all parties that it was only interested in allowing access to its photos, not making text editions or facsimiles. Further, Moffett noted, he was not sympathetic to Tov, who had suggested that competition was beneficial only after *editiones princepes* were completed. Neither was Moffett sympathetic to young scholars who had just received their allotments while others had stood by for decades to see material. Mostly, he was convinced that the editors should get to work finishing their editions instead of "policing the activities of others."[536] In releasing the library's scrolls Moffett announced, "When you free the scrolls, you free the scholars. If we had sat quietly we would have violated our own policy of unrestricted access."[537] The Oxford Centre's reply to Moffett was similar to HUC-JIR's: It was bound by written agreement not to give access to its negatives until the IAA lifted the restrictions.[538]

Abegg and Wacholder were against Gottschalk participating in the meeting for two reasons. First, they were concerned that the meeting would create a situation in which the IAA and the editors could seek retribution for the College having supported the bootleg edition. After all, Puech had already threatened to sue. Second, they saw the meeting as another attempt by the IAA and the editors to reassert control over the negatives that the various institutions possessed. As far as they were concerned, the only "happy result could be the official release of the Dead Sea Scrolls to the world."[539] There was general concern that if HUC-JIR stood by its agreement, remaining committed to the contents of its September press release,[540] the institutions collectively would backtrack and lose support of all those scholars who had applauded them for helping to break the monopoly.[541]

A Busy October

In mid-October Harman approached Gottschalk with the hope of resolving the situation. According to Harman, in looking back at his files over the past twenty years, he was "surprised" to see the changes that had taken place in the implementation of his 1969 agreement with Glueck. He understood that the original agreement referred to "high quality negatives of all the Dead Sea Schools [sic] in the custody of the Shrine of the Book. This meant precisely what it said, namely the seven Dead Sea Scrolls in the custody of the Shrine of the Book."[542] Harman blamed Broshi for the situation. In contrast to the original agreement, Broshi, for some unexplainable reason, had sent copies of negatives of all the scrolls and fragments in the custody of both the Shrine of the Book and the Department of Antiquities (now the IAA). Harman's letter of 1989 gave permission to open the original seven scrolls discussed explicitly in the 1969 letter to Glueck, since these were the only ones for which the board of the Shrine of the Book could give permission. According to Harman, Broshi's error explained why the $10,000 was so quickly spent without positives having been made. Harman's clear implication was that from the beginning Broshi mishandled the situation: "The people in charge of the Shrine of the Book went way beyond the undertaking I gave in my letter to Nelson Glueck." Harman hoped that this would end any dispute between HUC-JIR and the Hebrew University.[543] Gottschalk in responding, likewise showed surprise since it had never been made clear to him that there were two authorities HUC-JIR was dealing with—The Shrine of the Book on the one hand, and the IAA on the other.

In attempting to keep the historical record straight, Harman later laid the blame completely on Broshi:

> He apparently interpreted the agreement [between Harman and Glueck] as being that he had to send to H.U.C.-J.I.R. negatives not only of the scrolls in the Shrine of the Book, but also all the scrolls and scroll fragments which were in the custody of the Department of Antiquities at the Rockefeller Museum. He had access to these owing to his relations with the Department of Antiquities.[544]

Neither Gottschalk nor Zafren agreed with Harman's explanation of the events. Gottschalk responded to Harman with a rather sarcastic tone. He found it mysterious that HUC-JIR had received its materials in error. Had Claremont and Oxford received their materials by accident as well?[545] Zafren's reading was far more pointed. For one, he could not understand why, if the purpose of sending the original negatives to HUC-JIR was security, there would have been a need to only send copies of the published material. It was precisely the unpublished materials that needed a complete backup set in storage away from Israel. Further, every letter between 1969 and 1989 suggested to him that all parties understood and operated as if HUC-JIR was responsible for safeguarding copies of all the scrolls. The 1989 letter from Harman was the first to suggest otherwise. Everything depended on whether one believed that Broshi had erred two decades earlier and never corrected the error.[546] Given that the earliest letters from Broshi to the College had even been copied to Harman and Yadin, Harman's position is difficult to accept. In fact, it appears that Zafren and Gottschalk were operating without all the available documentation that could impugn Harman. Neither of their archival files includes a June 1969 letter from Harman to Glueck explaining how the sum of $10,000 was calculated, nor do they ever make reference to it. It is now preserved only in Glueck's general correspondence files. Most important, Harman notes in the letter that two thousand negatives were to be made and that HUC-JIR's $10,000 would cover the entire cost. The letter states explicitly that it is a "breakdown of the costs of the work of photographing *the scrolls and fragments*"[547] (emphasis added). Further, in Glueck's diary entry about his meeting with Harman in July 1969, he summarized his understanding of the agreement. He noted that at the meeting he,

> took the occasion to tell the President of the University [Harman] that [he] had gotten the generous agreement of Mr. Philip D. Sang to give the Hebrew Union College $10,000 which would be turned over to the Hebrew University for the copies of the photographs and negatives of *all the Dead Sea Scroll material*, which would be deposited in our great Library at Cincinnati, with various reservations about their future use (emphasis added).[548]

Finally, Harman wrote to Glueck's donor, Philip Sang, thanking him for his help as the Shrine of the Book undertook the "necessary project of photographing in both negative and positive all the *Dead Sea Scrolls and Fragments*… As a result of this, Hebrew Union College will be the repository in the United States of a *complete set of negatives and positives of all the Dead Sea Scrolls and Fragments*." (emphasis added)[549]

However, whether Harman was being entirely honest about his recollections had little role in the ongoing process of making the negatives available to the scholarly community. In mid-October, Hershel Shanks contacted Gottschalk to inform him of his intentions to release, on 19 November 1991, a facsimile edition of the scrolls made from negatives from a confidential source. He invited HUC-JIR to join a Dead Sea Scroll consortium with the Biblical Archaeology Society in support of the publication. Gottschalk indicated that he was not ready to participate in a consortium to publish what may have been "bootlegged" materials.[550] Participating in Shanks's efforts could only serve to further upset the Israelis, given Wacholder and Abegg's activities and the concern that HUC-JIR might release its negatives.

Also in October, Avraham Biran at HUC-JIR in Jerusalem took it upon himself as a former director of IAA to approach Amir Drori, the then-current director, to have him release the scrolls to all scholars for "the sake of Israel's good name."[551] Drori hoped that the 4 December meeting would allow for the adoption of a formula that would satisfy the "need of the public to know."[552] Following up on the meeting, he faxed a copy of a *Jerusalem Post* article, "Antiquities Authority Reverses Its Policy on Dead Sea Scrolls Photos," to Gottschalk. The IAA then faxed a press release to HUC-JIR dated 27 October 1991, titled "The Israel Antiquities Authority to Permit Access to Judean Desert Scroll Photos."[553] By this point, Oxford, the Ancient Biblical Manuscript Center, and HUC-JIR had accepted the IAA's invitation for the meeting on 4 December. Moffett at the Huntington Library had not yet responded, but neither had he released his photos.[554] The issue was moot, though, since the change in the Israeli position meant that the meeting was cancelled. The *Jerusalem Post* article noted that the IAA intended to make the scroll photographs available to scholars through HUC-JIR, the Ancient Biblical Manuscript Center, and the Centre for Post-Graduate Hebrew Studies at Oxford.[555] On 27 October 1991, Gottschalk announced publicly (at the HUC-JIR associates dinner)[556] that very soon the College would make the negatives available to those who would like to view them, although it had no authority to allow publication.[557] Wacholder publicly stated, "We welcome the new guidelines"; but, with the restriction that those accessing them could not publish editions and could only cite limited portions, he was convinced the new policy would not be effective.[558]

On Monday 28 October the material became available for viewing, but only the media were immediately interested.[559] When the press asked how the public had responded, David Gilner, the Klau librarian replied, "The response has not exactly been overwhelming."[560] Gilner suggested that a number of explanations were possible but that the biggest issue was that there was no clear index of the material and "scholars can't ask for what they don't know."[561] The other institutions faced similar problems.[562]

Under these circumstances, Wacholder and Abegg were committed to the particular importance of their reconstructions: "Our work provides a transcribed, readable text. You have to be able to interpret the photos.... [The publication of the photos] increases the reliability of our work [and makes it] less speculative."[563]

The media interest provided another forum for Gottschalk and Wacholder. Gottschalk credited Wacholder for providing the impetus for finally making the photographs public: "The painful part was that we couldn't let him use what was at HUC." Gottschalk's statement is significant for two reasons. First, by highlighting Wacholder's efforts, he attempted to place HUC in a leadership role in breaking the monopoly rather than its role in keeping the negatives secured and away from other scholars. Second, scholars accused Wacholder and Abegg of having had access to materials other than the concordance to aid their reconstruction efforts. In writing about their edition's accuracy, Hartmut Stegemann suggested the reconstructions were simply too accurate: "In general, everything is perfectly done. I wonder if the editors, indeed, used the concordance only, or whether they also had Milik's transcription or some photos."[564] As early as November 1989, Broshi suggested that HUC-JIR had released copies of negatives to Wacholder.[565] As Gottschalk made clear, and Abegg and Wacholder maintained, they made no use of HUC-JIR's negatives because they were never given access to them.[566]

Interest in HUC-JIR's scroll collection might have increased, but the school was caught in a strange situation, as Gilner reported:

> We were given this in trust to hold safely, but nothing came with it to fund us as a scroll institute, so we don't have the staff or the funds to go about doing the things we're being asked to do.... This is not something we have much experience with, but we're learning.[567]

It was clear, though, that HUC-JIR was not in a position to make the negatives useful to inquiring scholars. Gilner noted of the negatives, "It was intended to be an archive.... We don't have a light table to use the negatives."[568] In fact, in the only photograph of Gilner examining the negatives, he is holding one up in the air so that the ceiling light shines through it, making it readable.[569] The College needed equipment to study the negatives. Zafren was raising funds to help support research and preservation efforts. He received a $5,000 donation from Oliver Birckhead, retired CEO of Central Bancorporation, to be used in these matters.[570]

Despite the difficulties, HUC-JIR and Gilner were pleased the material had finally been opened. "No librarian," Gilner

Scan of original halftone plate of David Gilner examining negative, Cincinnati, October 1991

(©*The American Israelite*, reprinted with permission)

commented, "could be happy with keeping this hidden away.... The first rule for librarians is that books are for use."[571] Gilner's response was consistent with the comments of Patricia Glass Schuman, president of the American Library Association, and John A. Fleckner, chief archivist at the Smithsonian Institution's National Museum of American History. In response to the Huntington Library's offer to release its diapositives, Glass noted, "As librarians we strongly believe that all information should be affordable, available, and accessible." Fleckner concurred: "We have a commitment to the notion of equal access, the philosophical idea that the more eyes you get looking at a document, the more likely you are to come to truth." Regarding the meeting of the philosophical ideal and the actuality of contracts and restrictions, Fleckner commented, "It can often be a difficult balancing act."[572]

In November 1991, Gilner asked the IAA how he was to proceed with handling requests for access to the negatives. The IAA had announced the release of the material two weeks previous, in the press release of 27 October 1991. The first request, by Martin Abegg, had been honored, but HUC-JIR was seeking a clear explanation of the procedure.[573] The HUC-JIR form Abegg used was quite specific that the user requested access and that the negatives "would not be used for the production of a text edition," thus protecting the rights of the editorial team to produce the *editio princeps*.[574] The only response Gilner received was that the photographic images were to be stamped "Copyright of the Israel Antiquities Authority" to prevent unlawful publishing.[575]

The Final Chapter

Although HUC-JIR's negatives were released, the story was not quite over. On 19 November 1991 Shanks announced the publication of the two-volume facsimile edition that had previously been contracted with Brill.[576] The volumes were coming at a good time. HUC-JIR's material remained in negatives, which made it difficult to access. The Huntington Library announced that it would be at least another month before it could share its photographs with other libraries.[577] The source of the pictures Shanks used remained anonymous. This led to the suggestion that HUC-JIR and the other institutions had leaked their negatives, but they were ultimately cleared.[578] The facsimile edition proved to be the final straw, and on 26 November Emanuel Tov officially announced that all restrictions were removed from use of the scrolls, including production of text editions.[579]

Unfortunately, Shanks's facsimile edition led to the first legal action involving HUC-JIR. Included in the editors' preface to the volume was a reproduction of a transcription of 120 lines of the unpublished text 4QMMT. Elisha Qimron of the Hebrew University, who, along with John Strugnell, had produced the transcription, sued Shanks for copyright infringement.[580] On 30 March 1993 the Jerusalem District Court ruled in Qimron's favor and awarded him approximately $55,000 USD in damages.[581] Although the case had no direct impact on HUC-JIR, Qimron had his attorneys assert his copyright over any edition of 4QMMT—and this affected Wacholder and Abegg, who were at work on the third volume of their preliminary edition series:

> It has come to our attention that you might be in possession of Professor Qimron's composite text of MMT. Moreover, we have been informed that you might be using portions of Professor Qimron's reconstruction in a publication planned by you and Professor Abegg.
>
> On behalf of Professor Qimron, please accept this letter as notification that any use of Professor Qimron's reconstructed text is a violation of his copyright and Professor Qimron will take all steps available to him under both American and Israeli law to protect that copyright.[582]

Qimron essentially asserted that Wacholder and Abegg would have to clear any knowledge of his reconstruction from their mind before reconstituting the texts themselves—a difficult task, to say the least. Legal scholar Cindy Carson comments on this particular issue:

> With regard to Professors Wacholder and Abegg, there is no intent to copy, although it is likely that their work will be very similar if not virtually identical [to Qimron's]. To avoid infringement, then Professors Wacholder and Abegg will need to ensure that their wording is at least slightly different from Professor Qimron's. However, if Professor Qimron's work is accurate, Professors Wacholder and Abegg will be forced to be less accurate merely to avoid infringement.... If the first interpolator is allowed to obtain protection, the fear of rushed and haphazard scholarship voiced by those who object to open access may be realized in a different context.[583]

In May, Abegg and Wacholder were still at work on the materials for the third fascicle, but because of the threat of legal action, they were concerned about including a reconstruction of the text. As *BAR* noted in reporting on the case, Abegg and Wacholder, like most other scholars in the field, had seen Qimron's reconstruction and agreed with the majority of it.[584] Even though their reconstruction would be done independently, they still risked the accusation. According to Abegg, he spent hundreds of hours comparing the bootlegged version of Qimron's text, which Kapera made available in 1988 and which Shanks had published, with the facsimile edition. Abegg established that in 95 percent of cases, Qimron agreed with the original transcription work Milik did, which had served as the basis for the concordance.[585] Abegg and Wacholder hoped to use this material to demonstrate that Qimron did not hold the copyright for the text, and on 29 July 1993, in response to the letter and with the hope of preempting action by Qimron, they took him to federal court in Philadelphia, where he was visiting the Annenberg Research Institute.[586] In essence, they were "asking the court to break Qimron's stranglehold on one of the most important still-unpublished Dead Sea Scrolls."[587] Abegg and Wacholder's legal team included David Nimmer, a copyright specialist who also served on the legal team defending Shanks. The previous February, Shanks had turned to the same Philadelphia court for declaratory relief.[588] The lawsuits were certainly intertwined, as Shanks himself later noted:

> We are going to appeal. The principal reason for [this] is the courageous action of two American scholars—Professor Ben Zion Wacholder of Hebrew Union College–Jewish Institute of Religion in Cincinnati, Ohio, and Professor Martin Abegg of Grace Theological Seminary in Winona Lake, Indiana—who have instituted their own suit against Qimron.[589]

Shanks, who was a well established and connected lawyer before turning his attention to publishing, certainly had a role to play in both cases. Ultimately, both Philadelphia suits were dropped. Shanks continued his appeal through the Israeli Supreme Court. For Abegg and Wacholder, the situation had simply changed. Because Qimron was an Israeli, the court system in Philadelphia proved a complicated locus of legal action to fight this particular battle.[590] Further, they became convinced that Qimron would not come after them.[591] The likelihood is that they had only been targeted because of their relationship with Shanks and not for their own work in reconstructing the text. Finally, Qimron's official publication of the text appeared in 1994[592] and their "preliminary edition" followed soon after.[593] The case, and the story of HUC-JIR 's participation in the freeing of the scrolls, was put to rest.

Conclusion

From 1948 until 1993, HUC-JIR, its faculty, and its administration devoted significant resources to studying, teaching, and preserving the Dead Sea Scrolls. Their efforts showed various commitments, from supporting the State of Israel, to preserving its cultural heritage and that of the Western religions, to the importance of archaeology in the teaching of Bible and ancient Jewish history, to fully participating in international academe. As a seminary, the College considered the scrolls both in the context of its desire to participate in the life of the academy and also for exploring the place of these types of discoveries in modern Jewish life. As Glueck noted in his second review in the *New York Times*, the ability to establish the antiquity of the biblical text had profound implications for the beliefs of those committed to it and the ability to inspire others.

Additionally, exploring the study of the scrolls on campus provides insight into the scholarly life of the HUC-JIR community, the debates and concerns of its members, and its dedication to scholarly freedom. Faculty members were committed to appearing in public forums of all sorts, to writing for the public press, and to sharing their honest evaluation of the scrolls with the Jewish community and the public at large. These efforts highlight the role of the faculty as American spiritual leaders who used the newest scientific findings to help maintain the religious commitments of those who otherwise might perceive them as dangerous or be misled by those who sought to undermine their faith.

Although this story ends in 1993, the story of HUC-JIR and the scrolls has certainly not ended. Its faculty continues to research and teach about the scrolls. The critical views of Ellis Rivkin and Samuel Sandmel have been replaced by those of faculty who have had access to more of the material—in part due to the efforts of Wacholder and Abegg—and students who continue to explore the implications of these ancient texts for their understanding of the Jewish past and of the present.

Notes

Unless otherwise indicated, all archival material cited is from the Jacob Rader Marcus Center of the American Jewish Archives, Cincinnati, Ohio, or the Klau Library, Hebrew Union College–Jewish Institute of Religion, Cincinnati, Ohio.

[1] HUC-JIR president Alfred Gottschalk to Hebrew University president Avraham Harman, 24 October 1991, Administrative File: Dead Sea Scrolls, Klau Library. HUC-JIR.

[2] The earliest group of Jewish scholars in the United States to publish articles or to give scholarly conference presentations about the scrolls included Isaiah Sonne and Harry Orlinsky of HUC-JIR; Saul Lieberman, H.L. Ginsberg, and Robert Gordis at the Jewish Theological Seminary; Sydney Hoenig at Yeshiva University; and Solomon Zeitlin at Dropsie College. Among the major non-Jewish scholars first attached to the scrolls were William Albright of The Johns Hopkins University and Millar Burrows of Yale University. For a recent survey of the history of Dead Sea Scroll research see Dimant, *The Dead Sea Scrolls in Scholarly Perspective* (2012).

[3] On the discovery and sale see the overview provided by Frank, "How the Dead Sea Scrolls Were Found," 1, 7–16, 28–30. A thorough account of the discovery, sale, and study of the scrolls between 1947 and 1960 is found in Fields, *The Dead Sea Scrolls* (2009).

[4] Kando (1910–1993) was a Syrian Orthodox Christian who, although he began as a cobbler, later opened an antiquities shop. In addition to arranging these sales, he eventually acted as the intermediary between the Bedouin and the Jordanian Department of Antiquities for the sale of the ancient materials discovered in other caves. See Briend, "Shahin, Khalil Iskander (Kando)," 869–870.

[5] Samuel (1907–1995) was the Turkish-born archbishop of Jerusalem until he left for the United States, settling in New Jersey in 1949. He eventually sold his scrolls in 1954. They were purchased for the State of Israel by Yigael Yadin (1917–1984), son of the eminent Hebrew University scholar Eleazar Sukenik. Samuel recounts the tale of his involvement with the scrolls in his autobiography, *Treasure of Qumran* (1966).

[6] Sukenik (1889–1953), a Lithuanian-born, American-trained archaeologist, joined the faculty of Hebrew University in the late 1920s and became involved with the scrolls as the curator of the National Museum of Antiquities at the Hebrew University. See Silberman, "Sukenik, Eleazar L.," 902–903.

[7] Sukenik describes the events in *The Dead Sea Scrolls of the Hebrew University*, 13–21. He does not mention the antiquities dealer by name. This information is taken from Silberman, "Sukenik," 902. See also Silberman, *The Hidden Scrolls*, 43–46.

[8] The Bedouin discovered Cave 2 in February 1952. Although archaeologists found Caves 3 and 5, the Bedouin discovered Caves 4 and 6, also in 1952. The interchange of discovery between archaeologists and Bedouin, indicated by the naming of the caves by number in sequence of discovery, clearly reveals the close race between the discoverers to find additional caves. Archaeologists discovered Caves 7, 8, 9, and 10 in 1954; but Cave 11, again a source of significant and relatively intact material, was discovered by the Bedouin, in 1956.

[9] See Trever, *The Untold Story of Qumran*, 1–76.

[10] They receive mention in passing in his *Rivers in the Desert*, 143.

[11] Wise to Orlinsky, 3 May 1948, MS 19, Jewish Institute of Religion/29/2. Orlinsky, Harry M., Correspondence 1945–1948.

[12] Magnes, *A Treatise as to 1) Necessary Existence* (1904); and, Nelson Glueck, *Das Wort hesed* (1927). For a biography of Magnes see Bentwich, *Judah L. Magnes* (1955) and Kotzin, *Judah L. Magnes* (2010).

[13] Glueck described their similar paths in a tribute commemorating the tenth anniversary of Magnes's death. See Glueck, *Lion of Judah*, 7–8.

[14] Glueck served three times as director of ASOR Jerusalem: 1932–1933, 1936–1940, and 1942–1947.

[15] The May 1988 interview is cited in Brown and Kutler, *Nelson Glueck*, 73. In his biography of Magnes, Norman Bentwich reports that during this period Glueck often took Magnes along to visit archaeological sites throughout Israel and Trans-Jordan. See Bentwich, *Judah L. Magnes*, 137.

[16] Brown and Kutler, *Nelson Glueck*, 112.

[17] "Dr. Judah Magnes, Dead at Age 71," *The New York Times* (28 October 1948): 29.

[18] Glueck to Albright, 8 November 1948, MS 20/A1a-8/26, Albright, Wm.

[19] "The Thayer Fellowship, 1924–25," 14–15. See also Bentwich, *Judah L. Magnes*, 137.

[20] See Kiraz, *Anton Kiraz's Dead Sea Scroll Archive*, xxi; Samuel, *Treasure of Qumran*, 155–156.

[21] Yadin, *The Message of the Scrolls*, 27.

[22] Ibid., 29.

[23] Burrows to Magnes, 9 June 1948, MS 20/A1a-8/26, Albright, Wm.

[24] Ibid.

[25] Ibid.

[26] Magnes to Burrows, 17 June 1948, MS 20/A1a-8/26, Albright, Wm.

[27] Magnes to Burrows, 2 July 1948, MS 20/A1a-8/26, Albright, Wm.

[28] Kiraz, *Anton Kiraz's Archive*, xvii–xxxiv.

[29] Burrows to Magnes, 19 June 1948, MS 20/A1a-8/26, Albright, Wm. For Samuel's account of these activities and the trouble stirred by Kiraz's claims see his, *Treasure of Qumran*, 167–169.

[30] Ibid.

[31] Burrows to Magnes, 6 July 1948, MS 20/A1a-8/26, Albright, Wm.

[32] Magnes to Glueck, 12 July 1948, MS 20/A1a-8/13, M, General.

[33] Magnes to Glueck, 3 September 1948 (erroneously dated 3.IX.49), MS 20/A1a-8/13, M, General.

[34] Landesberg to Glueck, 22 October 1948, MS 20/A1a-8/26, Albright, Wm.

[35] Glueck to Albright, 8 November 1948, MS 20/A1a-8/26, Albright, Wm.

[36] Ibid.

[37] Albright to Glueck, 12 November 1948, MS 20/A1a-8/26, Albright, Wm.

[38] Sukenik to Kiraz, 1 October 1948, reprinted in Kiraz, *Anton Kiraz's Archive*, 2.

[39] Nelson Glueck, "Judah Leon Magnes," 3.

[40] Cited in Yadin, *The Message of the Scrolls*, 29.

[41] Burrows, Trever, and Brownlee, *The Dead Sea Scrolls of St. Mark's Monastery* (1950).

[42] Nelson Glueck, "Light From a Dim Past," *The New York Times* (20 November 1955): BR54–BR55. Quote on BR55.

[43] Blank to Glueck, 16 November 1948, MS 20/J1-5/2, Society of Biblical Literature (SBL).

[44] Marx to Glueck, 19 January 1949, MS 20/A1a-8/13, M, General.

[45] "Proceedings, December 28th to 30th, 1948," v.

[46] Milton Robertson, "Hebrew Union College to be Host to National Meetings of Bible Instructors and Society of Biblical Literature," for release 23 December 1949, MS 20/J1-5/2, SBL.

[47] The proceedings of the SBL meeting are recorded in "Proceedings, December 28th to 30th, 1949," i–xli; and the ASOR proceedings are recorded in Pfeiffer, "The Annual Meeting of the Corporation," 6–8. The AOS held its meeting from 4 to 6 April 1950.

[48] Milton Robertson, "American Bible Instructors Convene at Hebrew Union College Dec. 27–28," for release 20 December 1949, MS 20/J1-5/2, SBL.

[49] Milton Robertson, "Hebrew Union College to be Host to National Meetings of Bible Instructors and Society of Biblical Literature," for release 23 December 1949, MS 20/J1-5/2, SBL.

[50] Milton Robertson, "Jewish Messiah and Pauline Christ Will be the Subject of Biblical Society Symposium at Hebrew Union College," for release 26 December 1949, MS 20/J1-5/2, SBL.

[51] This was not the first SBL conference where the scrolls were discussed. A panel, "The Jerusalem Hebrew Scrolls," was presented at the 1948 annual meeting and included Millar Burrows, William H. Brownlee, and John C. Trever. See Saunders, *Searching the Scriptures*, 44.

[52] Pfeiffer, "The Annual Meeting of the Corporation," 7.

[53] A copy of the abstracts of the papers is preserved in: Society of Biblical Literature and Exegesis (SBLE, later SBL), Nearprint File.

[54] For public discussion see, *inter alia*, William G. Weart, "Bible Scroll 'Find' Suspected as Hoax; Dr. Zeitlin of Dropsie College Splits With Other Scholars on Dead Sea Discovery," *The New York Times* (4 March 1949): 19; Eleazer L. Sukenik, "Antiquity of Hebrew Scrolls: Scholar Presents Evidence for View That Manuscripts are Authentic," *The New York Times* (19 March 1949): 14; and, Solomon Zeitlin, "Origin of Hebrew Scrolls; Authenticity of Manuscript Said Not to Be Established," *The New York Times* (2 April 1949): 14. For the academic discussion see the articles collected in *JQR* between 1949 and 1964. Although Zeitlin wrote many of the articles against the antiquity of the scrolls and was editor of the journal, he freely made space available to scholars who disagreed with his views and wished to debate them. This pattern continued well into the 1960s. In March 1967 Ben Zion Wacholder, a member of the HUC-JIR faculty, sent Zeitlin an offprint of an article he had recently published on the scrolls. Zeitlin replied, "I read it with interest. A detailed reply will appear shortly in the *Jewish Quarterly Review*." MS 829/1/Correspondence – 1960s. The biting reply is found in Zeitlin, "The Word BᵉTalmud and the Method of Congruity of Words," 78–80.

[55] The first news of the St. Mark's Scrolls appeared in "Ancient MSS. Found in Palestine: Earliest Known Copy of Isaiah," *Times of London* (12 April 1948): 4. Formal news of Israel's purchase followed in "Isaiah Find Described: Bible manuscript 2,000 Years Old," *Palestine Post* (27 April 1948): 3. See also Julius Louis Meltzer, "10 Ancient Scrolls Found in Palestine," *The New York Times* (25 April 1948): 6.

[56] That SBL, ASOR, and NABI agreed to meet in Cincinnati was even more prestigious because they had traditionally met only in New York. In 1948 SBL voted to hold meetings outside New York once every four years. See "Proceedings, December 28th to 30th, 1948" iv.

[57] "Bible 'Find' Discussed: Pottery Containing Manuscripts Held of 1st Century B.C.," *The New York Times* (29 December 1949): 46.

[58] "Experts Dispute Age of Bible Documents," *The New York Times* (30 December 1949): 4.

[59] Ibid.

[60] "Scroll Comment Denied: Biblical Scholar Says Date of Text Was Not at Issue," *The New York Times* (8 January 1950): 149. Orlinsky's remarks should be contrasted with those of Gordis, from the same conference, who suggested:

> The extraordinary discoveries of ain Feshka, particularly the Isaiah Scroll, shed most welcome light on Hebrew Orthography and other aspects of the Biblical text and suggest a radical revision with regard to the date and origin of the early Masoretes. Evidence from

Rabbinic sources previously overlooked or ignored also substantiates the conclusion that the beginnings of Masoretic activity are to be sought in the period before the destruction of the Second temple in 70 C.E. [From the abstract preserved in SBLE, Nearprint File.]

[61] A copy of the conference papers abstracts is preserved in MS 20/J1-1/6, 1948–1955, AOS.

[62] See previous note.

[63] Berg and Goldberg, "The Dead Sea Scrolls: A Chronological Bibliography" (1949).

[64] After his death in 1985, HUC-JIR acquired Yadin's personal library for its Jerusalem campus. The collection included more than seven thousand books, many on the Dead Sea Scrolls and many containing Yadin's marginal notes. See "HUC Gains Yadin's Personal Library," *The American Israelite* (3 July 1986): 1.

[65] Ross Parmenter, "World of Music: Dead Sea Scrolls Hint that Hebrew had an Early System of Notation," *The New York Times* (6 January 1957): D9. Werner's findings were published in "Musical Aspects of the Dead Sea Scrolls," 21–37.

[66] The syllabus is preserved in MS 20/L5/15. The primary readings for the course included Millar Burrows's two volumes, *The Dead Sea Scrolls* (1955) and *More Light on the Dead Sea Scrolls* (1958); and Theodore Gaster's *The Dead Sea Scriptures* (1956).

[67] See, for example, "Rule of the Community III," 239–243.

[68] See Meyer, "The Refugee Scholars Project of the Hebrew Union College," 359–375.

[69] See MS 513, Isaiah Sonne/2343b/Dead Sea Scrolls.

[70] Sanders, *The Psalms Scroll of Qumrân Cave 11* (1965). A second expanded edition also appeared, *The Dead Sea Psalms Scroll* (1967). Sanders's contribution to scroll scholarship continued for the next four decades. In addition to his work on the Psalms Scroll, he published the first catalogs and indices to the scroll material in "Palestinian Manuscripts, 1947–1967," 431–440; and "Palestinian mss. 1947–1972," 74–83. His work on the development of the biblical canon has also relied heavily on scroll research. See, for example, Sanders, "The Judaean Desert Scrolls and the History of the Text of the Hebrew Bible," 1–17; and "The Scrolls and the Canonical Process," 1–23. In 1977, Sanders founded the Ancient Biblical Manuscript Center in Claremont, California. He remained director until his retirement in 1997.

[71] Email communication with James Sanders, 24 May 2008.

[72] The joint meeting of the Mid-West Sections of the AOS and the SBLE was held on 15 and 16 April 1949. Along with Sonne's paper, David Noel Freedman spoke on "'The House of Absalom' in the Habakkuk Scroll." A copy of the program is preserved in MS 20/J1-1/6, 1948–1955, AOS. For a brief overview of Sonne's contribution to scroll scholarship, see also Barth, "Rabbinics," 345–346.

[73] Undated notes to prepare the talk included with his manuscript for the annual SBLE meeting in December 1949 are preserved in MS 513/2343b/Dead Sea Scrolls.

[74] Trever to Glueck, 21 December 1949, MS 20/J1-5/2, SBL.

[75] Rivkin to Orlinsky, 30 November 1949, Harry Orlinsky, HUC-JIR, Unprocessed Material/ Ellis Rivkin.

[76] From the text of Sonne's presentation to the SBLE annual meeting preserved in MS 513/2343b/ Dead Sea Scrolls. Trever discusses the two Daniel fragments in *The Untold Story of Qumran*, 123–133.

[77] Trever to Sonne, 28 February 1950, MS 513/2343g/Correspondence, 1950. According to his report published more than a decade later, the archbishop offered Trever the scrolls at a meeting in New Jersey. See Trever, *The Untold Story of Qumran*, 123.

[78] Trever to Sonne, 13 March 1950, MS 513/2343g/Correspondence, 1950.

[79] Trever to Sonne, 6 April 1950; Sonne to Trever, 10 April 1950; and, Trever to Sonne 19 April 1950, MS 513/2343g/Correspondence, 1950.

[80] Sonne, "A Hymn Against Heretics in the Newly Discovered Scrolls," 275–313.

[81] Just over half were written by HUC-JIR faculty. Among the other contributors were Emanual Tov, the editor-in-chief of the Cave 4 editorial team, and Esther Eshel, an important Israeli scroll scholar.

[82] Burrows to Sonne, 23 May 1952, MS 513/2343h/Correspondence, 1952.

[83] Sonne, "Remarks on 'Manual of Discipline,' Col. VI, 6–7," 405–408.

[84] Ibid., 406.

[85] See Burrows to Sonne, 30 January 1957; Sonne to Burrows, 5 February 1957; Burrows to Sonne, 12 February 1957, all included in MS 513/2343h/Correspondence, 1957.

[86] Davies to Sonne, 12 December 1952, MS 513/2343h/Correspondence, 1952; Davies to Sonne, 4 February 1953, MS 513/2343h/Correspondence, 1953; and an undated copy of Sonne's reply is preserved in MS 513/2343/Articles on Essenes, Dead Sea Scrolls.

[87] Jeffery to Sonne, 18 April 1951; Jeffery to Sonne, 29 April 1951; Sonne to Jeffrey, 4 May 1951, all preserved in MS 513/2343h/Correspondence, 1951; and Jeffery to Sonne, 20 May 1952, MS 513/2343h/Correspondence, 1952.

[88] From 1943 until 1948, Rosenthal was lecturer in Jewish art and assistant professor of Bible and Semitic languages on the HUC, Cincinnati campus. Like Sonne, Rosenthal had been brought to the United States by HUC as part of its Refugee Scholars Project. See Meyers, "The Refugee Scholars Project," 359–375.

[89] Rosenthal to Sonne, 9 January 1955, MS 513/2343h/Correspondence, 1955.

[90] Halkin, "Isaiah Sonne," 15.

[91] Sonne, "A Hymn Against Heretics in the Newly Discovered Scrolls," 275–276.

[92] Ibid., 276–277.

[93] Birnbaum to Sonne, 1 December 1952, MS 513/2343h/Correspondence, 1952.

[94] A draft of the talk with copyediting in pencil is preserved in MS 513/2343b/Dead Sea Scrolls. See p. 4.

[95] Sonne, "Final Verdict on the Scrolls," 37–44.

[96] Ibid., 44.

[97] Sonne to Dentan, 15 September 1950, MS 513, Isaiah Sonne, 2343g/Correspondence, 1950.

[98] Zeitlin, "The Hebrew Scrolls and the Status of Biblical Scholarship," 133–192. On Sonne specifically, see 156–162.

[99] Ibid., 156.

[100] Sonne, "The Newly Discovered Bar Kokeba Letters," 75–108.

[101] Zeitlin, "The Propaganda of the Hebrew Scrolls and the Falsification of History," 25.

[102] Ibid., 34.

[103] Ibid.

[104] Ibid., 19.

[105] Halkin, "Isaiah Sonne," 9.

[106] Wolfgang Saxon, "Dr. Harry Orlinsky, 84, Professor Specializing in Biblical Literature," *The New York Times* (24 March 1992): D22.

[107] Orlinsky, "An Analysis of the Relationship Between the Septuagint and Masoretic Text of the Book of Job" (1935).

[108] Orlinsky began studying with Zeitlin in October 1931. See Orlinsky, "The Masorah," 46. Orlinsky went to Dropsie to work with Max Margolis who died soon after his arrival. See Orlinsky, "Margolis' Work in the Septuagint," 35–44. Despite the limited contact, Margolis had a tremendous influence on Orlinsky's scholarly trajectory.

[109] See Sperling, *Students of the Covenant*, 78–80. On Orlinsky's relationship with Albright and his students, see Long, *Planting and Reaping Albright*, 71–109.

[110] Orlinsky to Albright, 25 October 1945, Harry Orlinsky, HUC-JIR, Unprocessed Material/ Albright, W. F.

[111] Orlinsky published eight articles specifically on the scroll: "Studies in the St. Mark's Isaiah Scroll," 149–166; "Photography and Paleography in the Textual Criticism of St. Mark's Isaiah Scroll," 33–35; "Studies in the St. Mark's Isaiah Scroll II: yiswāhū in 42.11," 153–156; "Studies in the St. Mark's Isaiah Scroll III: Masoretic המח in Isaiah XLII, 25," 151–154; "Studies in the St. Mark's Isaiah Scroll IV (7.1; 14.4; 14.30)," 329–340; "Studies in the St. Mark's Isaiah Scroll V (15.9)," 5–8; "Studies in the St. Mark's Isaiah Scroll VI (34.16; 40.12)," 85–92; and, "Studies in the St. Mark's Isaiah Scroll VII (49:17)," 4–8.

[112] Orlinsky published close to a dozen popular reviews of books on the scrolls in *In Jewish Bookland* between 1950 and 1962. Collectively he published more than 140 reviews for that publication. A bibliography through 1982, along with a complete list of these reviews, is found in Miller, "A Selective Bibliography," xii–xxviii.

[113] "Proceedings of the American Oriental Society Meeting at New Haven, Connecticut, 1949," 185.

[114] Zeitlin, "A Commentary on the Book of Habakkuk," 235–247.

[115] For a summary of the paper see Orlinsky, "Studies in the St. Mark's Isaiah Scroll," 151–152.

[116] Ibid., 164–165.

[117] On the merger see Meyer, "A Centennial History," 185–192.

[118] Orlinsky to Glueck, 5 January 1950 (misdated 1949), MS 661, Harry Meyer Orlinsky/6/14, Glueck, Nelson, 1950–1974.

[119] See note marked * for discussion of the conference and the problems with the newspaper coverage of his comments (as also discussed above) in Orlinsky, "Studies in the St. Mark's Isaiah Scroll," 149.

[120] Ibid., 165, n. 21. In December 1949 he claimed that he had been shown two scrolls at St. Mark's Monastery: the Isaiah Scroll and a Haftarah Scroll used for liturgical readings on the Sabbath. He concluded, based on marginal notes in the latter scroll, that it was of late provenance and that the former, by relation to it, likewise could not be ancient. See his newspaper article, *"HaGenizah haGluyah v'ha Genizah haGnuzah,"* *Ha'Olam* (1 December 1949): 156–157; and Wechsler, "The 'Hidden Geniza' Once More," 247–250 and "The Origin of the So Called Dead Sea Scrolls," 121–139. Biographical information for Wechsler is quite limited. In secondary literature Wechsler is occasionally addressed as Doctor or Professor and more often as Mister. Sometimes he is described as a professor and at times as a journalist. According to his own account, he was a "researcher of ancient Israel history" born in Libau, Latvia, in 1889. Wechsler received his higher education in Tübingen and Hamburg and made aliyah to Israel in 1935. See Wechsler, "Wechsler, Tovia," 653.

[121] Orlinsky to Sonne, 29 June 1950, MS 513/2343g/Correspondence, 1949–1950.

[122] Ibid.

[123] Sonne to Orlinsky, 4 July 1950 (translated from the Hebrew), MS 513/2343g/Correspondence, 1949–1950.

[124] At the 1953 SBL meeting Orlinsky publicly accused Sonne of stealing ideas in his conference paper from the DHL thesis of one of the college's graduate students. Orlinsky to Glueck, 6 August 1953, MS 661/6/14, Glueck, Nelson, 1950–1971. Sonne only grew more aggravated with Orlinsky when, in 1956, Orlinsky published a critical review of the first volume of the official Dead Sea Scrolls publication. See Orlinsky, "Review: Barthelemy, D., and Milik, J. T., *Discoveries in the Judean Desert; I, Qumran Cave I*," 217. The review angered Sonne enough that he wrote to the editor, Salo Baron, to ask why he did not prevent the publication of the review. See Baron to Sonne, 24 September 1956, MS 513/2343h/Correspondence, 1957. Baron continued to maintain a friendly relationship with Sonne. See, Baron, "Isaiah Sonne 1887–1960," 130–132.

Sonne remained on guard for Orlinsky's book reviews. When Orlinsky wrote negatively about Kittel's *Biblia Hebraica* in the *JBL* ["Review: *The Text of the Old Testament, an Introduction to Kittel-Kahle's Biblia Hebraica*," 176–178], Sonne was so angered that he wrote a short article challenging the review (which he called an "unfair and intemperate attack") and sent it to the former *JBL* editor David Noel Freedman and his successor, Morton Enslin. When Enslin suggested that Sonne write directly to Orlinsky instead, because the journal could not publish replies to its articles and reviews, Sonne replied, "[R]egarding your suggestion to write directly to Dr. Orlinsky, I frankly do not see what purpose it could serve. Do you think Dr. Orlinsky could be persuaded to retract his attack?" See Sonne to Freedman, 22 January 1960; Sonne to Editor (*JBL*); 22 January 1960; Freedman to Sonne, 26 January 1960; Enslin to Sonne, 3 February 1960; and, Sonne to Enslin, 5 February 1956. These are preserved along with a draft of the article in MS 513/2343h/Correspondence, 1960.

Sonne was much in the habit of writing sharp reviews. As a result of his 1948 review of Cecil Roth's *The History of the Jews of Italy* (1946), he began what the prominent American Jewish historian Jonathan Sarna has called "one of the great literary exchanges in the history of book reviewing." [*JPS: The Americanization of Jewish Culture*, 203]. In the review Sonne critiqued Roth for ascribing the title "the circumciser" to the late ninth or tenth century Italian liturgical poet Menahem Corizzi and challenged him to provide a source for this information. [Sonne, "Review: *The History of the Jews of Italy by Cecil Roth*," 469–472]. Roth replied in a later volume that he had, in fact, taken the information from an Italian language article by Sonne himself! [Roth, "Critical Notes," 217].

[125] Orlinsky to Albright, 11 May 1949, MS 661/1/11, Albright, William F., 1941–1971.

[126] Albright to Orlinsky, 9 May 1949, MS 661/1/11, Albright, William F., 1941–1971.

[127] See Trever, "A Paleographic Study of the Jerusalem Scrolls," 16–17.

[128] Orlinsky to Albright, 11 May 1949, MS 661/1/11, Albright, William F., 1941–1971. With regard to Zeitlin's knowledge of this period's material, Orlinsky commented to Albright (already in 1945) that he had demonstrated "that he has no equal in the world today in historical perspective of the intertestamental period combined with a first-hand knowledge of the rabbinic material and a reliable knowledge of the hellenistic data. All his critics will pounce upon him ... but the fact always remains that their criticism is scarcely worth a hoot." Orlinsky to Albright, 25 October 1945, Harry Orlinsky, HUC-JIR, Unprocessed Material/Albright, W. F.

[129] Orlinsky, "The Masorah," 48.

[130] Orlinsky to Albright, 10 February 1949, Harry Orlinsky, HUC-JIR, Unprocessed Material/Albright, W. F.

[131] Although the discussion here relies heavily on the correspondence with Albright, among Orlinsky's papers are letters discussing the scrolls with Millar Burrows, John Trever, Eugene Ulrich, Michael Klein, Lawrence Schiffman, and many others. See MS 661/Harry Meyer Orlinsky, Sub-series 1: Correspondence. The reliance on Albright has to do with his stature and the extensiveness of the correspondence. Albright's influence on scrolls scholarship is rarely discussed but should not be overlooked. See Du Toit and Kalman, "Albright's Legacy?," 23–48.

[132] Orlinsky to Albright, 9 October 1950, MS 661/1/11, Albright, William F., 1941–1971. Orlinsky made a similar comment to H.H. Rowley of the University of Manchester: "I am very dubious that the Scrolls are at all Karaitic. I read them with that in mind, and then reread Karaite commentaries on some biblical Books and Karaite polemics against Jewish Orthodoxy. It was my judgment that no connection could be found." Orlinsky to Rowley, 29 September 1950, Harry Orlinsky, HUC-JIR, Unprocessed Material/R.

[133] Weis, "The Date of the Habbakuk Scroll," 125–154. Weis suggested that variant spellings and the like found in the scroll resulted from the influence of Arabic.

[134] Harold Henry Rowley (1890–1969) was Weis's colleague as professor of Hebrew at University of Manchester from 1945 until 1959. Beginning in the early 1940s Orlinsky corresponded with Rowley as the editor of the *Journal of Semitic Studies* and as secretary of the International

Organization for the Study of the Old Testament. In August 1950 Rowley informed Orlinsky that Weis had an article in press on the relationship between the scrolls and the Karaites. Rowley to Orlinsky, 18 August 1950, Harry Orlinsky, HUC-JIR, Unprocessed Material/R. Orlinsky replied the next month with his doubts about Karaite origins for the scrolls but looked forward to seeing Weis's work (see n. 132 above). Rowley replied that, at least with the Isaiah Scroll, "I am reacting against the pre-Christian date . . . though I think the limit of lateness would be about the seventh century A.D." Rowley to Orlinsky, 15 October 1950, Harry Orlinsky, HUC-JIR, Unprocessed Material/R. In 1952 Rowley published *The Zadokite Fragments and the Dead Sea Scrolls* wherein he concluded that the nonbiblical scroll materials certainly predated 131 BCE.

[135] Orlinsky to Rivkin, 8 November 1950, Harry Orlinsky, HUC-JIR, Unprocessed Material/ Ellis Rivkin. Orlinsky made a near-identical claim to Nelson Glueck earlier that same week: "As I see it now, unless and until some one can prove Weis wrong, a pre-Islamic date can scarcely be assumed for the Scrolls." Orlinsky to Glueck, 3 November 1950, Harry Orlinsky, HUC-JIR, Unprocessed Material/Glueck, Nelson.

[136] As late as 1957 Rivkin wrote to Orlinsky asking, "Are you taking any definite stand as yet with respect to the scrolls?" Rivkin to Orlinsky, 18 January 1957, Orlinsky, HUC-JIR, Unprocessed Material/Ellis Rivkin. Concerning Orlinsky's position on the text of the St. Mark's Scroll, S. David Sperling has noted, "It was Orlinsky who demonstrated the textual unreliability of the St. Mark's Isaiah scroll at a time when most scholars were hailing it as an important source of valuable variants to the received Hebrew texts of Isaiah." Sperling, *Students of the Covenant*, 80.

[137] Albright to Orlinsky, 19 December 1949, MS 661/1/11, Albright, William F., 1941–1971.

[138] Albright's only public disagreement with Orlinsky on the matter appeared in his "The Dead Sea Scrolls of St. Mark's Monastery," 5–6. On the fact that the Isaiah Scroll would not undermine the value of other early textual witnesses, Albright noted: "In this respect Dr. H.M. Orlinsky . . . is certainly correct (though his second example, Is. 43:19, is unhappy...)" (p.6). Orlinsky later wrote to Albright to thank him for his comments: "I am sorry that I cannot agree with your statement that "the textual value of the Scroll" will become increasingly clear. I appreciate very much your fair attitude towards my June JBL article . . . and I wish most heartily that I could agree with your estimate of the value of the scroll." Orlinsky to Albright, 1 October 1950, MS 661/1/11, Albright, William F., 1941–1971.

[139] Albright to Orlinsky, 3 December 1952, MS 661/1/11, Albright, William F., 1941–1971.

[140] Long, *Planting and Reaping Albright*, 98–99, n. 72. Orlinsky was well aware of the schism with Albright, and in his correspondence with Nelson Glueck he noted the impact the scrolls debate was having on the relationship: "And yet, with all our disagreements, I believe that Albright and I will yet come to common ground in the evaluation of the scrolls. Certainly I am the happiest person that our relationship is once again as cordial as it had always been." Orlinsky to Glueck, 9 October 1950, Harry Orlinsky, HUC-JIR, Unprocessed Material/Glueck, Nelson.

[141] Orlinsky to Albright, 22 November 1953, MS 661/1/11, Albright, William F., 1941–1971. In April 1953 Orlinsky referred publicly to the St. Mark's scrolls as "garbage." His comment was cited in a newspaper article with others by Zeitlin. Thus the two men's opinions were bound more tightly together. See Samuel, *Treasure of Qumran*, 196.

[142] Ibid.

[143] Albright to Orlinsky, 26 February 1954, and Albright to Orlinsky, 22 May 1954, MS 661/1/11, Albright, William F., 1941–1971.

[144] Albright to Orlinsky, 11 June 1954, MS 661/1/11, Albright, William F., 1941–1971. In the 1970s Orlinsky was still quite critical of Cross. Describing one of Cross's students, Orlinsky suggested that he knew he was a Cross student because he was "subservient and uncritical (to Cross) . . . [and] that he is superficial and knows little about methodology." Orlinsky to Wacholder, 30 June 1973, MS 661/15/32, Wacholder, Ben Zion. By the 1990s Orlinsky's position on Cross had softened rather significantly. In 1990 Orlinsky reported that when he was working on translating the *Revised Standard Version* of the book of Samuel in the mid-1970s, Cross gave him access to his unpublished allotment of Dead Sea Samuel texts. Cross's act received

acknowledgement in the *RSV* (note to 1 Sam. 1:23), and Orlinsky commented that he wanted to repeat the story because people were largely unaware of Cross's graciousness in this matter. See Orlinsky, "Closing Remarks," 411.

[145] Albright to Orlinsky, 20 April 1951; Orlinsky to Albright, 21 April 1951; MS 661/1/11, Albright, William F., 1941–1971.

[146] Albright to Orlinsky, 12 May 1951; Albright to Orlinsky, 11 June 1954; MS 661/1/11, Albright, William F., 1941–1971.

[147] See Long, *Planting and Reaping Albright*, 98–99.

[148] Orlinsky to Glueck, 12 April 1953, MS 661/6/14, Glueck, Nelson, 1950–1974. John Bright, also an Albright student, came out in support of Orlinsky's view: "While I am no specialist in textual criticism, as you know, I think that your general verdict on DSIa is correct. May it prevail." Bright to Orlinsky, 27 February 1957, Harry Orlinsky, HUC-JIR, Unprocessed Material/B.

[149] "The New Scrolls from the Judaean Desert," 3–4, 6–8. Throughout his career Orlinsky took the opportunity to share scroll scholarship with the lay public. Frequently his synagogue or Jewish Community Center talks included the scrolls, and he was often interviewed for newspaper articles. In 1956, he gave a long interview for broadcast in early 1957 on the BBC, which was rebroadcast by the University of Wisconsin Radio. Orlinsky to Bridson, 25 April 1957, Harry Orlinsky, HUC-JIR, Unprocessed Material/B. The text of the interview is included in this same file. Much of the discussion points to the importance of the Masoretic text and the integrity of its transmission: "Most of the Dead Sea Scroll fragments by far, even though they be a thousand years older than the oldest dated manuscript of the Hebrew Bible known to us . . . are inferior in their text to our traditional text; they were received and copied and transmitted by far less careful and learned and interested scribes."

[150] Ibid., 5–6.

[151] Gordon to Orlinsky, 3 March 1959, MS 661/6/22, Gordon, Cyrus, 1940–1959, 1981–1990. Orlinsky added his own note to the margin of the letter, indicating that he wanted the title of the course changed to "The Masoretic Text of the Old Testament and the Dead Sea Scrolls."

[152] Orlinsky to Brickman, 18 June 1957, Harry Orlinsky, HUC-JIR, Unprocessed Material/B.

[153] What follows summarizes the story as recounted by Orlinsky in "The Dead Sea Scrolls and Mr. Green," 245–256.

[154] Orlinsky knew the volume well, having sat on the publication committee of ASOR, which approved the publication, and having carried on a long correspondence with Burrows concerning it and especially the Isaiah Scroll. E.g., Burrows to Orlinsky, 9 January 1950; and Orlinsky to Burrows, 13 January 1950, Harry Orlinsky, HUC-JIR, Unprocessed Material/B.

[155] Ibid., 255.

[156] Orlinsky to Belliveau, 25 June 1956, Harry Orlinsky, HUC-JIR, Unprocessed Material/B.

[157] A transcription of the statement is found in Orlinsky, "The Dead Sea Scrolls and Mr. Green," 255.

[158] "Israel Acquires Ancient Scrolls," *The New York Times* (14 February 1955): 21.

[159] Orlinsky to Albright, 15 June 1954, and Albright to Orlinsky, 23 June 1954, MS 661, Harry Meyer Orlinsky Papers/1/11, Albright, William.

[160] In the article Orlinsky specifically attacked the carbon 14 dating of the scrolls, which had actually been done on fabric coverings and not the scrolls themselves. In 1957 the issue was brought up again in correspondence with Ellis Rivkin. Additionally, in 1956–1957, the topic of carbon 14 dating had been in the news as a result of an article in the *New York Times* that argued that the magnetic force of the Earth had diminished over time, thus throwing off carbon 14 dating by up to two hundred years. See John Hillaby, "Earth As Magnet Said to Weaken," the *New York Times* (26 December 1956): 24. Ellis Rivkin drew Orlinsky's attention to the issue. Rivkin to Orlinsky, 18 January 1957, Harry Orlinsky, HUC-JIR, Unprocessed Material/Ellis Rivkin.

Sonne was displeased with the published interview and what he perceived as an attack by Orlinsky on the scrolls. When Millar Burrows wrote to the magazine in response to the article laying out why he believed the scrolls were important and significant ancient documents [*American Judaism* 5, no.3 (1956): 2], Sonne wrote to Burrows to thank him for taking a stand against Orlinsky's "presumptuous statements regarding the Dead Sea Scrolls." Sonne to Burrows, 29 January 1956, MS 513/2343h/Correspondence, 1956.

[161] Brodsky, "The Case of the 7 Dead Sea Scrolls," 16. In his recent account of the discovery and purchase of the Dead Sea Scrolls, Weston Fields implies that Orlinsky's effort to help Israel acquire these scrolls was hypocritical in light of his previous negative comments about them. He writes: "Once the details of the contract had been formalized, Professor Orlinsky (who had just the year before called the scrolls 'st. Mark's garbage'), took on a pseudonym ('Mr. Green') and he and several other Hebrew scholars were called in to authenticate the scrolls" (*The Dead Sea Scrolls*, 245–246). Fields does not appear to appreciate Orlinsky's distinction between their value for scholarship and their value as antiquities (or as national treasures).

[162] For Yadin's description of the events surrounding the purchase, see his *The Message of the Scrolls*, 39–52. The archbishop provides his version of the events in *Treasure of Qumran*, 197–201.

[163] See note 153 above.

[164] Rabbi Richard F. Steinbrink, New York class of 1961, recalled Orlinsky telling his class the story. Email communication, 16 May 2008. Rabbi Professor Marc Saperstein recalls being told the story in 1968. Email communication, 8 June 2008.

[165] "Failure to Publish Dead Sea Scrolls is Leitmotif of New York University Scroll Conference," 4.

[166] Harman to Orlinsky, 7 September 1981, MS 661/1/10, Harman, Avraham, 1982–1989.

[167] Orlinsky, "The Bible Scholar Who Became an Undercover Agent," 26–29.

[168] A copy of the invitation is preserved in Harry M. Orlinsky—Nearprint Biography. Orlinsky coordinated a similar event as president of the American Academy of Jewish Research. On 22 October 1980 the academy hosted a seminar on "The Temple Scroll and Halachah," which also included Ben Zion Wacholder, Joseph Baumgarten, and Baruch Levine. Orlinsky to Wacholder, 23 July 1980, MS 661/15/32, Wacholder, Ben Zion.

[169] By 1990 a number of voices were raised against the Essene hypothesis. See, for example, Schiffman, "The New Halakhic Letter (4QMMT) and the Origins of the Dead Sea Sect," 64–73. For a history of research concerning the identity of the community see, White Crawford, "The Idenitification and History of the Qumran Community in American Scholarship," 13–29.

[170] Orlinsky, "Closing Remarks," 411–415.

[171] Orlinsky to Wacholder, 18 December 1989, MS 661/15/32, Wacholder, Ben Zion.

[172] "Abraham in Normative and Hellenistic Traditions" (1949).

[173] Sandmel, "Judaism, Jesus and Paul," 220–250.

[174] Professor Norman Golb indicated in a conversation on 25 May 2008 that when he arrived at the college as a new faculty member in 1958 no courses on the scrolls were offered and he volunteered to fill the lacuna.

[175] For Sandmel's affirmation of the antiquity of the scrolls see, for example, *A Jewish Understanding of the New Testament*, 201, and "The Jewish Scholar and Early Christianity," 478.

[176] In more sober terms he published a similar idea the same year: "The Dead Sea Scrolls serve conspicuously in undermining the limitations on, and the uncertainties in, our knowledge [of first century Judaism]; they do not materially increase our specific knowledge, but only offer some corroboration of what was already known." Sandmel, *A Jewish Understanding of the New Testament*, 201.

[177] "Dead Sea Scrolls: Sharp Divergences in Scholarly Views," *The Montreal Star* (9 February 1956): 12; and, Douglas J. Wilson, "Biblical Study Intensified: Debate Goes on About the Dead Sea Scrolls," *The Montreal Star* (11 February 1956): 10. For discussion of the impact of his comments on McGill University's acquisition of Cave 4 material see Du Toit and Kalman, *Canada's Big Biblical Bargain*, 77.

[178] "Dead Sea Scrolls Held Overvalued," *The New York Times* (6 February 1956): 25. The same article was reprinted in the Canadian national press as, "Caution Urged by Theologians," *The Globe and Mail* (7 February 1956): 10. Sandmel was not the only HUC-JIR faculty member to publicly criticize Wilson. In reviewing Wilson's book, Harry Orlinsky noted, "If you want to know the whole truth about how, when, where and by whom the Dead Sea Scrolls were discovered, Wilson's Chapter I . . . is not recommended; it is incomplete and misleading in several important matters. If you want to know what Jewish group, or groups, wrote these scrolls, you had better not rely on what he has to say in his chapter II." He continues chapter by chapter, liking only chapter III on the monastery at Qumran "because Wilson knows how to describe men and things and nature." Harry Orlinsky, "Author Wilson Played the Role of Advocate," *In Jewish Bookland* (May 1956): 2.

[179] Wilson, "A Reporter at Large: The Scrolls from the Dead Sea," 45–121.

[180] Wilson, *The Scrolls from the Dead Sea* (1955).

[181] Schiffman, "Inverting Reality: The Dead Sea Scrolls in the Popular Media," 27. On the publications' reception by scholars see Goldman, "A Long Affair," 119–120.

[182] On 6 February 1956, references appeared in *The Des Moines Tribune, The Baltimore Sun, The New York Times,* and *The Rochester Times Union.* In the days following they were reported in *The Springfield Ohio News, The Omaha Morning World-Herald, The Two-Rivers Wisconsin Reporter,* Canada's *Globe and Mail, The Worcester Massachusetts Gazette, The Flint, Michigan Journal, The Montreal Jewish Chronicle,* Cincinnati's *The American Israelite,* Philadelphia's *Jewish Exponent,* and Baltimore's *The Jewish Times.*

[183] John Hillaby, "Christian Bases Seen in Scrolls," *The New York Times* (5 February 1956): 2.

[184] On McGill's purchase see Du Toit and Kalman, *Canada's Big Biblical Bargain* (2010).

[185] Until recently the only preserved copy of the lecture was found in the library of Christ the King Seminary in East Aurora, New York. I am grateful to the seminary for making a copy of the lecture available to me.

[186] "The Dead Sea Scrolls and the New Testament," 2.

[187] Ibid., 2–3.

[188] Andre Dupont-Sommer (1900–1983) was a French scholar who greatly influenced Wilson. Dupont-Sommer argued that the unidentified "Teacher of Righteousness" in the scrolls prefigured Jesus in that, as a result of his teachings, he was put to death by the Romans, and his followers—in fact, his church—awaited his return. See his *The Dead Sea Scrolls: A Preliminary Survey* (1952).

[189] Stanley Edgar Hyman, "Review: *The Dead Sea Scrolls* by Millar Burrows, *The Scrolls from the Dead Sea* by Edmund Wilson," 409.

[190] John Haverstick, "The Battle of the Dead Sea Scrolls," *Saturday Review* (3 March 1956): 28–29. Quotation on 29.

[191] Sandmel to Cousins, 2 March 1956, MS Col. 101, Samuel Sandmel/1/1, A-K, General. Cf., Sandmel's letter to the editor and Haverstick's correction, *Saturday Review* (31 March 1956): 25. In the letter Sandmel made clear that while he disagreed with Dupont-Sommer, he respected him as a serious scholar who published his works in a scholarly forum where they could be legitimately debated by his peers. He also lauded Millar Burrows: "The lay person may find it more difficult to read Burrows' book than Wilson. But then let him know that the choice is between authenticity and romance." In an unpublished essay, Sandmel also showed appreciation for Theodore Gaster's work on the scrolls, noting that, "Broad and acute scholarship distinguish it from many other writings in the field, and Dr. Gaster writes with a grace that Edmund Wilson might well envy." Samuel Sandmel, "Theodore H. Gaster's *The Dead Sea Scrolls*" preserved in, MS 101, Samuel Sandmel/15/6, Draft Articles.

[192] In this Sandmel followed his doctoral supervisor, Erwin Goodenough, who noted that by definition two parallel lines could never meet. For discussion see Fitzmyer, *Responses to 101 Questions on the Dead Sea Scrolls,* 101.

[193] Sandmel, "Parallelomania," 4–5.

[194] John Wicklein, "Scrolls Doubted as Link to Jesus: Biblical Scholar says They Represent an Exaggeration," *The New York Times* (31 December 1961): 17.

[195] Ibid., 17.

[196] Goodenough, *Jewish Symbols in the Greco-Roman Period*, 13 volumes (1953–1965).

[197] Samuel Sandmel, "Review: *Jewish Symbols in the Greco-Roman Period, Volume Four*," 380. In volume nine, on the artwork in the ancient synagogue at Dura-Europus, Goodenough adopted Sandmel's view of the relationship between his work and the scrolls, noting, for example, "The synagogue had quite as radical implications for our knowledge of Judaism as the Dead Sea Scrolls, if not far deeper; but whereas hundreds of people were prepared to read the Scrolls, no one alive knew how to read the language of the murals." Goodenough, *Jewish Symbols in the Greco-Roman Period,* vol. 9, 4.

[198] Sandmel, "Erwin Ramsdell Goodenough," 3.

[199] Ibid., 13.

[200] Sandmel likewise called the scrolls a fad in *The Genius of Paul*, 227.

[201] Sandmel, "Jesus in World History" (1966): 188.

[202] Seven of the twenty-four essays by Sandmel written between 1956 and 1967 and included in his *Two Living Traditions* include passages downplaying the importance of the scrolls.

[203] "Parallelomania," 12.

[204] New York: Schocken, 1970.

[205] Rollins, "Review: *The Genius of Paul: A Study in History* by Samuel Sandmel," 388.

[206] Brown, "Review: *The First Christian Century in Judaism and Christianity: Certainties and Uncertainties* by Samuel Sandmel," 235.

[207] Sandmel, *The First Christian Century*, 82.

[208] Ibid., 83.

[209] Ibid., 84–85.

[210] Sandmel's unpublished lecture, "Palestinian and Hellenistic Judaism and Christianity: The Question of the Comfortable Theory," takes issue with Albright's "Recent Discoveries in Palestine and the Gospel of John," 153–171. The lecture is found in MS 101/15/6, Draft Articles.

[211] According to James Sanders, whose HUC-JIR dissertation, "Suffering as Divine Discipline in the Old Testament and Post-Biblical Judaism" (1954) was written under the supervision of Sandmel and Sheldon Blank, Sandmel never discussed the scrolls in class or in private consultation with him. Further, Sanders excluded analysis of the scrolls from his dissertation, although he continued to study them on his own for the sake of his scholarly career. Sanders had previously studied the scrolls with J. Phillip Hyatt at Vanderbilt University and André Dupont-Sommer at the École des Hautes Études. In conjunction with the work he did with Sonne, these studies prepared him to continue to work on the scrolls independently. Email communications from James Sanders, 14 May 2008 and 28 August 2008.

[212] Rivkin, "Leon da Modena" (1946).

[213] For a biography of Rivkin see Silberg, "Aspects of the Life and Work of Ellis Rivkin: An Intellectual Biography with Annotated Bibliography" (2004).

[214] Weiner, "The Dead Sea Scrolls as Historical Sources," 177–178. Weiner has since concluded that the scrolls are ancient:

> The Dead Sea Scrolls "give us firsthand insights into the [era] that produced Christianity and the Judaism we know today," said Rabbi Daniel Weiner of Temple De Hirsch Sinai in Seattle and Bellevue. "It provides a grounding for our faith. . . . For Jews to have literally texts that are not only ancient in their content but in terms of their existence is extremely meaningful to a people who bind themselves to God through text."

Janet I. Tu, "A Rare Window into Biblical Times," *The Seattle Times* (17 September 2006): B1.

[215] Orlinsky taught Rivkin at Baltimore Hebrew College in the mid-1930s. From there a friendship and mentorship developed, as is shown by dozens of letters about research and family that Orlinsky—whom Rivkin always addressed as "Doc"— preserved. Rivkin's unfortunately unpublished monograph on Zeitlin (discussed below) was begun with the encouragement of Orlinsky, who wanted it for inclusion in the SBL's centenary publication series. Although Silberg notes their relationship, he does not give adequate attention to Orlinsky's influence on Rivkin or, for that matter, Rivkin's reliance on Orlinsky. See Silberg, 23.

[216] In a subsequent letter to Orlinsky, Rivkin described Trevor rather unflatteringly:

> What did you think of Zeitlin's latest article on the scrolls? It seems to me that he had many excellent points among which was the evidence that the various peculiar spellings can be duplicated in later manuscripts. When I spoke to Albright he was convinced as ever that there could be only one answer to the problem. What annoyed me immensely was the way in which he elevated Trevor [*sic*]—a complete am ha-aretz if there ever was one into an authority not only on paleography but on comparisons of manuscripts. How anyone so ignorant could dare right [*sic*] the article that he wrote in the last issue of the Quarterly is hard to imagine.

Rivkin to Orlinsky, 17 October 1950, Harry Orlinsky, HUC-JIR, Unprocessed Material/Ellis Rivkin.

[217] Rivkin to Orlinsky, 30 November 1949, Harry Orlinsky, HUC-JIR, Unprocessed Material/ Ellis Rivkin.

[218] In 1957 he noted to Orlinsky that he was "becoming more and more convinced of the strength of Zeitlin's case." Rivkin to Orlinsky, 18 January 1957, Harry Orlinsky, HUC-JIR, Unprocessed Material/Ellis Rivkin.

[219] Orlinsky to Rivkin, 8 November 1950, Harry Orlinsky, HUC-JIR, Unprocessed Material/ Ellis Rivkin.

[220] Phone conversation with Ellis Rivkin, 3 June 2008.

[221] Rivkin, "Solomon Zeitlin's Contribution," 360.

[222] See Weiner, "The Dead Sea Scrolls as Historical Sources," 156–157.

[223] From Rivkin's unpublished intellectual biography of Solomon Zeitlin, 123. I am grateful to Professor Rivkin for permitting me to read the manuscript.

[224] Cohen, "Review: *A Hidden Revolution* by Ellis Rivkin," 628.

[225] Seltzer and Bemporad, "Ellis Rivkin on Judaism and the Rise of Christianity," 4.

[226] Bailey's defense of Rivkin's method is understandable in light of his having been Rivkin's student while earning his doctorate at HUC-JIR in the 1960s. In his doctoral dissertation he credits Rivkin, who "completely revolutionized my thinking with respect to the Documentary Hypothesis, and several of his ideas have been utilized in the study." Bailey, "The God of the Fathers," iii.

[227] Bailey, "The Pharisees," 55.

[228] Rivkin, Unpublished intellectual biography of Solomon Zeitlin, 130.

[229] Although Rivkin attempts in the monograph to avoid dating the scrolls, trying to simply highlight the methodological issues Zeitlin raised, he certainly works hard to demonstrate that Zeitlin convincingly argued that they could not be from the Second Temple period. First, he notes that Zeitlin proved that the line-by-line commentaries found in the *pesharim* are atypical of the period and only appeared for the first time among the Karaites. Second, technical terms such as "Teacher of Righteousness" are only found outside the scrolls in Karaite writings. Third, certain terms used to designate the scroll community appear nowhere else in the extant Second Temple writings. Fourth, during the Second Temple period there were no messianic ascetic communities. Fifth, Zeitlin demonstrated that various orthographic and scribal practices in the scrolls were not attested before the Karaites. Sixth, Zeitlin proved that Josephus's Essenes and the Qumran community could not be the same, as they disagreed on fundamental beliefs such as immortality of the soul. As Rivkin notes, "These facts—and facts they are—are vital

for Dead Sea Scroll studies." Rivkin, Unpublished intellectual biography of Solomon Zeitlin, 129. Rivkin's point-by-point summary of Zeitlin's conclusions is found on 128–129.

[230] Ibid.

[231] According to Rivkin's biographer, Barry Silberg, "Sandmel questioned Rivkin's confidence in Ben Sira as a control text, doubted his synagogue hypothesis, and dismissed in a footnote the weight Rivkin assigned to Paul's self-affirmation in Philippians and his reference to paradosis in Galatians." Silberg, "Aspects of the Life," 77.

[232] The language that the two use in describing this problem is so similar it is difficult to imagine they did not discuss the issue. Sandmel wrote, for example, "Several years ago I wrote that to identify the Qumran community with the Essenes is to explain one unknown by another..." Sandmel, "Parallelomania," 8. Rivkin wrote, "[A] principle that affirms that since unknown can only be made known by the known, the first order of scholarly business is to compare the unknown with the known." Unpublished intellectual biography of Solomon Zeitlin, 130.

[233] Phone conversation with Ellis Rivkin, 3 June 2008. James Sanders, who studied with Rivkin in the early 1950s, recalled that Rivkin "never mentioned the Scrolls except to ridicule them as of any importance to Ancient Judaism. It was to me rather irritating that he wouldn't even engage them in any way." Email correspondence from James Sanders, 28 August 2008.

[234] See "Students of Philology," *The New York Times* (28 December 1894): 10; "Society of Biblical Literature," *The New York Times* (15 June 1895): 9; and, "Society Split Over Babylonian Tablets," *The New York Times* (27 November 1910): 5.

[235] See "Experts Dispute Age of Bible Documents," *The New York Times* (30 December 1949): 4; "Theologian Warns of Pressure Groups," *The New York Times* (29 December 1955): 26; "Scholars Dispute Scrolls' Validity," *The New York Times* (28 December 1956): 14; Farnsworthe Fowle, "Recent Discoveries Of Biblical Texts Hailed by Scholars," *The New York Times* (30 December 1958): 37; John Wicklein, "Scrolls Doubted as Link to Jesus," *The New York Times* (31 December 1961): 17; and, Peter Steinfels, "Dead Sea Scrolls Free of Last Curb," *The New York Times* (27 November 1991): A22.

[236] Orlinsky did not speak on the Dead Sea Scrolls but gave a paper titled, "Diviner vs. Prophet in Ancient Israel." See "Proceedings, December 29–31, 1958," iv.

[237] Glueck to Albright, 4 November 1968, MS 20/A1a-156/3, Albright, Wm.

[238] Nelson Glueck, "New Light on the Dim Past," *The New York Times* (20 November 1955): BR54–BR55.

[239] Ibid., BR54.

[240] Ibid., BR55.

[241] "Unearthing the Past: A Decade of Discoveries," *Time Magazine* (13 December 1963): 50–60. Quote on 60.

[242] Glueck, "New Light," BR54.

[243] Glueck, *Rivers in the Desert*, 31.

[244] Nelson Glueck, "Out of Yesterday, A Symbol for Today," *The New York Times* (11 May 1958): BR6.

[245] Brown and Kutler, *Nelson Glueck*, 130–131.

[246] Samuel Johnson Woolf, "To Teach 'Not Science, but Eternal Laws,'" *The New York Times* (7 March 1948): SM15.

[247] Orlinsky to Sonne, 21 December 1955, MS 513/2343h/Correspondence, 1955; and Orlinsky to Blank, Lewy, and Sandmel, 27 January 1956; MS 513/2343h/Correspondence, 1956. The list is preserved in MS 20/Aia-53/4, O, General.

[248] Sonne was pushed into retirement at the end of the 1955–1956 school year, which may explain his decision not to participate in organizing a conference for 1957. It is also plausible

that Sonne preferred not to work with Orlinsky in matters relating to the scrolls in light of their previous relationship.

[249] Press release, "Reform Rabbinic School Schedules International Scholarly Symposium on Dead Sea Scrolls," 10 November 1955, MS 20/A1a-45/3, O, General.

[250] Ibid.

[251] Orlinsky to Blank, Lewy, and Sandmel, 27 January 1956; MS 513/2343h/Correspondence, 1956.

[252] Sonne to Orlinsky, 2 February 1956, MS 513/2343h/Correspondence, 1956.

[253] Dinur to Orlinsky, 19 February 1956, MS 20/A1a-45/3, O, General. See also Orlinsky to Glueck, 25 September 1956, and Glueck to Dinur, 30 March 1956, MS 661/6/14, Glueck, Nelson.

[254] The papers from the session are published in Rabin and Yadin, *Scripta Hierosolymitana Volume IV* (1958).

[255] Dinur to Orlinsky, 19 February 1956, MS 20/A1a-45/3, O, General. Orlinsky to Glueck, 25 September 1956, and Glueck to Dinur, 30 March 1956, MS 661/6/14, Glueck, Nelson.

[256] See Golb, "The Second World Congress of Jewish Studies," 30–36.

[257] Orlinsky to Glueck, 25 September 1956, MS 661/6/14, Glueck, Nelson.

[258] Orlinsky to Glueck, 25 September 1956, and Glueck to Van Dusen, 18 December 1956, MS 661/6/14, Glueck, Nelson.

[259] Albright to Glueck, undated response to letter of 11 April 1956, MS 661/6/14, Glueck, Nelson.

[260] Orlinsky to Glueck, 20 April 1956, MS 661/6/14, Glueck, Nelson.

[261] Orlinsky to Glueck, 20 April, 1956, MS 661/6/14, Glueck, Nelson.; and, Orlinsky to Glueck, 2 May 1956, MS 20/Aia-45/3, O, General.

[262] Orlinsky to Glueck, 2 May 1956, MS 20/Aia-45/3, O, General.

[263] Glueck to Albright, 25 April 1956, MS 20/A1a-41/7, Albright, Wm.

[264] Albright to Glueck, 30 April 1956, MS 20/A1a-41/7, Albright, Wm.

[265] Ibid.

[266] Orlinsky to Glueck, 10 May 1956, MS 20/Aia-45/3, O, General.

[267] Glueck to Orlinsky, 14 May 1956, MS 661/6/14, Glueck, Nelson.

[268] Orlinsky to Glueck, 3 October 1956, MS 661/6/14, Glueck, Nelson. His pushing does not appear to have caused any particular ill will. In July 1956 Dinur invited Glueck to chair the closing session of the congress, which would be used as an opportunity to sum up deliberations from the sessions. Dinur to Glueck, 21 July 1956, MS 20/Aia-50/1, D, General. Glueck accepted the invitation. (See Ostrov to Dinur, 17 August 1956, and Glueck to Dinur, 17 September 1956, MS 20/Aia-50/1, D, General.) Golb describes Glueck's participation in the congress, "Second World Congress," 32.

[269] Glueck to Van Dusen, 18 December 1956, MS 661/6/14, Glueck, Nelson.

[270] Albright highlighted this conflict in his response to Glueck having informed him of the conference's indefinite deferral: "I think it very wise to defer the Dead Sea Scroll conference for next September. The direct conflict between it and the Munich Congress of Orientalists, which you did not mention, should be alone enough to make the postponement necessary." Albright to Glueck, 4 February 1956, MS 20/Aia-47/9, Albright, Wm.

[271] Glueck to Van Dusen, 1 February 1957, MS 661/6/14, Glueck, Nelson.

[272] See Zeitlin, "The Dead Sea Scrolls: Fantasies and Mistranslations," 71–85 especially 75–76; and, Kutscher, "Dating the Language of the Genesis Apocryphon," 288–292.

[273] By December 1956 Orlinsky had already prepared the full program. He planned to have Yigael Yadin and William Albright speak on the discovery, recovery, and archaeology of the scrolls;

Patrick Skehan, James Muilenberg, Harry Orlinsky, H.L. Ginsberg, and Frank Cross to speak on the scrolls and the Hebrew Bible. On the scrolls and the Second Jewish Commonwealth he hoped to have Samuel Sandmel, Isaiah Sonne, Saul Lieberman, Solomon Zeitlin, Isaac Rabinowitz, Millar Burrows, and Joseph Baumgarten. Millar Burrows, William Brownlee, Frank Cross, H.H. Rowley, Andre Dupont-Sommer, Oscar Cullman, and Morton Enslin were to be invited to speak on the scrolls and the New Testament. On the scrolls and linguistics he hoped Isaac Rabinowitz, Ezekiel Kutscher, H.L. Ginsberg, Henoch Yalon, and G.R. Driver might speak. On the scrolls and later Christianity he wanted Paul Kahle, Josef Milik, and Leonhard Rost; on the scrolls and Jewish history he hoped to have Pinkas Weis, Joseph Baumgarten, and Leon Nemoy. Orlinsky also wanted to encourage the active participation of Dominique Barthelemy, Roland de Vaux, G. Lankester Harding, A.M. Habermann, Samuel Birnbaum, John Allegro, Erwin Goodenough, Otto Eissfeldt, David Noel Freedman, and Jacob Licht. See "Symposium, Dead Sea Scroll, September 17, 1957," 12 December 1956, MS 20/Aia-53/4, O, General. Even casually surveying the list, the inclusion of people not normally identified as Dead Sea Scroll scholars is apparent (e.g., Saul Lieberman). For an insightful discussion of the contributions made by this early generation see Jassen, "American Scholarship on Jewish Law in the Dead Sea Scrolls," 101–154 .

[274] Harry Orlinsky, undated manuscript, MS 661/4/18, Dead Sea Scrolls Intro. Orlinsky reminisced about the seminar (including repeating his joke about covering everything from A to Z) in his closing remarks at the Second International Congress on Biblical Archaeology held in Jerusalem during the summer of 1990. Orlinsky, "Closing Remarks," 412.

[275] Glueck did manage to attract some publicity for the College when he arranged two speaking events for Yigael Yadin in New York and Cincinnati in November 1956. Yadin had recently made known the contents of the Genesis Apocryphon, and in New York on 29 November and Cincinnati on 30 November, he gave lectures titled, "Tales of Genesis: An Illustrated Lecture on the Newly-Deciphered Dead Sea Scroll." The invitations are preserved in Nearprint–Yigael Yadin. The lectures came out of a discussion between Glueck and Yadin that September. Yadin was disappointed that they had not been able to see each other in either Tel Aviv or at his Hazor excavation while Glueck was in Israel, and he informed Glueck that he would be in New York in November and December. Yadin to Glueck, 6 September 1956, MS 20/A1a-155/10, XY, General.

[276] Samuel Sandmel, "Theodore H. Gaster's *The Dead Sea Scrolls*," unpublished manuscript, preserved in MS 101/15/6, Draft Articles. Here Sandmel appears to be referring to John Allegro. Allegro, a member of the team assigned to edit the scrolls found in later caves, particularly Cave 4, broadcast on the BBC in January 1956 his conclusion that the scrolls discussed a crucified leader of the sect similar to, or perhaps inspiring, the story of Jesus and his crucifixion. The other team members were dismayed by his having shared this news based on manuscripts no one else had seen or evaluated. Allegro's comments and the editorial team's response were carried in the international press. For discussion of the events see Brown, *John Marco Allegro*, 76–97. Allegro's conclusions were discussed in *The New York Times* just a few days before Sandmel gave his lecture in Montreal (See above).

[277] Phone conversation with Norman Golb, 25 May 2008. For Golb's biography and a survey of his contributions to scholarship see Kraemer, "Portrait of the Scholar," 1–9.

[278] *JQR* 47, no.4 (1957): 354–374.

[279] *JJS* 8 (1957): 51–69.

[280] Golb, "Literary and Doctrinal Aspects of the Damascus Document," 374.

[281] Glueck informed Golb of his employment on 21 February 1958. The board appointed him officially in late May or early June. See Glueck to Golb, 4 June 1958, MS 20/Aia-59/2, G, General.

[282] Phone conversation with Norman Golb, 25 May 2008.

[283] The course catalogue was for the two academic years, and there is no clear indication of when the course was actually offered. In conversation, Golb was relatively certain that he actually taught the course in 1959–1960.

[284] Conversation with Norman Golb, 25 May 2008.

[285] A copy of the proposal is found in MS 20/Aia-67/5, G, General.

[286] Glueck, reference letter regarding Dr. Norman Golb, 1 May 1959, MS 20/Aia-67/5, G, General.

[287] Golb provided a summary of his activities and research in England during the Summer of 1959 in "Grant No. 2574 (1959), $1,200," 488–491.

[288] The conference presentations included: "The Qumran Sectarians, the 'Maġārīya', and the Qaraites," at the 1958 SBL Meeting [see "Proceedings, December 29–31, 1958," v.]; "The Redactions of the Damascus Covenant and Their Importance for the Problem of the Sect's Migration to Damascus," at the 1959 SBL Meeting [see "Proceedings December 29–31, 1959," iv]; "The Cairo Genizah and its Bearing on the Qumran Problem," at the 1960 Middle West Branch of the AOS Meeting [see "Proceedings of the Middle West Branch American Oriental Society April 22–23, 1960," 296]; and, "Who Were the Maġārīya?," at the 1960 AOS Meeting [see "Proceedings of the American Oriental Society, Meeting at New Haven, Connecticut, 1960," 285]. The articles included: "Who Were the Maġārīya?," 347–359; and, "The Qumran Covenanters and the Later Jewish Sects," 38–50.

[289] "Dead Sea Scrolls Subject of Talk," *Montreal Star* (7 February 1961): 13.

[290] Phone conversation with Norman Golb, 25 May 2008. For Rivkin's response to this "insult," see Silberg, "Aspects of the Life," 78–79.

[291] In conversation Golb recalled that the rabbinical students were rather docile about the scrolls. However, they had very limited contact with the material.

[292] Golb to Glueck, 18 February 1963, File: Golb, Norman—Correspondence, SC-3986.

[293] Conversation with Norman Golb, 25 May 2008.

[294] On the history of the Shrine of the Book see Roitman, "Shrine of the Book," 874–875.

[295] He discusses his effort in Trever, *The Untold Story of Qumran*, 1–76.

[296] On the photographic work of the Bieberkrauts see Broshi, "The Negatives Archive of the Shrine of the Book," 135–136.

[297] On Albina's efforts see Cross, "On the History of the Photography," 121–122 and, Strugnell, "On the History of Photographing the Discoveries," 123–134.

[298] Harman (1915–1992) served as university president from 1968 until 1983, and later as chancellor.

[299] The volume in Albright's honor is *Eretz-Israel 9: W.F. Albright Volume* (1969).

[300] Jerusalem mayor Teddy Kollek discussed publicly the difficulty of translating the Hebrew title when the award was presented to Albright. See James Feron, "Jerusalem Hails U.S. Archaeologist: Names Albright a 'Worthy' for Long Scholarship," *The New York Times* (24 March 1969): 11.

[301] Glueck's Jerusalem Diary, 30, MS 20/A1a-149/10, Diary, Jerusalem.

[302] Meeting of the Board of Governors, 90, 5 June 1969, MS 20/B1/13, 1969–1970.

[303] Harman to Glueck, 14 April 1969, Administrative File: Dead Sea Scrolls, Klau Library.

[304] Ibid.

[305] Glueck to Harman, 2 May 1969, Administrative File: Dead Sea Scrolls, Klau Library.

[306] Glueck to Sang, 28 April 1969, MS 20/A1a-154/1, S, General. Sang (1902–1975) was president of Goldenrod Ice Cream Co. of Chicago. He collected rare manuscripts of Americana and Judaica Americana, as well as art and jazz memorabilia. He was also a board member of the Jewish Publication Society. A long-term friendship between Sang and Glueck is attested by the materials collected in the AJA, Cincinnati. See Sang, Philip D., Nearprint Box—Biographies. Sang's donations to HUC began in 1946 and continued until his death. He particularly supported the building program of the Jerusalem campus and early efforts to introduce the students to computers and the "computerization" of rabbinic texts. Martin Holstein to Jacob Rader Marcus, 20 June 1972, Sang, Philip D., Nearprint Box—Biographies. For his financial

support and service to the college, HUC-JIR awarded Sang a doctor of humane letters, *honoris causa*, in 1973. A biography can be found in Walton, "Philip David Sang, 1902–1975," 429–434.

[307] Sang is referred to as chairman in several of the reports to the committee preserved in MS 20/G-1/ Reports of the Libraries, 1944–1991.

[308] Glueck to Sang, 14 May 1969, MS 20/A1a-154/1, S, General. In June, Harman wrote to Glueck explaining that the $10,000 would cover the entire cost of making the two thousand negatives of the scrolls and fragments, duplicate copies of the negatives, and several sets of positives. As such, HUC-JIR was funding the entire project. Harman to Glueck, 18 June 1969, MS 20/A1a-151/3, H, General.

[309] Glueck to Harman, 15 May 1969, Administrative File: Dead Sea Scrolls, Klau Library.

[310] Glueck to Sang, 28 April 1969, MS 20/A1a-154/1, S, General.

[311] Glueck to Sang, 14 May 1969, MS 20/A1a-154/1, S, General.

[312] Ibid.

[313] The records of the purchase are not preserved, but Glueck discusses it and the assessment of the vessel when it reached the Los Angeles campus of HUC-JIR in 1969. Glueck to Berkowitz, 10 July 1969, MS 20/K2-2/1969 July. The jar is exhibited in the Skirball Museum at HUC-JIR in Cincinnati. Accession number: 1982 49.1A+B/A0869A+B. A color photograph appears on the cover and also accompanies Jerry Stein, "Hebrew Union's Little Gem: Museum a Treasury of Jewish Art," *The Cincinnati Post* (5 February 1996): 1B.

[314] Only a few days after writing Glueck with the details of the proposed scroll transaction, Harman wrote to Harold P. Manson of the American Friends of Hebrew University (copying Glueck and HUC-JIR Jerusalem dean Ezra Spicehandler) for help in arranging housing for between twenty-six and forty HUC-JIR students. Harman to Manson, 17 April 1969, MS 20/A1a-151/3, H, General. This correspondence might be interpreted as encouraging Glueck to find the funds for the work on the scrolls.

[315] Presumably Glueck was referring to "writing tables." These were found in what Roland de Vaux identified as the "scriptorium" at the settlement of Qumran; as early as 1958, their description as "writing tables" for scribes copying scrolls was challenged. See *inter alia*, Metzger, "The Furniture in the Scriptorium at Qumran," 509–515. The problem of identifying these items and explaining their use remains. See Magness, *The Archaeology of Qumran*, 60–61.

[316] Glueck's diary entry for 21 June 1967. See Glueck, *Dateline: Jerusalem*, 26–27. William G. Dever was then the executive officer of the HUC-JIR Biblical Archaeology School and was preparing to begin the excavation at Gezer. He provides a first-hand description of the events in Jerusalem in "Archaeology and the Six Day War," 73, 102–107. Glueck was in Jerusalem from 12 June to 27 August 1967. The topic of the scrolls came up frequently during the visit, first regarding the exploration and repair of the Rockefeller Museum. During the visit Glueck met with Israeli Supreme Court justice Haim Cohn, who was judging the case of a journalist who had been denied a permit to excavate at Qumran (*Dateline: Jerusalem*, 65). Since the discovery of the scrolls there had been rumors of an eighth intact scroll circulating among scholars and collectors. On 23 June Glueck visited with Kando, the antiquities dealer who had helped arrange the original sale of scrolls to Athanasius Samuel. During the visit Glueck was informed that some of Kando's merchandise—the rumored scroll, Glueck supposed—had been confiscated by Israeli authorities (*Dateline: Jerusalem*, 29–30). In the last part of the diary, on 22 August 1967, Glueck noted, "One of my favorite diversions since coming here this June has been to pursue the story of the missing Dead Sea Scroll." (*Dateline: Jerusalem*, 116). What follows the statement is five pages of Glueck recounting his discussions about the scroll with Kando and his advice to the dealer that he approach the Israelis for compensation as provided for in the Israeli antiquities law. (*Dateline: Jerusalem*, 116–120). The scroll turned out to be the longest one found and is identified as the Temple Scroll. See Yadin, *Temple Scroll* (1985), 39–55 for an account of the confiscation of the scroll from Kando. Clearly, from the time of their discovery until the years immediately preceding his death, Glueck was very much caught up in the adventure of the scrolls.

[317] Glueck, diary entry for 14 July 1969, MS 20/A1a-158/11, Diary. The conversation was followed with a letter from Harman and a confidential memorandum about the project. Cataloguing and microfilming the approximately three thousand manuscripts was expected to last though 1972 with a budget of $100,000. The idea was that the costs would be split evenly between Hebrew University and a single donor institution, which would then receive a complete copy of the films. Harman to Glueck, 14 July 1969, with attached document "CONFIDENTIAL: Monastery of Mount Sinai Manuscripts," MS 20/K2-2/1969 July.

[318] In 1961 a new library building was constructed on the Cincinnati campus. The library was named for David W. Klau, who supported the construction of the new building and who died three months preceding its dedication in June 1961.

[319] Glueck to Zafren, 15 August 1969, MS 20/A1a-164/6, X, Y, Z, General.

[320] Broshi to Glueck, 23 February 1970, negative enclosed, Administrative File: Dead Sea Scrolls, Klau Library.

[321] Cross reference to the inventory list indicates that it is negative number 42.553, photographed by Albina in December 1958. See Tov and Pfann, *Companion Volume*, 161.

[322] Benoit, Milik, de Vaux, *Les Grottes de Murabba'at*, v.1: 155–159, v.2: Plate XLV.

[323] He is described thusly by Meyer, "A Centennial History," 220.

[324] Bamberger to Zafren, 3 November 1970, Administrative File: Dead Sea Scrolls, Klau Library.

[325] Zafren to Glueck, 17 November 1970; Glueck to Broshi, 20 November 1970, Administrative File: Dead Sea Scrolls, Klau Library.

[326] Broshi to Glueck, 2 December 1970, Administrative File: Dead Sea Scrolls, Klau Library.

[327] For a brief overview see Cross, *The Ancient Library of Qumran*, 35–40. A position on the editorial team was also offered to some of the institutions that funded the acquisition of Cave 4 fragments. See Du Toit and Kalman, *Canada's Big Biblical Bargain*, 56. While many accounts of the history of the discoveries and early Dead Sea Scrolls scholarship ignore or downplay Harding's role, in the most recent he is a central figure. See, Fields, *The Dead Sea Scrolls* (2009). On the history of the museum see Ibrahim, *West Meets East* (2006).

[328] See Schiffman, *Reclaiming the Dead Sea Scrolls*, 21–22. Yadin described his discussions with de Vaux following the change in authority in *The Temple Scroll* (1985), 45–46.

[329] Broshi to Glueck, 18 December 1970, Administrative File: Dead Sea Scrolls, Klau Library.

[330] Cited from a draft response to Broshi by Glueck, enclosed with Zafren to Glueck, 31 December 1970, Administrative File: Dead Sea Scrolls, Klau Library.

[331] Zafren to Glueck, 31 December 1970, Administrative File: Dead Sea Scrolls, Klau Library.

[332] Glueck to Broshi, 11 January 1971, Administrative File: Dead Sea Scrolls, Klau Library.

[333] Gottschalk to Board of Directors, Shrine of the Book Fund, 23 November 1971, Administrative File: Dead Sea Scrolls, Klau Library. Gottschalk (1930–2009) was ordained by HUC-JIR in 1957 and appointed acting dean (1958) and then dean (1959) of its Los Angeles campus. He received his Ph.D from the University of Southern California in 1965 and succeeded Nelson Glueck as president of HUC-JIR (1971–1996).

[334] Ibid.

[335] Zafren to Gottschalk, 6 March 1972, Administrative File: Dead Sea Scrolls, Klau Library.

[336] Air Waybill, El Al Israel Airlines LTD., 114–574234 3, 24 March 1972, Administrative File: Dead Sea Scrolls, Klau Library.

[337] Broshi to Gottschalk, 11 April 1972, Administrative File: Dead Sea Scrolls, Klau Library.

[338] Zafren to Broshi, 20 April 1972, Administrative File: Dead Sea Scrolls, Klau Library.

[339] Broshi to Zafren, 7 May 1972, Administrative File: Dead Sea Scrolls, Klau Library.

[340] Broshi to Zafren, 12 June 1972; Zafren to Gottschalk, 16 June 1972, Administrative File: Dead Sea Scrolls, Klau Library. The first complete catalogue of the material was not published until 1994: Reed, Lundberg, and Phelps, *The Dead Sea Scrolls Catalogue*.

[341] Zafren to Gottschalk, 25 January 1973, Administrative File: Dead Sea Scrolls, Klau Library.

[342] Zafren to Gottschalk, 27 October, 1975; and Klein to Zafren, 24 August 1976, Administrative File: Dead Sea Scrolls, Klau Library.

[343] Zafren to Gottschalk, 17 January 1980, Administrative File: Dead Sea Scrolls, Klau Library.

[344] Gottschalk to Zafren, 4 November 1975, Administrative File: Dead Sea Scrolls, Klau Library.

[345] Zafren to Gottschalk, 3 June 1976, Administrative File: Dead Sea Scrolls, Klau Library.

[346] Zafren to Broshi, 13 July 1976, Administrative File: Dead Sea Scrolls, Klau Library.

[347] Broshi to Zafren, 25 July 1976, Administrative File: Dead Sea Scrolls, Klau Library.

[348] Ibid.

[349] Zafren to Gottschalk, 30 July 1976, Administrative File: Dead Sea Scrolls, Klau Library.

[350] Summary of meeting in Broshi to Gottschalk, 22 August 1976; Klein to Zafren, 24 August 1976, Administrative File: Dead Sea Scrolls, Klau Library.

[351] Klein to Zafren, 24 August 1976, Administrative File: Dead Sea Scrolls, Klau Library.

[352] Letter cited in Shanks, "Silence, Anti-Semitism, and the Scrolls," 56.

[353] Ibid., 55–57. On the complex relationship between scholars of the ancient Near East and Zionism see Sherrard, "American Biblical Archaeologists and Zionism" (2011).

[354] Marcus to Zafren, 11 January 1980, Administrative File: Dead Sea Scrolls, Klau Library. On Skehan's anti-Israel bias, see also Vermes, *Providential Accidents*, 191.

[355] Zafren to Gottschalk, 15 January 1980, Administrative File: Dead Sea Scrolls, Klau Library.

[356] Upon his retirement in 2003, James Sanders provided in his final presidential report a record of the first twenty-five years of the Ancient Biblical Manuscript Center's activities. I am grateful to Professor Sanders for sharing his unpublished report with me.

[357] Sanders to Harman, 27 December 1979, Administrative File: Dead Sea Scrolls, Klau Library.

[358] Biran to Gottschalk, 30 December 1979, Administrative File: Dead Sea Scrolls, Klau Library.

[359] Zafren to Gottschalk, 17 January 1980, Administrative File: Dead Sea Scrolls, Klau Library.

[360] Ibid.

[361] On 17 May 1992, Sanders gave the second annual Lily Rosman lecture, "The Dead Sea Scrolls: New Perspectives for Christians and Jews," at the HUC-JIR Skirball Museum in Los Angeles. From 5–9 November 2001, Sanders was graduate-alumnus-in-residence at HUC-JIR, Cincinnati.

[362] See VanderKam and Flint, *The Meaning of the Dead Sea Scrolls*, 71.

[363] Zafren to Gottschalk, 17 January 1980, Administrative File: Dead Sea Scrolls, Klau Library.

[364] Zafren to Broshi, 12 June 1980, Administrative File: Dead Sea Scrolls, Klau Library.

[365] Gottschalk's handwritten note to Zafren added at the bottom of Zafren to Gottschalk, 15 January 1980, Administrative File: Dead Sea Scrolls, Klau Library.

[366] Ibid.

[367] Qimron completed his doctorate at the Hebrew University on the Hebrew of the Dead Sea Scrolls in 1976. In 1980 Emanuel Tov and Qimron were the first Israelis appointed to the Cave 4 editorial team.

[368] Broshi to Zafren, 29 June 1980, Administrative File: Dead Sea Scrolls, Klau Library.

[369] Zafren to Gottschalk, 10 July 1980, Administrative File: Dead Sea Scrolls, Klau Library.

[370] Gottschalk to Zafren, 19 August 1980, Administrative File: Dead Sea Scrolls, Klau Library.

[371] Hoter, "Biran, Avraham," 710–711.

[372] For an overview of the events surrounding the scrolls during the war see Yadin, *The Temple Scroll* (1985), 44–46. For Biran's description of the events see his comments in "Captured

Museum Yields Scrolls Bits," *The New York Times* (17 June 1967): 19, and James Feron, "Israel Repairing Ravaged Museum," *The New York Times* (9 July 1967): 11.

[373] "New Wind in the Scrollery," *The Jerusalem Post International Edition* (Week ending 26 October 1991): 10–11. Quote on 10.

[374] Zafren to Gottschalk, 8 September 1980, Administrative File: Dead Sea Scrolls, Klau Library.

[375] Sanders to Zafren, 22 August 1980, Administrative File: Dead Sea Scrolls, Klau Library.

[376] Zafren to Sanders, 2 September 1980, Administrative File: Dead Sea Scrolls, Klau Library.

[377] Zafren to Broshi, 4 February 1981, Administrative File: Dead Sea Scrolls, Klau Library.

[378] Broshi to Zafren, 19 July 1981, Administrative File: Dead Sea Scrolls, Klau Library.

[379] Although there is no letter of confirmation of receipt, in Zafren to Broshi, 7 July 1981, the former indicates that he planned to be in Jerusalem at the HUC campus between 11 and 23 August. Administrative File: Dead Sea Scrolls, Klau Library. The follow-up letter, Broshi to Zafren, 19 July 1981, indicates Broshi wanted to hand the material over in person. Administrative File: Dead Sea Scrolls, Klau Library.

[380] Gottschalk to Harman, 20 October 1982, Administrative File: Dead Sea Scrolls, Klau Library.

[381] John Noble Wilford, "Keepers of the Dead Sea Scrolls Accused of Blocking Research," *The New York Times* (26 June 1989): A6.

[382] Shanks, "Jerusalem Rolls out Red Carpet for Biblical Archaeology Congress," 12–18.

[383] For a survey of Shanks's efforts and a discussion of his motivations see Silberman, *The Hidden Scrolls*, 213–245. Shanks describes his role in the Dead Sea Scrolls story in his recent autobiography *Freeing the Dead Sea Scrolls* (2010).

[384] Zafren to Broshi, 28 September 1989, Administrative File: Dead Sea Scrolls, Klau Library.

[385] Ibid.; Zafren to Gottschalk, 19 October 1989, Administrative File: Dead Sea Scrolls, Klau Library. Although in the latter letter Zafren indicates that he did not think Wacholder's evidence for the rumors was reliable, he used the suggestion in his earlier letter to Broshi with the hope of pushing HUC-JIR's case.

In fact, during the previous July one of Wacholder's graduate students wrote to Zafren explaining that while studying at the Hebrew University in 1986–1987 he had been granted access to unpublished material by Emanuel Tov. Other students in the seminar even visited the vaults at the Rockefeller Museum to view the unpublished material "first hand." Along with the letter he included a copy of another student's term paper with citations from unpublished fragments to support his claim. See Abegg to Zafren, 24 July 1989, MS 829/3/Biblical Archeology Society.

On 15 September Wacholder requested that Gottschalk and Zafren make the security copy of the negatives available for consultation (not publication) by faculty and students. He reasoned that the access should be granted because the official editors were already releasing materials for consultation to scholars they favored. He provided citations from several publications which included acknowledgment of such preferred access. Wacholder to Gottschalk, 15 September 1989, MS 829/3/Biblical Archeology Society.

[386] Wacholder (1924–2011) was brought to the Los Angeles school as a librarian to prepare the library for review by the Western College Association. At the time he was working on his doctorate at UCLA. The original appointment had been limited to two and a half months, but he was hired full time by Nelson Glueck beginning in January 1957. See Zeldin to Zafren, November 1956, MS 20/A1a-49/1, Faculty; and Lyons to Glaser, 23 January 1957, MS 20/A1a-49/2, California School. He was appointed assistant professor in Los Angeles in January 1962. Glueck to Wacholder, 14 February 1962, MS 20/A1a-90/11, Faculty. In June 1963 Wacholder was promoted to associate professor of Jewish history and rabbinics (untenured with a renewable three-year contract) and moved to the Cincinnati campus. Glueck to Wacholder, 14 June 1963; and Wacholder to Glueck, 25 June 1963, MS 20/Aia-96/10, Faculty.

[387] Wacholder, "How Long Did Abram Stay in Egypt," 43–56; and, "A Qumran Attack on the Oral Exegesis?," 575–578.

388 The two Qumran-related books are *The Dawn of Qumran* (1983) and *The New Damascus Document* (2007). For his publications through 1993 see Cohen Selavan and Wolfson, "A Bibliography of the Works of Ben Zion Wacholder," 410–412. Between 1994 and 2007 his Qumran-related publications include: "Jubilees as the Super Canon: Torah-Admonition versus Torah-Commandment," 195–211; "Historiography of Qumran," 347–377; "The Preamble to the Damascus Document," 31–47; "Deutero-Ezekiel and Jeremiah (4Q384–4Q391)," 445–461; "The Righteous Teacher in the Pesherite Commentaries," 1–27; and, together with Sholom Wacholder, "Patterns of Biblical Dates and Qumran's Calendar: the Fallacy of Jaubert's Hypothesis," 1–40.

389 *The Temple Scroll* (Heb.; 1977).

390 See his acknowledgments page in *The Dawn of Qumran*, xi.

391 His 1987 syllabus for "Introductory Readings in the Dead Sea Scrolls" concentrated on the sectarian texts including the Community Rule and the Damascus Document, and Qumranic biblical interpretation as found in the Pesharim. Wacholder's 1994 class "Hellenistic Literature 5: Introduction to the Dead Sea Scrolls" offered extensive readings from the newly published computer-reconstructed texts on which he worked with Martin Abegg. The syllabi are on record with the HUC-JIR registrar's office in Cincinnati.

392 Abegg, "The War Scroll From Qumran Caves 1 and 4: A Critical Edition" (1992). Abegg is currently co-director with Peter Flint of the Dead Sea Scrolls Institute at Trinity Western University in Langley, British Columbia, Canada. Among numerous academic articles and digital resources he is responsible for editing, with James E. Bowley and Edward M. Cook, multiple volumes of the *Dead Sea Scrolls Concordance* (Vol. 1 parts 1 and 2; Vol 3 parts 1 and 2; 2003–2010). He has also published popular translations of biblical and non-biblical Dead Sea Scrolls texts. See, Abegg, Flint, and Ulrich, *The Dead Sea Scrolls Bible* (1999); and, Wise, Abegg, and Cook, *The Dead Sea Scrolls: A New Translation* (1996, rev. ed. 2005).

Abegg arrived at HUC-JIR in Cincinnati to work with Wacholder in 1987. His memories of studying and working with him for the next decade are available at: http://www.amotherinisrael. com/ben-zion-wacholder/#Marty. Accessed 15 September 2012. Abegg was the HUC-JIR Graduate School alumnus-in-residence from 5–7 March 2012. On 7 March he devoted his talk to recounting the experience of studying with Wacholder.

393 Bowley, "Traditions of Abraham in Greek Historical Writings" (1992). Bowley has published a number of articles on scrolls-related topics and edited the *Dead Sea Scrolls Concordance* with Martin Abegg (see previous note).

394 Kampen, "The Hasideans and the Origins of Pharasaism" (1985). Kampen has written numerous academic articles and edited several volumes of essays devoted to the scrolls. His most recent book on this topic is *Wisdom Literature* (2011).

395 Wacholder was involved in the supervision of almost all graduate students working on the scrolls (sometimes as second reader). Other students included Oliver S. Howard, "The Greek Text of Job in Light of the Ancient Qumran Targum" (1978); and Wave E. Nunnally, "The Fatherhood of God at Qumran" (1992). Steven L. Jacobs wrote a dissertation for a DHL degree under the supervision of David S. Weisberg, "The Biblical Masorah and the Temple Scroll (11QTorah)" (1990).

396 VanderKam, "Review: *The Dawn of Qumran*," 127.

397 Martinez, "Temple Scroll," 933.

398 For a comparison of Wacholder's views with those of his contemporaries see the summary provided in Jacobs, *The Biblical Masorah and the Temple Scroll*, 92–99.

The Dawn of Qumran unfortunately drew the ire of a rather significant supporter of HUC-JIR, Yigael Yadin. He accused Wacholder of plagiarizing the volume from his Hebrew edition of the Temple Scroll. Wacholder wrote a long defense of his work, and the matter was settled when Jacob Neusner, an independent third party, reviewed Yadin's claim and Wacholder's defense and concluded that the work was not plagiarized. See Yadin to Gottschalk, 10 October 1983; Wacholder to Gottschalk, 9 December 1983; Neusner to Wacholder, 17 December 1983;

Wacholder to Neusner, 27 December 1983; and Neusner to Wacholder, 30 December 1983. Preserved in SC-12641, Wacholder, Ben Zion. Wacholder had heard a rumour of Yadin's accusation even before he received an official letter. He quickly sent a brief note to Gottschalk defending himself by pointing out that the scholars who read his manuscript before publication were also familiar with Yadin's work and had found no problematic content. Wacholder to Gottschalk, 3 October 1983; Sanders to Wacholder, 31 January 1984, MS 829/1/Correspondence – 1980s.

[399] See, for example, "A Qumran Attack," 578.

[400] *The Dawn of Qumran*, xi.

[401] Wacholder, "The Ancient Judaeo-Aramaic Literature (500–164 BCE)," 257–281.

[402] Strugnell, "Moses Pseudepigrapha at Qumran," 248–254.

[403] Shanks, "BARview: Failure to Publish Dead Sea Scrolls," 4, 6, 66–72.

[404] In fact, Wacholder knew Strugnell was working on these fragments several years before the conference. In April 1981 Strugnell sent Wacholder a long letter describing all the copies of the Temple Scroll. He outlined which plates they were on and the differences from Yigael Yadin's manuscript. Additionally he described a seminar that he taught about the scroll and the results which his students were soon to publish. Strugnell to Wacholder, 28 April 1981, MS 829/1/ Correspondence – 1980s. See, also, *The Dawn of Qumran*, xiv. Wacholder's relationship with Strugnell began in the late 1960s. Strugnell was the reviewer for Wacholder's manuscript on Eupolemus which he had submitted to Harvard University Press for publication. Although the volume was approved, financial troubles at the press prevented its publication. The two men carried on friendly correspondence through the 1990s. See Strugnell to Wacholder, 8 July 1968; and, Orlov to Wacholder, 30 July 1968, MS 829/1/Correspondence – 1960s. See too, Strugnell to Wacholder, 25 May 1972, and, Wacholder to Strugnell, 2 November 1972, MS 829/1/ Correspondence – 1970s. Frequently Strugnell replied to Wacholder from Jerusalem and the letters include updates on his scrolls-editing activities. Strugnell also served as external reviewer for *The Dawn of Qumran*. See Strugnell to Meyer, 16 September 1980, MS 829/1/ Correspondence – 1980s.

[405] Shanks, "BARview: Failure to Publish Dead Sea Scrolls," 68, 70.

[406] Silberman, *The Hidden Scrolls*, 215. Interview 27 July 1993. The East European Scholar was Wacholder, see Shanks, "BARview: Failure to Publish Dead Sea Scrolls," 66.

[407] Ben. L. Kaufman, "Secrets of Dead Sea Scrolls Uncovered," *The Cincinnati Enquirer* (4 September 1991): A1, A10. Quote on A10.

[408] Broshi to Zafren, 11 October 1989, Administrative File: Dead Sea Scrolls, Klau Library.

[409] Zafren to Gottschalk, 21 November 1989, Administrative File: Dead Sea Scrolls, Klau Library.

[410] Ibid.

[411] Isaiah A and B, the Manual of Discipline, the War Scroll, the Thanksgiving Hymns, Pesher Habakkuk, and the Genesis Apocryphon.

[412] Harman to Gottschalk, 7 December 1989, Administrative File: Dead Sea Scrolls, Klau Library.

[413] Drori to Harman, 25 December 1989, Administrative File: Dead Sea Scrolls, Klau Library.

[414] Shanks to HUC-JIR Librarian, 27 December 1989, Administrative File: Dead Sea Scrolls, Klau Library. Shanks does not seem to have been aware of HUC-JIR's collection much before this. In an early article written when he began his efforts to have Israel release the scrolls, he mentions only the negatives held by the Ancient Biblical Manuscript Center in Claremont, California. See "Israeli Authorities Now Responsible for Delay in Publication of Dead Sea Scrolls," 71.

[415] Shanks was at the University of Cincinnati to discuss "The Bible and Archaeology in Jerusalem." However, it was his discussion of the Dead Sea Scrolls that caught the audience's attention. See Scott Burgins, "Dead Sea Scrolls being kept secret, lecturer says," *The Cincinnati Enquirer* (31 October 1989): A-9.

[416] Shanks, "Michael L. Klein, 1940–2000," 18.

[417] Ibid.

[418] Klein to Zafren, 5 November 1989, Administrative File: Dead Sea Scrolls, Klau Library.

[419] Zafren to Shanks, 16 January 1990, Administrative File: Dead Sea Scrolls, Klau Library.

[420] Zafren to Gottschalk, 18 January 1990, Administrative File: Dead Sea Scrolls, Klau Library.

[421] Zafren to Gottschalk, 8 January 1990, Administrative File: Dead Sea Scrolls, Klau Library.

[422] Draft included in Zafren to Gottschalk, 3 January 1990, Administrative File: Dead Sea Scrolls, Klau Library.

[423] Gottschalk to Harman, 22 January 1990, Administrative File: Dead Sea Scrolls, Klau Library.

[424] Ibid.

[425] Gottschalk to Harman, 10 May 1990, Administrative File: Dead Sea Scrolls, Klau Library.

[426] Zafren to Gottschalk, 13 August 1991, Administrative File: Dead Sea Scrolls, Klau Library.

[427] Shanks, "New Hope for the Unpublished Dead Sea Scrolls," 55–56, 74. Shanks reported, "But the agreements with the depositories—the Institute of Antiquity and Christianity in Claremont, California, and Hebrew Union College in Cincinnati—forbid their giving access to outside scholars. One prominent HUC scholar has written his administration that this restriction is no longer binding because of the selective access given to outside scholars by members of the publication team" (56). Given the content of the communication from an HUC-JIR faculty member, it is likely that Wacholder shared with Shanks his discussion with Zafren and Gottschalk about rumors of access in Jerusalem and California. See above n.385.

[428] Zafren to Rosenberg, 15 January 1991, Administrative File: Dead Sea Scrolls, Klau Library.

[429] Shanks, "New Hope for the Unpublished Dead Sea Scrolls," 56.

[430] See Abegg, Phelps, and Shanks, "Will Marty Abegg Ever Find A Job?," 37. The conference proceedings are available. See Dimant and Rappaport, *The Dead Sea Scrolls* (1992).

[431] See Shanks, "Leading Dead Sea Scroll Scholar Denounces Delay," 22–25. The concordance was published as: Brown, et al., *A Preliminary Concordance to the Hebrew and Aramaic Fragments from Qumran Caves II–X* (1988). For a description of how the concordance was compiled see Fitzmyer, "More Computer-Generated Scrolls," 62–63; and, Steudel, "Basic Research, Methods and Approaches to the Qumran Scrolls," 572–574.

[432] Shanks, "Antiquities Director Confronts Problems and Controversies," 38.

[433] Strugnell to Wacholder, 12 October 1989, "Release" enclosed, Administrative File: Dead Sea Scrolls, Klau Library; and, MS 829/1/Correspondence – 1980s.

[434] Wacholder, *The Dawn of Qumran*, xi.

[435] "for B.Z. Wacholder" is inserted in Strugnell's hand.

[436] In 1989 Gilner was deputy librarian of Cincinnati's Klau Library. Herbert Zafren was the head librarian in Cincinnati, as well as the national director of HUC-JIR's libraries. In July 1991 Gilner was promoted to head librarian in Cincinnati. Following Zafren's retirement in 1994, Gilner was promoted to national director of libraries.

[437] The cost to the college was $551.72. See Lesley to Gilner, 2 November 1990.

[438] Gilner to Zafren, 24 September 1991, Administrative File: Dead Sea Scrolls, Klau Library.

[439] Gilner to Baumgarten, 1 December 1989, Administrative File: Dead Sea Scrolls, Klau Library.

[440] Baumgarten to Gilner, 6 December 1989, Administrative File: Dead Sea Scrolls, Klau Library.

[441] "Dead Sea Scroll Concordance Now Available for Use by Scholars," 23.

[442] Ibid.

[443] Gilner to Verba, 21 March 1990, Administrative File: Dead Sea Scrolls, Klau Library.

[444] Gilner to Zafren, 24 September 1991, Administrative File: Dead Sea Scrolls, Klau Library.

[445] Silberman, *The Hidden Scrolls*, 221. See *BAR* 16, no. 2, March/April 1990.

[446] "Quotes from the Fleas," 25.

[447] Kaufman has made his own significant contribution to Qumran scholarship. See, for example, "The Temple Scroll and Higher Criticism," 29–43. Additionally, Kaufman was appointed to the editorial team following the Israeli change in policy and the promotion of Tov to editor-in-chief. Although assigned Aramaic texts to edit, the actual texts were never found, having likely been incorporated into other allotments. As a result Kaufman never participated in the editing process. Conversation with Stephen Kaufman, 2 June 2008.

[448] "More Fleas," 6. As far as Wacholder was concerned this information was confidential and should not have been shared. Wacholder to Kaufman, 21 March 1990, MS 829/1/Dead Sea Scrolls.

[449] Durocher to Wacholder, 5 March 1990, with bill dated 9 March 1990 for $56 dollars, to be cancelled in lieu of copy of publication. Administrative File: Dead Sea Scrolls, Klau Library.

[450] Ben Zion Wacholder with Martin Abegg, "The Fragmentary remains of 11QTorah (Temple Scroll)," 1–116. The first line of the references includes an acknowledgement: "I thank the Israel Department of Antiquities and its archivist Sophie Durocher for their prompt and efficient service in furnishing all the plates requested along with the authorization to publish. The department's photographer, Mrs. Tsila Sagiv, deserves special attention for her beautiful facsimiles. Professor J.P.M. van der Ploeg made his plate of 11QT^t available and was instrumental in providing me the authorization to use the copyrighted material from the Dutch Academy of Arts and Sciences." See, also, Van der Ploeg to Wacholder, 29 June 1989, MS 829/3/Biblical Archeology Society.

At age 80 van der Ploeg still had unpublished texts for which he was responsible but, as he noted to Wacholder in slightly garbled English,

> Years ago I had proposed [Adam Simon] van der Woude to publish the Qumran text of the [Royal Netherlands] Academy in one volume. At that time van der Woude did not agree, having too much work of various kinds. Some time ago it was he who proposed me the same thing, but now I had to refuse because of my age (80) and reasons of health.
>
> Yigael Yadin has published the texts of 11QT he could find without asking permission from the Academy. The publication of those texts had been entrusted to me. Now I am not more interested in a publication by me of those texts. For this reason it is equal to me who publishes them, provided the publication is no longer delayed. [van der Ploeg to Wacholder, 3 March 1990, MS 829/3/Biblical Archeology Society]

Van der Woude was less cooperative than van der Ploeg, granting Wacholder only the right to publish photographs of previously published material. See Sussmann to Wacholder, 21 July 1991, MS 829/3/Biblical Archeology Society.

The Royal Netherlands Academy of Arts and Sciences had good reason to enforce their copyright and control access to their materials. According to van der Ploeg, the Academy, "had to pay the sum of ƒ250,000 for publishing the documents of 11Q entrusted to her…The primary intention of the Academy had been to buy the various mss, but when they were nationalised by Jordan, it could only buy the right to publish them. The sum to be paid for that was the same sum the trustees of the then "Palestine Museum" had paid to acquire them….There was some criticism that such a big sum was used for a 'Copyright.'" See van der Ploeg to Wacholder, 15 March 1990. On the Dutch acquisition see van der Ploeg, et al., *Le Targum de Job*, 1–2; and, Shepherd, *Targum and Translation*, 2–3.

[451] Martinez, "Temple Scroll," 928.

[452] Gilner to Baumgarten, 24 May 1990, Administrative File: Dead Sea Scrolls, Klau Library.

[453] Lesley to Gilner, 7 August 1990, Administrative File: Dead Sea Scrolls, Klau Library.

[454] Lesley to Gilner, 2 November 1990, Administrative File: Dead Sea Scrolls, Klau Library.

[455] Abegg, "The War Scroll from Qumran Caves 1 and 4" (1992).

[456] Gilner to Zafren, 24 September 1991, Administrative File: Dead Sea Scrolls, Klau Library.

[457] See *Abstracts AAR/SBL*, 378.

[458] Ben Zion Wacholder and Martin G. Abegg, "After 30 Years of Yearning, We Saw the Texts Suddenly Appear," *Los Angeles Times* (29 September 1991): 3.

[459] Shanks, "When 5,613 Scholars Get Together in One Place," 63.

[460] Email communication with Martin Abegg, 2 May 2008. Milik's publication is, "Milkî-sedeq et Milkî-resha' dans les anciens écrits juifs et chrétiens," 95–144.

[461] Email communication with Martin Abegg, 2 May 2008. See also Abegg, "'Rabbi Computer' Recreates Unpublished Texts," 51–52.

[462] Ben. L. Kaufman, "Secrets of Dead Sea Scrolls Uncovered," *The Cincinnati Enquirer* (4 September 1991): A1, A10. Quote on A10.

[463] Martin Abegg, "'Rabbi Computer' Recreates Unpublished Texts," 52.

[464] "Focus on: The Dead Sea Scrolls – The Textbusters," 54.

[465] Ibid.

[466] Kaufman, "Secrets of Dead Sea Scrolls Uncovered,"A1, A10.

[467] Ibid., A10.

[468] Cook was a staff member of the Comprehensive Aramaic Lexicon Project housed at HUC-JIR, Cincinnati from 1988 until 1997. He participated in editing *The Dead Sea Scrolls Concordance* with Abegg and Bowley. He is the author of *Solving the Mysteries of the Dead Sea Scrolls: New Light on the Bible* (1994). In Chapter 4, "The Rediscovery of the Dead Sea Scrolls," he provides a brief account of the reconstruction of the Cave 4 texts based, at least in part, on conversations with Martin Abegg and his own recollection of events.

[469] Email communication with Martin Abegg, 10 May 2008.

[470] Following the release of the volumes, Kaufman editorialized against their work, offering (1) that he thought the result of their efforts created a problematic text from a scholarly perspective, and (2) that the action was immoral in that it "scooped" scholars who had devoted much of their lives to preparing texts for publication and had been promised the rights to publish first editions. See "The Ethical Issues: A Position Statement," 1, 5.

[471] Kaufman, "Secrets of the Dead Sea Scrolls Uncovered," A1, A10.

[472] Abegg, Phelps, and Shanks, "Will Marty Abegg Ever Find A Job?" 38.

[473] According to Kaufman ("Secrets of the Dead Sea Scrolls Uncovered," A10), Wacholder was so enthusiastic about the project that he acted to financially support the work himself, mortgaging his home for $26,000. From a discussion with Wacholder and his family it appears that this was not the case, and the details were erroneously reported. Interview with Ben Zion Wacholder and his daughter Nina Wacholder, 25 October 2008. Following the interview, email communications from other Wacholder children showed surprise at the report.

[474] Email communication with Martin Abegg, 10 May 2008.

[475] Wernberg-Møller, *The Manual of Discipline: Translated and Annotated with an Introduction* (1957).

[476] For a fuller discussion of the activities surrounding the Eisenman-Brill arrangement, see Silberman, *The Hidden Scrolls*, 231–234.

[477] Wacholder and Abegg, *A Preliminary Edition of the Unpublished Dead Sea Scrolls: Fascicle 1* (1991).

[478] Wacholder and Abegg, "After 30 Years of Yearning," 3.

[479] John Noble Wilford, "Computer Breaks Monopoly on Study of the Dead Sea Scrolls," *The New York Times* (5 September 1991): A1, A7.

[480] Ibid.

[481] Ibid.

[482] Noam M.M. Neusner, "Scholars Feud Over Bootlegged Scroll," *Detroit Jewish News* (13 September 1991): 32–33. Quote on 32.

[483] The italicized portion is added by hand to the typed letter. It is signed by "Professor John Strugnell, Editor-in-Chief, Discoveries in the Judaean Desert," 12 October 1989.

[484] Gilner, "H.U.C. Violated No Trust," 17.

[485] Fitzmyer, "Reply to Gilner," 17–18.

[486] Ibid., 18.

[487] "Bootleg Volume of Long-Secret Dead Sea Scrolls Is Published," *The Los Angeles Times* (5 September 1991): 18.

[488] Ellen K. Coughlin, "Biblical Scholars Construct Bootleg Version of Some Unpublished Dead Sea Scrolls," *The Chronicle of Higher Education* (11 September 1991): A9, A12. Quote on A12.

[489] Wilford, "Computer Breaks Monopoly," A7.

[490] Neusner, "Scholars Feud Over Bootlegged Scroll," 32.

[491] Abraham Rabinovich, "Bootleg Scrolls," *The Jerusalem Post International Edition* (week ending 26 October 1991): 11. Tov had been Abegg's first teacher of the scrolls during a seminar at the Hebrew University in 1986–1987. Of his relationship with Tov following the publication of the unauthorized reconstructions, Abegg wrote:

> You might wonder what my relationship with Emanuel Tov is these days. After all, he is not only the editor in chief of the scroll publication team, but he is the man who introduced me to the scrolls back in 1986. The first time I talked to him after the publication by Ben Zion and me was at the book exhibit of the SBL meeting in Kansas City. He walked up to me and simply quoted part of Isaiah 1:2 in Hebrew: Banim Gidalti v'romumti, which is roughly, "I have raised up children." And he left it at that. He was doing a very Rabbinic thing. He wanted to lead me on to his point, but without being specific. It took me by surprise. I recognized that it was from Isaiah, but that's all. Only in my hotel that night did I realize his point. It is in the completion of the verse, *v'hem pashu vi*, "And they have rebelled against me." I was crestfallen.

> That's where Emanuel and I were in the fall of 1991. That's all changed, however... Emanuel is now my editor in chief and we are very good friends.

Abegg, Phelps, and Shanks, "Will Marty Abegg Ever Find A Job?" 38–39. For Tov's own account of his activities as scholar and editor see "Some Academic Memoirs," 1–28.

[492] Wilford, "Computer Breaks Monopoly," A7.

[493] The *Tribune* contributed to the story in the Cincinnati paper. See also Ron Grossman (*Chicago Tribune*), "Computer Gives Life to Ancient Texts. Dead Sea Scrolls, Unseen, Were Pieced Together From Phrase List," *The Kansas City Star* (5 September 1991): A1.

[494] Email communication with Martin Abegg, 2 May 2008.

[495] Jonathan Schachter, "Scholars Issue Unauthorized Version of 'secret' Scrolls," *The Jerusalem Post* (5 September 1991): 1 and back page. Reprinted in, "A Tale of an Unauthorized Scroll," *Jewish Exponent* (Philadelphia) (13 September 1991): 5, 79. Abegg's suggestion is on 79. Also reprinted in "Exposing the 'secret Scrolls,'" *The Jewish Journal of Greater Los Angeles* (13–19 September 1991): 19–20.

[496] Schachter, "A Tale of an Unauthorized Scroll," 5, 79.

[497] Ibid., 79.

[498] "Breaking the Scroll Cartel," *The New York Times* (7 September 1991): 22.

[499] Yehuda Lev, "Our Town—Dead Sea Scrolls," *The Jewish Journal of Greater Los Angeles* (13–19 September 1991): 4.

[500] W. Gunther Plaut, "Dead Sea Scrolls are Taking too Long to Decifer [sic]," *Canadian Jewish News* (24 October 1991): 11.

[501] Ibid.

[502] "Focus on the Dead Sea Scrolls," *Reform Judaism* 20, no.3 (Spring 1992): 42–56. In addition to recounting Wacholder and Abegg's reconstruction of the Dead Sea Scrolls from the concordance, other articles include: excerpts from Edmund Wilson's works (43); Orlinsky describing his adventure as Mr. Green (46); discussion of Hershel Shanks publishing a facsimile edition of the scrolls (49); and Wacholder explaining the significance of the scrolls for understanding the history of Judaism and Christianity (52). On the reception of the scrolls by the Reform Movement, its rabbis, members, and institutions, see Freund, "The Dead Sea Scrolls, Hebrew Union College, and Reform Judaism 1948–2008," 621–647; Freund, "How the Dead Sea Scrolls Influenced Reform Judaism," 115–143; and, Kalman and Saperstein, "A Spiritually Powerful Sect of Judaism," 144–161.

[503] Neusner, "Scholars Feud Over Bootlegged Scroll," 32. The following month Schiffman outlined the contribution made by the texts reconstructed by Wacholder and Abegg for understanding the Jewish community that produced the scrolls, especially regarding their calendar, ritual practices, and even the Sadducean origins of the sect. Lawrence Schiffman, "Piecing together the saga of the scrolls," *The Jewish World* (11–17 Oct. 1991): 3, 14.

[504] Stegemann, "Computer-Generated Dead Sea Scrolls Texts 98% Accurate," 70. In a long letter to Shanks, Stegemann described comparing the reconstructions to original photographs and transcriptions in his possession. He also asked to be added to the subscription list for acquiring the three planned fascicles. He insisted that they were necessarily going to be important resources even for scholars who had authorized access to the original material. Stegemann to Shanks, 5 October 1991, MS 829/1/Correspondence – 1990s.

[505] "BAS Publishes Fascicle Two of DSS Transcripts," 70.

[506] Phyllis Singer, "Wacholder's Work on Scrolls Sparks Controversy," *The American Israelite* (5 September 1991): A3, A24. The projected budget for preparing the first two fascicles was $212,990.00. See, Budget for the Institute of Mediterranean Studies, undated, MS 829/1/Dead Sea Scrolls.

[507] "Help Needed for Dead Sea Scrolls," 4.

[508] Wacholder and Abegg, *A Preliminary Edition of the Unpublished Dead Sea Scrolls: Fascicle 2*, v, xvi.

[509] Email communication with Martin Abegg, 6 May 2008.

[510] VanderKam and Flint, *The Meaning of the Dead Sea Scrolls*, 70.

[511] Ibid., 391–393. Bechtel left the Center in December 1980 and Sanders became president.

[512] For a thorough discussion of the arrangements and the agreement that forbade anyone from consulting the negatives without official permission see Vermes, *Providential Accidents*, 196–199. On the actions of the Oxford Centre for Hebrew and Jewish Studies see Vermes, *The Story of the Scrolls*, 80–84.

[513] Russel Chandler, "Library Lifts Veil on Dead Sea Scrolls," *The Los Angeles Times* (22 September 1991): A1, A30–A31. The article also discusses Wacholder and Abegg although there is no suggestion of their having motivated the Huntington Library to act.

[514] Wacholder and Abegg, "After 30 Years of Yearning," 3.

[515] Yehuda Lev, "Dead Sea Scroll Furor: HUC Scholar Defends Huntington Library," *The Jewish Journal of Greater Los Angeles* (27 September–3 October 1991): 7.

[516] "Flash! From 200 B.C.," *The New York Times* (24 September 1991): A30.

[517] "Opening the Scrolls," *The Cincinnati Post* (26 September 1991): A14.

[518] "New Wind in the Scrollery," *The Jerusalem Post International Edition* (Week ending 26 October 1991): 10–11.

[519] Ben L. Kaufman, "HUC Won't Release Its Copies of Scrolls," *The Cincinnati Enquirer* (25 September 1991): B4.

[520] Ibid.

[521] Ibid.

[522] Drori and Tov to Director, HUC, Cincinnati, 25 September 1991, Administrative File: Dead Sea Scrolls, Klau Library.

[523] Hugh Orel and Tom Tugend, "Israel Invites Scrolls Scholars to End Dispute," *The American Israelite* (3 October 1991): 1, 24.

[524] Gottschalk to Drori and Tov, 9 October 1991, MS 20/A2b-4/1968-1991, Dead Sea Scrolls.

[525] Undated handwritten notes.

[526] Reiley to Gilner, 30 September 1991, Administrative File: Dead Sea Scrolls, Klau Library.

[527] Zafren to Gottschalk, 3 October 1991, Administrative File: Dead Sea Scrolls, Klau Library.

[528] Wacholder to Gottschalk, 27 September 1991, Administrative File: Dead Sea Scrolls, Klau Library.

[529] Orel and Tugend, "Israel Invites Scrolls Scholars to End Dispute," 24.

[530] Patterson to Moffett, 23 October 1991, Administrative File: Dead Sea Scrolls, Klau Library.

[531] Gottschalk to Patterson, 4 October 1991, MS 20/A2b-4/1968–1991, Dead Sea Scrolls.

[532] Moffett to Patterson, 18 October 1991, Administrative File: Dead Sea Scrolls, Klau Library.

[533] Ibid.

[534] Gottschalk to Moffett, 4 October 1991, Administrative File: Dead Sea Scrolls, Klau Library.

[535] Gottschalk to Rosensaft, 2 October 1991, MS 20/A2b-4/1968–1991, Dead Sea Scrolls.

[536] Moffett to Patterson, 18 October 1991, Administrative File: Dead Sea Scrolls, Klau Library.

[537] Clyde Haberman, "Israel Angry as Library Opens Access to Scrolls," *The New York Times* (23 September 1991): A8.

[538] Patterson to Moffett, 23 October 1991, MS 20/A2b-4/1968–1991, Dead Sea Scrolls.

[539] Wacholder and Abegg, "After 30 Years of Yearning," 3.

[540] Kaufman, "HUC Won't Release Its Copies of Scrolls," B4; and, "College to Keep Scrolls Secret," *Cincinnati Post* (25 September 1991): A5.

[541] Gottschalk to Moffett, 4 October 1991, Administrative File: Dead Sea Scrolls, Klau Library.

[542] Harman to Gottschalk, 10 October 1991, Administrative File: Dead Sea Scrolls, Klau Library.

[543] Ibid.

[544] Harman to Gottschalk, 13 November 1991, Administrative File: Dead Sea Scrolls, Klau Library.

[545] Gottschalk to Harman, 25 November 1991, Administrative File: Dead Sea Scrolls, Klau Library.

[546] Draft letter composed by Zafren for Gottschalk to send to Harman, enclosed with Zafren to Gottschalk, 27 November 1991, Administrative File: Dead Sea Scrolls, Klau Library.

[547] Harman to Glueck, 18 June 1969, MS 20/A1a-151/3, H, General.

[548] Glueck, Diary entry for 14 July 1969, MS 20/A1a-158/11, Diary.

[549] The letter was copied to Glueck as well. Harman to Sang, 14 July 1969, MS 20/K2-2/1969 August.

[550] Gottschalk, Confidential notes, dated 18 October 1991, MS 20/A2b-4/1968–1991, Dead Sea Scrolls.

[551] Biran to Gottschalk, 22 October 1991, MS 20/A2b-4/1968–1991, Dead Sea Scrolls.

[552] Ibid.

[553] MS 20/A2b-4/1968–1991, Dead Sea Scrolls.

554 John Noble Wilford, "Officials in Israel Ease Stand on Access to Ancient Scrolls," *The New York Times* (27 September 1991): A14.

555 Abraham Rabinovich, "Antiquities Authority Reverses Its Policy on Dead Sea Scrolls Photos," *The Jerusalem Post* (28 October 1991): 55.

556 Phyllis Singer, "HUC Opens Access to Photos of Dead Sea Scrolls," *The American Israelite* (31 October 1991): 1, 25.

557 Molly Kavanaugh, "Public, as Well as Scholars, Soon to View Ancient Scrolls," *The Cincinnati Post* (28 October 1991): 1B.

558 Larry Yudelson, "Group Relinquishes Some Control over Access to Dead Sea Scrolls," *JTA Daily News Bulletin* (29 October 1991): 4.

559 Singer, "HUC Opens Access to Photos of Dead Sea Scrolls," 25.

560 Laurie Petrie, "Ancient Secrets Stirring: Hebrew Union College Unlocks Door to Past," *The Cincinnati Post* (4 November 1991): 6a–7a. Quote on 7a.

561 Ibid.

562 John Noble Wilford, "Officials in Israel Ease Stand On Access to Ancient Scrolls," A14.

563 Larry Yudelson, "Photographs of the Dead Sea Scrolls to be Published," *The American Israelite* (5 December 1991): A29.

564 "Computer-Generated Dead Sea Scrolls Texts 98% Accurate," 70.

565 Klein to Zafren, 5 November 1989, Administrative File: Dead Sea Scrolls, Klau Library.

566 See "Focus on: The Dead Sea Scrolls – The Text Busters," *Reform Judaism* 20, no.3 (1992): 54–55.

567 Petrie, "Ancient Secrets Stirring," 7a.

568 Yudelson, "Group Relinquishes Some Control ," 4.

569 Singer, "HUC Opens Access to Photos of Dead Sea Scrolls," 1.

570 Gottschalk to Zafren, 10 January 1992, MS 20/A2b-4/1968–1991, Dead Sea Scrolls.

571 Petrie, "Ancient Secrets Stirring," 6a.

572 Ellen R. Coughlin, "Opening the Dead Sea Scrolls Archive Underlines Problems That Can Complicate Access to Research Material," *The Chronicle of Higher Education* (2 October 1991): A6, A10, A11. Quotes on A10.

573 Gilner to IAA, 8 November 1991, Administrative File: Dead Sea Scrolls, Klau Library.

574 Sample form signed by Abegg, 7 November 1991, appended to Gilner to IAA, 8 November 1991.

575 Sussman to Gilner, 11 November 1991, Administrative File: Dead Sea Scrolls, Klau Library.

576 John Noble Wilford, "Dead Sea Scrolls to be Published: Two Scholars Report Access to 1,787 Documents That had not Been Issued," *The New York Times* (20 November 1991): A7.

577 Ibid. Ultimately, the Huntington Library never actually released their negatives, and they were turned over to the Ancient Biblical Manuscript Center in Claremont after Moffett's death in 1995. The center now keeps one copy in Claremont for research and another in a climatized vault near Tahoe City, California. Email correspondence from James Sanders, 28 August 2008.

578 Larry Yudelson, "Photographs of the Dead Sea Scrolls to be Published," *The American Israelite* (5 December 1991): A7, A29.

579 Peter Steinfels, "Dead Sea Scrolls Free of Last Curb," *The New York Times* (27 November 1991): A22.

580 For an overview of the case see the essays collected in Lim, et al., *On Scrolls, Artefacts and Intellectual Property* (2001). See, more recently, Israeli, *Piracy in Qumran* (2008). All of the legal documents, including draft settlements and correspondence, are preserved in MS 829/3.

[581] For discussion see Carson, "Raiders of the Lost Scrolls," 199–248. A copy of the court's ruling is translated in Lim et al., *On Scrolls, Artefacts and Intellectual Property*, 26–62. The case eventually ended up in the Supreme Court of Israel. The ruling with a summary of the previous court action is likewise found in *On Scrolls, Artefacts and Intellectual Property*, 233–258. For further discussion of the legal issues and the impact of the ruling on scholarship see Cohen, "Copyrighting the Dead Sea Scrolls," 380–423; Israeli, *Piracy in Qumran*, 71–175; MacQueen, "The Scrolls and the Legal Definition of Authorship," 723–748; and, Nimmer, "Copyright in the Dead Sea Scrolls," 1–222. On the growth of "copyright and the Dead Sea Scrolls" as a field of scholarship see Collins, "Examining the Reception and Impact of the Dead Sea Scrolls," 231.

[582] Zachary L. Grayson of Wolf, Block, Schorr and Solis-Cohen to B.Z. Wacholder, 16 February 1993, Ben-Zion Wacholder, Biography—Nearprint File. The letter is also cited in Nimmer, "Copyright in the Dead Sea Scrolls," 69–70.

[583] Carson, "Raiders of the Lost Scrolls," 335.

[584] "Bits & Pieces: Qimron Threatens More Scholars," 72.

[585] Email communication with Martin Abegg, 10 May 2008.

[586] "Dead Sea Scrolls Scholars Seek Protection From Suit," *St. Paul Pioneer Press* (1 August 1993): 16a. See also Nimmer, "Copyright in the Dead Sea Scrolls," 70.

[587] "American Professors Seek to Block Qimron's Control of MMT," 65.

[588] Nimmer, "Copyright in the Dead Sea Scrolls," 69.

[589] "BAR Decides to Appeal Qimron Decision, After All," 66.

[590] Email communication with Martin Abegg, 10 May 2008.

[591] Shanks, "Intellectual Property Law and the Scholar," 70.

[592] Qimron and Strugnell, *Qumran Cave 4, V - Miqsat Maase Ha-Torah* (1994).

[593] Abegg and Wacholder's edition was announced in March 1995, although they had completed their work by June 1994. See the advertisement for the volume in *BAR* 21, no.2 (March/Apr. 1995): 95; and Wacholder and Abegg, *A Preliminary Edition of the Unpublished Dead Sea Scrolls: Fascicle 3*, xxvi. *Fascicle 4* which includes a concordance to the first three volumes appeared in 1996. Despite the assumption of some that open access to the original texts would make these publications obsolete, they continue to be cited in academic articles and monographs.

Bibliography

Abegg, Martin G., Jr., "'Rabbi Computer' Recreates Unpublished Texts." *Biblical Archaeology Review* 33, no. 3 (2007): 51–52.

———. "The War Scroll From Qumran Caves 1 and 4: A Critical Edition". Ph.D diss., Hebrew Union College–Jewish Institute of Religion, 1992.

Abegg, Martin G., Jr., James E. Bowley, and Edward M. Cook. *The Dead Sea Scrolls Concordance, Volume 1*. 2 vols. Leiden: E. J. Brill, 2003.

———. *The Dead Sea Scrolls Concordance, Volume 3*. 2 vols. Leiden: E. J. Brill, 2009.

Abegg, Martin G., Jr., Peter W. Flint, and Eugene C. Ulrich. *The Dead Sea Scrolls Bible: The Oldest Known Bible*. San Francisco: HarperSanFrancisco, 1999.

Abegg, Martin G., Jr., Michael B. Phelps, and Hershel Shanks. "Will Marty Abegg Ever Find A Job? Scroll Scholar Thrives Despite Unauthorized Publication." *Biblical Archaeology Review* 29, no. 1 (2003): 37.

Abstracts AAR/SBL. Atlanta: Scholars Press, 1990.

Albright, William F. "The Dead Sea Scrolls of St. Mark's Monastery." *Bulletin of the American Schools of Oriental Research* 118 (1950): 5–6.

———. "Recent Discoveries in Palestine and the Gospel of John." In *The Background of the New Testament and Its Eschatology*, edited by David Daube and W. D. Davies, 153–171. Cambridge: Cambridge University Press, 1956.

"American Professors Seek to Block Qimron's Control of MMT." *Biblical Archaeology Review* 19, no. 6 (1993): 65.

Bailey, Lloyd R. "The God of the Fathers". Ph.D diss., Hebrew Union College–Jewish Institute of Religion, 1967.

———. "The Pharisees." In *The Historiographic Method of Ellis Rivkin: Structural Analysis*, edited by Allen Podet, 53–58. Potsdam: Abraham Geiger College, 2002.

"BAR Decides to Appeal Qimron Decision, After All." *Biblical Archaeology Review* 19, no. 6 (1993): 66.

Baron, Salo W. "Isaiah Sonne 1887–1960." *Jewish Social Studies* 23, no. 2 (1961): 130–132.

Barth, Lewis. "Rabbinics." In *Hebrew Union College–Jewish Institute of Religion at One Hundred Years*, edited by Samuel Karff, 317–382. Cincinnati: Hebrew Union College Press, 1976.

"BAS Publishes Fascicle Two of DSS Transcripts." *Biblical Archaeology Review* 18, no. 4 (1992): 70.

Benoit, Pierre, Józef T. Milik, and Roland de Vaux. *Les Grottes de Murabba'at. Discoveries in the Judaean Desert II*. 2 vols. Oxford: Clarendon Press, 1961.

Bentwich, Norman. *Judah L. Magnes: A Biography of the First Chancellor and First President of the Hebrew University of Jerusalem*. London: East & West Library, 1955.

Berg, Fanny K., and Isaac Goldberg. "The Dead Sea Scrolls: A Chronological Bibliography". Cincinnati, 1949.

"Bits & Pieces: Qimron Threatens More Scholars." *Biblical Archaeology Review* 19, no. 3 (1993): 72.

Bowley, James E. "Traditions of Abraham in Greek Historical Writings". Ph.D diss., Hebrew Union College–Jewish Institute of Religion, 1992.

Briend, Jacques. "Shahin, Khalil Iskander (Kando)." In *Encyclopedia of the Dead Sea Scrolls*, edited by Lawrence H. Schiffman and James C. VanderKam, 1:869–870. Oxford: Oxford University Press, 2000.

Brodsky, Edith. "The Case of the 7 Dead Sea Scrolls." *American Judaism* 5, no. 2 (1955): 14–16.

Broshi, Magen. "The Negatives Archive of the Shrine of the Book." In *Companion Volume to the Dead Sea Scrolls Microfiche Edition*, edited by Emanuel Tov and Stephen J. Pfann, 135–136. Leiden: E. J. Brill, 1995.

Brown, Jonathan M., and Laurence Kutler. *Nelson Glueck: Biblical Archaeologist and President of the Hebrew Union College–Jewish Institute of Religion*. Cincinnati: Hebrew Union College Press, 2006.

Brown, Judith Anne. *John Marco Allegro: The Maverick of the Dead Sea Scrolls*. Grand Rapids, MI: William B. Eerdmans, 2005.

Brown, Raymond E. "Review: *The First Christian Century in Judaism and Christianity: Certainties and Uncertainties* by Samuel Sandmel." *Journal of the American Academy of Religion* 39, no. 2 (1971): 234–236.

Brown, Raymond E., Joseph A. Fitzmyer, Willard G. Oxtoby, and Javier Teixidor. *A Preliminary Concordance to the Hebrew and Aramaic Fragments from Qumran Caves II–X, Including, Especially, the Unpublished Material from Cave IV: Arranged and Prepared for Printing by Hans-Peter Richter*. Göttingen: Distributed by H. Stegemann on behalf of J. Strugnell, 1988.

Burrows, Millar. *The Dead Sea Scrolls*. New York: Viking Press, 1955.

———. *More Light on the Dead Sea Scrolls: New Scrolls and New Interpretations, with Translations of Important Recent Discoveries*. New York: Viking Press, 1958.

Burrows, Millar, John C. Trever, and William H. Brownlee. *The Dead Sea Scrolls of St. Mark's Monastery*. New Haven, CT: The American Schools of Oriental Research, 1950.

Carson, Cindy Albert. "Raiders of the Lost Scrolls: The Right of Scholarly Access to the Content of Historic Documents." *Michigan Journal of International Law* 16 (1994–1995): 199–248.

Cohen, David L. "Copyrighting the Dead Sea Scrolls: Qimron v. Shanks." *Maine Law Review* 52, no. 2 (2000): 380–423.

Cohen Selavan, Ida, and Laurel Wolfson. "A Bibliography of the Works of Ben Zion Wacholder." In *Pursuing the Text: Studies in Honor of Ben Zion Wacholder on the Occasion of His Seventieth Birthday*, edited by John C. Reeves and John Kampen, 410–412. Journal for the Study of the Old Testament Supplement Series 184. Sheffield: Sheffield Academic Press, 1994.

Cohen, Shaye J. D. "Review: *A Hidden Revolution* by Ellis Rivkin." *Journal of Biblical Literature* 99, no. 4 (1980): 627–629.

Collins, Matthew A. "Examining the Reception and Impact of the Dead Sea Scrolls: Some Possibilities for Future Investigation." *Dead Sea Discoveries* 18, no. 2 (2011): 226–246.

Cook, Edward M. *Solving the Mysteries of the Dead Sea Scrolls: New Light on the Bible*. Grand Rapids, MI: Zondervan, 1994.

Cross, Frank Moore. *The Ancient Library of Qumran*. Garden City, NJ: Doubleday Anchor, 1961.

―――. "On the History of the Photography." In *Companion Volume to the Dead Sea Scrolls Microfiche Edition*, edited by Emanuel Tov and Stephen J. Pfann, 121–122. Leiden: E. J. Brill, 1995.

"Dead Sea Scroll Concordance Now Available for Use by Scholars." *Biblical Archaeology Review* 16, no. 2 (1990): 23.

Dever, William G. "Archaeology and the Six Day War." *Biblical Archaeologist* 30, no. 3 (1967): 73–108.

Dimant, Devorah, ed. *The Dead Sea Scrolls in Scholarly Perspective: A History of Research*. Studies on the Texts of the Desert of Judah 99. Leiden: E. J. Brill, 2012.

Dimant, Devorah, and Uriel Rappaport, eds. *The Dead Sea Scrolls: Forty Years of Research*. Studies on the Texts of the Desert of Judah 10. Leiden: E. J. Brill, 1992.

Dupont-Sommer, André. *The Dead Sea Scrolls: A Preliminary Survey*. Oxford: Blackwell, 1952.

"Failure to Publish Dead Sea Scrolls Is Leitmotif of New York University Scroll Conference." *Biblical Archaeology Review* 11, no. 6 (1985): 4.

Du Toit, Jaqueline S., and Jason Kalman. "Albright's Legacy?: Homogeneity in the Introduction of the Dead Sea Scrolls to the Public." *Journal of Northwest Semitic Languages* 36, no. 2 (2010): 23–48.

―――. *Canada's Big Biblical Bargain: How McGill University Bought the Dead Sea Scrolls*. Montreal and Kingston: McGill-Queen's University Press, 2010.

―――. "Great Scott! The Dead Sea Scrolls, McGill University, and the Canadian Media." *Dead Sea Discoveries* 12, no. 1 (2005): 6–23.

Fields, Weston W. *The Dead Sea Scrolls: A Full History – Volume One, 1947–1960*. Leiden: E. J. Brill, 2009.

Fitzmyer, Joseph A. "More Computer-Generated Scrolls." *Biblical Archaeology Review* 19, no. 1 (1993): 62–63.

―――. "Reply to Gilner." *Biblical Archaeology Review* 19, no. 3 (1993): 17–18.

―――. *Responses to 101 Questions on the Dead Sea Scrolls*. New York: Paulist Press, 1992.

"Focus on: The Dead Sea Scrolls – The Textbusters." *Reform Judaism* 20, no. 3 (Spring 1992): 54.

Frank, Harry Thomas. "How the Dead Sea Scrolls Were Found." *Biblical Archaeology Review* 1, no. 4 (1975): 1, 7–16, 28–30.

Freund, Richard. "The Dead Sea Scrolls, Hebrew Union College, and Reform Judaism 1948–2008." In *The Dead Sea Scrolls and Contemporary Culture: Proceedings of the International Conference Held at the Israel Museum, Jerusalem (July 6–8, 2008)*, edited by Adolfo D. Roitman, Lawrence H. Schiffman, and Shani Tzoref, 621–647. Studies on the Texts of the Desert of Judah 93. Leiden: E. J. Brill, 2011.

―――. "How the Dead Sea Scrolls Influenced Reform Judaism." *American Jewish Archives Journal* 61, no. 1 (2009): 115–143.

Garcia Martinez, Florentino. "Temple Scroll." In *Encyclopedia of the Dead Sea Scrolls*, edited by Lawrence H. Schiffman and James C. VanderKam, 2:933. Oxford: Oxford University Press, 2000.

Gilner, David J. "H.U.C. Violated No Trust Over Scrolls Concordance." *Biblical Archaeology Review* 19, no. 3 (1993): 17.

Glueck, Nelson. *Das Wort hesed im alttestamentlichen Sprachgebrauche als menschliche und göttliche gemeinschaftgemässe Verhaltungsweise*. Giessen: A. Töpelmann, 1927.

―――. *Dateline: Jerusalem*. Cincinnati: Hebrew Union College Press, 1968.

———. "Judah Leon Magnes." *Bulletin of the American Schools of Oriental Research* 114 (1949): 3.

———. *The Lion of Judah (Judah Leon Magnes) 1877–1948*. New York: American Friends of the Hebrew University, 1958.

———. *Rivers in the Desert: A History of the Negev*. New York: Farrar, Straus and Cudahy, 1959.

Golb, Norman. "The Dietary Laws of the Damascus Covenant in Relation to Those of the Karaites." *Journal of Jewish Studies* 8 (1957): 51–69.

———. "Grant No. 2574 (1959), $1,200. Relationship of Qumran Sectarianism to that of Later Jewish Sects." *Yearbook of the American Philosophical Society* (1960): 488–491.

———. "Literary and Doctrinal Aspects of the Damascus Covenant in the Light of Karaite Literature." *Jewish Quarterly Review* 47, no. 4. New Series (1957): 354–374.

———. "The Qumran Covenanters and the Later Jewish Sects." *Journal of Religion* 41, no. 1 (1961): 38–50.

———. "The Second World Congress of Jewish Studies." *Judaism* 7, no. 1 (1958): 30–36.

———. "Who Were the Maġārīya?" *Journal of the American Oriental Society* 80, no. 4 (1960): 347–359.

Goldman, Shalom. "A Long Affair: Edmund Wilson on Judaism, the Hebrew Language, and the American Jewish Community." *Modern Judaism* 21, no. 2 (2001): 108–124.

Goodenough, Erwin R. *Jewish Symbols in the Greco-Roman Period*. 13 vols. New York: Bollingen Foundation, 1953.

Gordis, Robert, ed. *Max Leopold Margolis: Scholar and Teacher*. Philadelphia: Dropsie College, 1952.

Halkin, Abraham S. "Isaiah Sonne (1887–1960), the Historian." *Proceedings of the American Academy for Jewish Research* 29 (1960): 9–15.

"Help Needed for Dead Sea Scrolls." *Biblical Archaeology Review* 17, no. 5 (1991): 4.

Hoenig, Sidney B., ed. *Solomon Zeitlin: Scholar Laureate: An Annotated Bibliography, 1915–1970, with Appreciations of his Writings*. New York: Bitzaron, 1971.

Hoter, Elaine. "Biran, Avraham." In *Encyclopaedia Judaica*. 2nd rev.; 3:710–711. Detroit: Macmillan, 2007.

Howard, Oliver S. "The Greek Text of Job in Light of the Ancient Qumran Targum". Ph.D diss., Hebrew Union College–Jewish Institute of Religion, 1978.

Hyman, Stanley Edgar. "Review: *The Dead Sea Scrolls* by Millar Burrows, *The Scrolls from the Dead Sea* by Edmund Wilson." *Journal of American Folklore* 69, no. 274 (1956): 406–409.

Ibrahim, Fawzi. *West Meets East: The Story of the Rockefeller Museum*. Jerusalem: The Israel Museum, 2006.

"Israeli Authorities Now Responsible for Delay in Publication of Dead Sea Scrolls." *Biblical Archaeology Review* 11, no. 6 (1985): 71.

Israeli, Raphael. *Piracy in Qumran: The Battle Over the Scrolls of the Pre-Christ Era*. New Brunswick, NJ: Transaction Publishers, 2008.

Jacobs, Steven L. "The Biblical Masorah and the Temple Scroll (11QTorah): Some Problems and Solutions". D.H.L. thesis, Hebrew Union College–Jewish Institute of Religion, 1990.

———. *The Biblical Masorah and the Temple Scroll: An Orthographical Inquiry*. Lanham, MD: University Press of America, 2002.

Jassen, Alex P. "American Scholarship on Jewish Law in the Dead Sea Scrolls." In *The Dead Sea Scrolls in Scholarly Perspective*, edited by Devorah Dimant, 101–154. Studies on the Texts of the Desert of Judah 99. Leiden: E. J. Brill, 2012.

Kalman, Jason. "Optimistic, Even with the Negatives: The Hebrew Union College–Jewish Institute of Religion and the Dead Sea Scrolls, 1948–1993." *American Jewish Archives Journal* 61, no. 1 (2009): 1–114.

Kalman, Jason, and Marc Saperstein. "A Spiritually Powerful Sect of Judaism: Two Sermons on the Dead Sea Scrolls by Rabbi Harold I. Saperstein." *American Jewish Archives Journal* 61, no. 1 (2009): 144–161.

Kampen, John. "The Hasideans and the Origins of Pharasaism". Ph.D diss., Hebrew Union College–Jewish Institute of Religion, 1985.

———. *Wisdom Literature*. Eerdmans Commentaries on the Dead Sea Scrolls. Grand Rapids, MI: William B. Eerdmans, 2011.

Kaufman, Stephen A. "The Ethical Issues: A Position Statement." *Newsletter of the Comprehensive Aramaic Lexicon* 9 (1992): 1, 5.

———. "The Temple Scroll and Higher Criticism." *Hebrew Union College Annual* 53 (1982): 29–43.

King, Philip J. *American Archaeology in the Mideast : A History of the American Schools of Oriental Research*. Philadelphia: American Schools of Oriental Research, 1983.

Kiraz, George A., ed. *Anton Kiraz's Archive on the Dead Sea Scrolls*. Piscataway, NJ: Gorgias Press, 2005.

Kotzin, Daniel P. *Judah L. Magnes: An American Jewish Nonconformist*. Syracuse, NY: Syracuse University Press, 2010.

Kraemer, Joel L. "Portrait of the Scholar." In *Pesher Nahum: Texts and Studies in Jewish History and Literature from Antiquity Through the Middle Ages Presented to Norman (Nahum) Golb*, edited by Joel L. Kraemer and Michael G. Wechsler, 1–9. Chicago: The Oriental Institute of the University of Chicago, 2012.

Kraemer, Joel L., and Michael G. Wechsler, eds. *Pesher Nahum: Texts and Studies in Jewish History and Literature from Antiquity Through the Middle Ages Presented to Norman (Nahum) Golb*. Chicago: The Oriental Institute of the University of Chicago, 2012.

Kutscher, Ezekiel Y. "Dating the Language of the Genesis Apocryphon." *Journal of Biblical Literature* 76, no. 4 (1957): 288–292.

Levey, Samson H. "Rule of the Community III." *Revue de Qumran* 5, no. 2 (1965): 239–243.

Levine, Baruch A., and Abraham Malamat, eds. *Eretz-Israel 16: Harry M. Orlinsky Volume*. Jerusalem: Israel Exploration Society and Hebrew Union College–Jewish Institute of Religion, 1982.

Lim, Timothy H., Hector L. MacQueen, and Calum M. Carmichael, eds. *On Scrolls, Artefacts and Intellectual Property*. Journal for the Study of the Pseudepigrapha Supplement Series 38. Sheffield, England: Sheffield Academic Press, 2001.

Long, Burke O. *Planting and Reaping Albright: Politics, Ideology, and Interpreting the Bible*. University Park, PA: Pennsylvania State University Press, 1997.

MacQueen, Hector L. "The Scrolls and the Legal Definition of Authorship." In *The Oxford Handbook of the Dead Sea Scrolls*, edited by Timothy H. Lim and John J. Collins, 723–748. Oxford: Oxford University Press, 2010.

Magnes, Judah L. *A Treatise as to 1) Necessary Existence, 2) the Procedure of Things from the Necessary Existence, 3) the Creation of the World, by Joseph ibn Aknin. Edited and Translated into English*. Berlin: H. Itzkowski, 1904.

Magness, Jodi. *The Archaeology of Qumran and the Dead Sea Scrolls*. Grand Rapids, MI: William B. Eerdmans, 2002.

Malamat, Abraham. *Eretz-Israel 9: William F. Albright Volume*. Jerusalem: Israel Exploration Society, 1969.

Metzger, Bruce M. "The Furniture in the Scriptorium at Qumran." *Revue de Qumran* 1, no. 4 (1959): 509–515.

Meyer, Michael A. "A Centennial History." In *Hebrew Union College–Jewish Institute of Religion At One Hundred Years*, edited by Samuel Karff, 3–283. Cincinnati: Hebrew Union College Press, 1976.

———. "The Refugee Scholars Project of the Hebrew Union College." In *A Bicentennial Festschrift for Jacob Rader Marcus*, edited by Bertram Korn, 359–375. New York: Ktav/ American Jewish Historical Society, 1976.

Milik, Józef T. "Milkî-sedeq Et Milkî-resha' Dans Les Anciens Écrits Juifs Et Chrétiens." *Journal of Jewish Studies* 23 (1972): 95–144.

Miller, Philip E. "A Selective Bibliography of the Writings of Harry M. Orlinsky." In *Eretz-Israel 16: Harry M. Orlinsky Volume*, edited by Baruch A. Levine and Abraham Malamat, xii–xxviii. Jerusalem: Israel Exploration Society and Hebrew Union College–Jewish Institute of Religion, 1982.

"More Fleas." *Biblical Archaeology Review* 16, no. 4 (1990): 6.

Nimmer, David. "Copyright in the Dead Sea Scrolls: Authorship and Originality." *Houston Law Review* 38, no. 1 (2001): 1–222.

Nunnally, Wave E. "The Fatherhood of God at Qumran". Ph.D diss., Hebrew Union College–Jewish Institute of Religion, 1992.

Orlinsky, Harry M. "An Analysis of the Relationship Between the Septuagint and Masoretic Text of the Book of Job". Ph.D diss., Dropsie College, 1935.

———. "The Bible Scholar Who Became an Undercover Agent." *Biblical Archaeology Review* 18, no. 4 (1992): 26–29.

———. "Closing Remarks." In *Biblical Archaeology Today 1990*, edited by Avraham Biran and Joseph Aviram, 411–415. Jerusalem: Israel Exploration Society, 1993.

———. "The Dead Sea Scrolls and Mr. Green." In *Essays in Biblical Culture and Bible Translation*, 245–256. New York: Ktav, 1974.

———. "Margolis' Work in the Septuagint." In *Max Leopold Margolis: Scholar and Teacher*, edited by Robert Gordis, 35–44. Philadelphia: Dropsie College, 1952.

———. "Masorah." In *Solomon Zeitlin: Scholar Laureate: An Annotated Bibliography, 1915–1970, with Appreciations of His Writings*, edited by Sidney B. Hoenig, 46–48. New York: Bitzaron, 1971.

———. "The New Scrolls from the Judaean Desert." *Reshith* 1, no. 3 (1950): 3–4, 6–8.

———. "Photography and Paleography in the Textual Criticism of St. Mark's Isaiah Scroll, 43:19." *Bulletin of the American Schools of Oriental Research* 123 (1951): 33–35.

———. "Review: Barthelemy, D., and J. T. Milik, *Discoveries in the Judean Desert; I, Qumran Cave I*." *Jewish Social Studies* 18, no. 3 (1956): 217–220.

———. "Review: *The Text of the Old Testament: An Introduction to Kittel-Kahle's Biblia Hebraica*." *Journal of Biblical Literature* 78, no. 2 (1959): 176–178.

———. "Studies in the St. Mark's Isaiah Scroll." *Journal of Biblical Literature* 69, no. 2 (1950): 149–166.

———. "Studies in the St. Mark's Isaiah Scroll II. Masoretic yiswāhū in 42:11." *Journal of Near Eastern Studies* 11, no. 3 (1952): 153–156.

———. "Studies in the St. Mark's Isaiah Scroll III: Masoretic חמה in Isaiah XLII, 25." *Journal of Jewish Studies* 2 (1951): 151–154.

———. "Studies in the St. Mark's Isaiah Scroll IV (7.1; 14.4; 14.30)." *Jewish Quarterly Review* 43, no. 4. New Series (1953): 329–340.

———. "Studies in the St. Mark's Isaiah Scroll V (15.9)." *Israel Exploration Journal* 4 (1954): 5–8.

———. "Studies in the St. Mark's Isaiah Scroll VI (34.16; 40.12)." *Hebrew Union College Annual* 25 (1954): 85–92.

———. "Studies in the St. Mark's Isaiah Scroll VII (49:17)." *Tarbiz* 24 (1954): 4–8.

Pfeiffer, Robert H. "The Annual Meeting of the Corporation." *Bulletin of the American Schools of Oriental Research* 117 (1950): 6–8.

"Proceedings of the American Oriental Society Meeting at New Haven, Connecticut, 1949." *Journal of the American Oriental Society* 69, no. 3 (1949): 185–196.

"Proceedings of the American Oriental Society, Meeting at New Haven, Connecticut, 1960." *Journal of the American Oriental Society* 80, no. 3 (1960): 284–295.

"Proceedings of the Middle West Branch American Oriental Society April 22–23, 1960." *Journal of the American Oriental Society* 80, no. 3 (1960): 296–297.

"Proceedings, December 28th to 30th, 1948." *Journal of Biblical Literature* 68, no. 1 (1949): i–xli.

"Proceedings, December 28th to 30th, 1949." *Journal of Biblical Literature* 69, no. 1 (1950): i–xli.

"Proceedings, December 29–31, 1958." *Journal of Biblical Literature* 78, no. 1 (1959): i–xxxii.

"Proceedings, December 29–31, 1959." *Journal of Biblical Literature* 79, no. 1 (1960): i–xxiv.

Qimron, Elisha, and John Strugnell. *Qumran Cave 4, V - Miqsat Maase Ha-Torah. Discoveries in the Judaean Desert X.* Oxford: Clarendon Press; Oxford University Press, 1994.

"Quotes from the Fleas." *Biblical Archaeology Review* 16, no. 2 (1990): 25.

Rabin, Chaim, and Yigael Yadin, eds. *Scripta Hierosolymitana Volume IV: Aspects of the Dead Sea Scrolls.* Jerusalem: Magnes Press, Hebrew University, 1965.

Reed, Stephen A., Marilyn J. Lundberg, and Michael B. Phelps. *The Dead Sea Scrolls Catalogue: Documents, Photographs, and Museum Inventory Numbers.* Atlanta: Scholars Press, 1994.

Rivkin, Ellis. "Leon da Modena". Ph.D diss., The Johns Hopkins University, 1946.

———. "Solomon Zeitlin's Contribution to the Historiography of the Inter-Testamental Period (Review-Essay)." *Judaism* 14, no. 3 (1965): 354–365.

Roitman, Adolfo D. "Shrine of the Book." In *Encyclopedia of the Dead Sea Scrolls*, edited by Lawrence H. Schiffman and James C. VanderKam, 2:874–875. Oxford: Oxford University Press, 2000.

Roitman, Adolfo D., Lawrence H. Schiffman, and Shani Tzoref. *The Dead Sea Scrolls and Contemporary Culture: Proceedings of the International Conference Held at the Israel Museum, Jerusalem (July 6–8, 2008).* Studies on the Texts of the Desert of Judah 93. Leiden: E. J. Brill, 2011.

Rollins, Wayne G. "Review: *The Genius of Paul: A Study in History* by Samuel Sandmel." *Journal of the American Academy of Religion* 39, no. 3 (1971): 387–388.

Roth, Cecil. "Critical Notes: A Reply to a Reviewer." *Jewish Quarterly Review* 39, no. 2. New Series (1948): 215–217.

———. *The History of the Jews of Italy.* Philadelphia: Jewish Publication Society of America, 1946.

Rowley, Harold H. *The Zadokite Fragments and the Dead Sea Scrolls.* Oxford: Blackwell, 1952.

Samuel, Athanasius Yeshue. *Treasure of Qumran: My Story of the Dead Sea Scrolls.* Philadelphia: Westminster Press, 1966.

Sanders, James A. *The Dead Sea Psalms Scroll.* Ithaca, NY: Cornell University Press, 1967.

———. "The Judaean Desert Scrolls and the History of the Text of the Hebrew Bible." In *Caves of Enlightenment: Proceedings of the American Schools of Oriental Research Dead Sea Scrolls Jubilee Symposium (1947–1997)*, edited by James H. Charlesworth, 1–17. North Richland Hills, TX: Bibal Press, 1998.

———. "Palestinian Manuscripts 1947–1967." *Journal of Biblical Literature* 86, no. 4 (1967): 431–440.

———. "Palestinian Mss. 1947–1972." *Journal of Jewish Studies* 24, no. 1 (1973): 74–83.

———. *The Psalms Scroll of Qumran Cave 11. Discoveries in the Judaean Desert IV.* Oxford: Clarendon Press, 1965.

———. "The Scrolls and the Canonical Process." In *In The Dead Sea Scrolls After Fifty Years: A Comprehensive Assessment*, edited by Peter W. Flint and James C. VanderKam, 2:1–23. Leiden: E. J. Brill, 1999.

———. "Suffering as Divine Discipline in the Old Testament and Post-Biblical Judaism". Ph.D diss., Hebrew Union College–Jewish Institute of Religion, 1954.

Sandmel, Samuel. "Abraham in Normative and Hellenistic Jewish Traditions". Ph.D diss., Yale, 1949.

———. "Erwin Ramsdell Goodenough: An Appreciation." In *Religions in Antiquity*, edited by Jacob Neusner, 3–17. Studies in the History of Religions 14. Leiden: E. J. Brill, 1968.

———. "Jesus in World History." In *Two Living Traditions: Essays on Religion and the Bible*, 178–194. Detroit: Wayne State University Press, 1972.

———. "The Jewish Scholar and Early Christianity." *Jewish Quarterly Review* 57. New Series (1967): 473–481.

———. *A Jewish Understanding of the New Testament*. Cincinnati: Hebrew Union College Press, 1956.

———. "Judaism, Jesus and Paul: Some Problems of Method in Scholarly Research." In *Vanderbilt Studies in the Humanities*, edited by Richmond C. Beatty, J. Philip Hyatt, and Monroe K. Spears, 1:220–250. Nashville: Vanderbilt University Press, 1951.

———. "Parallelomania." *Journal of Biblical Literature* 81, no. 1 (1962): 1–13.

———. "Review: *Jewish Symbols in the Greco-Roman Period, Volume Four: The Problem of Method; Symbols from Jewish Cult; Jewish Symbols in the Greco-Roman Period, Volumes Five and Six: Fish, Bread, and Wine* by Erwin R. Goodenough." *Journal of Biblical Literature* 77, no. 4 (1958): 380–383.

———. *Two Living Traditions: Essays on Religion and the Bible*. Detroit: Wayne State University Press, 1972.

Sarna, Jonathan D. *JPS: The Americanization of Jewish Culture, 1888–1988*. Philadelphia: Jewish Publication Society, 1989.

Saunders, Ernest W. *Searching the Scriptures: A History of the Society of Biblical Literature, 1880–1980*. Chico, CA: Scholars Press, 1982.

Schiffman, Lawrence H. "Inverting Reality: The Dead Sea Scrolls in the Popular Media." *Dead Sea Discoveries* 12, no. 1 (2005): 24–37.

———. "The New Halakhic Letter (4QMMT) and the Origins of the Dead Sea Sect." *Biblical Archaeologist* 53, no. 2 (1990): 64–73.

———. *Reclaiming the Dead Sea Scrolls: The History of Judaism, the Background of Christianity, the Lost Library of Qumran*. Philadelphia: Jewish Publication Society, 1994.

Seltzer, Robert M., and Jack Bemporad. "Ellis Rivkin on Judaism and the Rise of Christianity." *CCAR Journal* 43, no. 3 (1996): 1–16.

Shanks, Hershel. "Antiquities Director Confronts Problems and Controversies." *Biblical Archaeology Review* 14, no. 4 (1986): 38.

———. "BARview: Failure to Publish Dead Sea Scrolls Is Leitmotif of New York University Scroll Conference." *Biblical Archaeology Review* 11, no. 6 (1985): 4, 6, 66–72.

———. *Freeing the Dead Sea Scrolls and Other Adventures of an Archaeology Outsider.* London: Continuum, 2010.

———. "Intellectual Property Law and the Scholar: Cases I Have Known." In *On Scrolls, Artefacts and Intellectual Property,* edited by Timothy H. Lim, Hector L. MacQueen, and Calum M. Carmichael, 63–72. Journal for the Study of the Pseudepigrapha Supplement Series 38. Sheffield: Sheffield Academic Press, 2001.

———. "Jerusalem Rolls Out Red Carpet for Biblical Archaeology Congress." *Biblical Archaeology Review* 10, no. 4 (1984): 12–18.

———. "Leading Dead Sea Scroll Scholar Denounces Delay." *Biblical Archaeology Review* 16, no. 2 (1992): 22–25.

———. "Michael L. Klein, 1940–2000." *Biblical Archaeology Review* 27, no. 2 (2001): 18.

———. "New Hope for the Unpublished Dead Sea Scrolls." *Biblical Archaeology Review* 15, no. 6 (1989): 55–56, 74.

———. "Silence, Anti-Semitism, and the Scrolls." *Biblical Archaeology Review* 17, no. 3 (1991): 54–60.

———. "When 5,613 Scholars Get Together in One Place: The Annual Meeting, 1990." *Biblical Archaeology Review* 17, no. 2 (1991): 62–66.

Shepherd, David. *Targum and Translation: A Reconsideration of the Qumran Aramaic Version of Job.* Studia Semitica Neerlandica 45. Assen: Royal Van Gorcum, 2004.

Sherrard, Brooke. "American Biblical Archaeologists and Zionism: The Politics of Historical Ethnography". Ph.D diss., Florida State University, 2011.

Silberg, Francis Barry. "Aspects of the Life and Work of Ellis Rivkin: An Intellectual Biography with Annotated Bibliography". Ph.D diss., University of Wisconsin-Milwaukee, 2004.

Silberman, Neil Asher. *The Hidden Scrolls: Christianity, Judaism, and the War for the Dead Sea Scrolls.* New York: G.P. Putnam's Sons, 1994.

———. "Sukenik, Eleazar L." In *Encyclopedia of the Dead Sea Scrolls,* edited by Lawrence H. Schiffman and James C. VanderKam, 2:902–903. Oxford: Oxford University Press, 2000.

Sonne, Isaiah. "Final Verdict on the Scrolls?" *Journal of Biblical Literature* 70, no. 1 (1951): 37–44.

———. "A Hymn Against Heretics in the Newly Discovered Scrolls and Its Gnostic Background." *Hebrew Union College Annual* 23 (1951): 275–313.

———. "The Newly Discovered Bar Kokeba Letters." *Proceedings of the American Academy for Jewish Research* 23 (1954): 75–108.

———. "Remarks on 'Manual of Discipline', Col. VI, 6–7." *Vetus Testamentum* 7, no. 4 (1957): 405–408.

———. "Review: *The History of the Jews of Italy* by Cecil Roth." *Jewish Quarterly Review* 38, no. 4. New Series (1948): 469–472.

Sperling, S. David. *Students of the Covenant: A History of Jewish Biblical Scholarship in North America.* Atlanta: Scholars Press, 1992.

Stegemann, Hartmut. "Computer-Generated Dead Sea Scrolls Texts 98% Accurate." *Biblical Archaeology Review* 18, no. 1 (1992): 70.

Steudel, Annette. "Basic Research, Methods and Approaches to the Qumran Scrolls in German-Speaking Lands." In *The Dead Sea Scrolls in Scholarly Perspective,* edited by Devorah Dimant, 565–599. Studies on the Texts of the Desert of Judah 99. Leiden: E. J. Brill, 2012.

Strugnell, John. "Moses Pseudepigrapha at Qumran: 4Q375, 4Q376, and Similar Works." In *Archaeology and History in the Dead Sea Scrolls: The New York University Conference in Memory of Yigael Yadin*, edited by Lawrence H. Schiffman, 248–254. JSOT/ASOR Monograph Series 2. Sheffield: JSOT Press, 1990.

———. "On the History of Photographing the Discoveries in the Judean Desert for the International Team." In *Companion Volume to the Dead Sea Scrolls Microfiche Edition*, edited by Emanuel Tov and Stephen J. Pfann, 123–134. Leiden: E. J. Brill, 1995.

Sukenik, Eleazar Lipa. *The Dead Sea Scrolls of the Hebrew University.* Jerusalem: Magnes Press, Hebrew University, 1955.

"The Thayer Fellowship, 1924–25." *Bulletin of the American Schools of Oriental Research* 13 (1924): 14–15.

Tov, Emanuel. "Some Academic Memoirs." In *Qumran and the Bible: Studying the Jewish and Christian Scriptures in Light of the Dead Sea Scrolls*, edited by Nora David and Armin Lange, 1–28. Contributions to Biblical Exegesis & Theology 57. Leuven: Peeters, 2010.

Trever, John C. *The Dead Sea Scrolls: A Personal Account*. Rev. Grand Rapids, MI: William B. Eerdmans, 1977.

———. "A Paleographic Study of the Jerusalem Scrolls." *Bulletin of the American Schools of Oriental Research* 113 (1949): 6–23.

———. *The Untold Story of Qumran*. Westwood, NJ: F.H. Revell Co., 1965.

VanderKam, James C. "Review: *The Dawn of Qumran* by Ben Zion Wacholder." *Biblical Archaeologist* 48, no. 2 (1985): 126–127.

VanderKam, James C., and Peter W. Flint. *The Meaning of the Dead Sea Scrolls: Their Significance for Understanding the Bible, Judaism, Jesus, and Christianity*. San Francisco: HarperSanFrancisco, 2002.

van der Ploeg, Jan P. M., Adam S. van der Woude, and Bastiaan Jongeling, *Le Targum de Job de la Grotte XI de Qumrân*. Leiden: E.J. Brill, 1971.

Vermes, Geza. *Providential Accidents: An Autobiography*. Lanham: Rowman & Littlefield Publishers, 1998.

———. *The Story of the Scrolls: The Miraculous Discovery and True Significance of the Dead Sea Scrolls*. New York: Penguin, 2010.

Wacholder, Ben Zion. "The Ancient Judaeo-Aramaic Literature (500–164 BCE): A Classification of Pre-Qumranic Texts." In *Archaeology and History in the Dead Sea Scrolls: The New York University Conference in Memory of Yigael Yadin*, edited by Lawrence H. Schiffman, 257–281. JSOT/ASOR Monograph Series 2. Sheffield: JSOT Press, 1990.

———. *The Dawn of Qumran: The Sectarian Torah and the Teacher of Righteousness*. Monographs of the Hebrew Union College 8. Cincinnati: Hebrew Union College Press, 1983.

———. "Deutero-Ezekiel and Jeremiah (4Q384–4Q391): Identifying the Dry Bones of Ezekiel 37 as the Essenes." In *The Dead Sea Scrolls: Fifty Years After Their Discovery 1947–1997*, edited by Lawrence H. Schiffman, Emanuel Tov, and James C. VanderKam, 445–461. Jerusalem: Israel Exploration Society and The Shrine of the Book, Israel Museum, 2000.

———. *Eupolemus: A Study of Judaeo-Greek Literature*. Monographs of the Hebrew Union College 3. Cincinnati: Hebrew Union College Press, 1974.

———. "Historiography of Qumran: The Sons of Zadok and Their Enemies." In *Qumran Between the Old and New Testaments*, edited by Frederick H. Cryer and Thomas L. Thompson, 347–377. Journal for the Study of the Old Testament Supplement 290. Sheffield: Sheffield Academic Press, 1998.

———. "How Long Did Abram Stay in Egypt: A Study in Hellenistic, Qumran, and Rabbinic Chronography." *Hebrew Union College Annual* 35 (1964): 43–56.

———. "Jubilees as the Super Canon: Torah-Admonition Versus Torah-Commandment." In *Legal Texts and Legal Issues*, edited by Moshe Bernstein, Florentino Garcia Martinez, and John Kampen, 195–211. Studies on the Texts of the Desert of Judah 23. Leiden: E. J. Brill, 1997.

———. *The New Damascus Document: The Midrash on the Eschatological Torah of the Dead Sea Scrolls: Reconstruction, Translation and Commentary.* Studies on the Texts of the Desert of Judah 56. Leiden: E. J. Brill, 2007.

———. "The Preamble to the Damascus Document: A Composite Edition of 4Q266–4Q268." *Hebrew Union College Annual* 69 (1998): 31–47.

———. "The Righteous Teacher in the Pesherite Commentaries." *Hebrew Union College Annual* 73 (2002): 1–27.

———. "A Qumran Attack on the Oral Exegesis? The Phrase 'Šr Btlmwd Šqrm in 4Q Pesher Nahum." *Revue de Qumran* 5, no. 4 (1966): 575–578.

Wacholder, Ben Zion, and Martin G. Abegg. *A Preliminary Edition of the Unpublished Dead Sea Scrolls: The Hebrew and Aramaic Texts from Cave Four, Fascicle 1.* Washington, DC: Biblical Archaeology Society, 1991.

———. *A Preliminary Edition of the Unpublished Dead Sea Scrolls: The Hebrew and Aramaic Texts from Cave Four, Fascicle 2.* Washington, DC: Biblical Archaeology Society, 1992.

———. *A Preliminary Edition of the Unpublished Dead Sea Scrolls: The Hebrew and Aramaic Texts from Cave Four, Fascicle 3.* Washington, DC: Biblical Archaeology Society, 1995.

———. "The Fragmentary Remains of 11QTorah (Temple Scroll): 11QTorah[b] and 11QTorah[c] Plus 4QparaTorah Integrated with 11QTorah[a]." *Hebrew Union College Annual* 62 (1991): 1–116.

Wacholder, Ben Zion, Martin G. Abegg, and James E. Bowley. *A Preliminary Edition of the Unpublished Dead Sea Scrolls: The Hebrew and Aramaic Texts from Cave Four, Fascicle 4, Concordance of Fascicles 1–3.* Washington, DC: Biblical Archaeology Society, 1996.

Wacholder, Ben Zion, and Sholom Wacholder. "Patterns of Biblical Dates and Qumran's Calendar: The Fallacy of Jaubert's Hypothesis." *Hebrew Union College Annual* 66 (1995): 1–40.

Walton, Clyde C. "Philip David Sang, 1902–1975." *Journal of the Illinois State Historical Society* 68, no. 5 (1975): 429–434.

Wechsler, Tovia. "The 'Hidden Geniza' Once More or Mr. Trever Versus Mr. Trever." *Jewish Quarterly Review* 41, no. 3. New Series (1951): 247–250.

———. "The Origin of the So Called Dead Sea Scrolls." *Jewish Quarterly Review* 43, no. 2. New Series (1952): 121–139.

———. "Wechsler, Tovia." *Who's Who in Israel, 1966–67.* Tel Aviv: Mamut, 1966.

Weiner, Daniel A. "The Dead Sea Scrolls as Historical Sources: The Zeitlin Critique and His Critics". Rabbinic thesis, Hebrew Union College–Jewish Institute of Religion, 1991.

Weis, Pinkas Rudolf. "The Date of the Habakkuk Scroll." *Jewish Quarterly Review* 41, no. 2. New Series (1950): 125–154.

Wernberg-Møller, Preben. *The Manual of Discipline: Translated and Annotated with an Introduction.* Studies on the Texts of the Desert of Judah 1. Leiden: E. J. Brill, 1957.

Werner, Eric. "Musical Aspects of the Dead Sea Scrolls: For Curt Sachs on His 75th Birthday." *The Musical Quarterly* 43, no. 1 (1957): 21–37.

White Crawford, Sidnie. "The Identification and History of the Qumran Community in American Scholarship." In *The Dead Sea Scrolls in Scholarly Perspective*, edited by Devorah Dimant, 13–29. Studies on the Texts of the Desert of Judah 99. Leiden: E. J. Brill, 2012.

Wilson, Edmund. "A Reporter at Large: The Scrolls from the Dead Sea." *The New Yorker* 31, no. 13 (May 14, 1955): 45–121.

———. *The Scrolls from the Dead Sea*. New York: Oxford University Press, 1955.

Wise, Michael O., Martin G. Abegg, and Edward M. Cook. *The Dead Sea Scrolls: A New Translation*. Revised and updated. New York: HarperSanFrancisco, 2005.

———. *The Dead Sea Scrolls: A New Translation*. San Francisco: HarperSanFrancisco, 1996.

Yadin, Yigael. *The Message of the Scrolls*. London: Weidenfeld and Nicolson, 1957.

———. *The Temple Scroll*. New York: Random House, 1985.

———. *The Temple Scroll*. 3 vols. Hebrew ed. Jerusalem: Israel Exploration Society, Institute of Archaeology of the Hebrew University of Jerusalem, Shrine of the Book, 1977.

Zeitlin, Solomon. "'A Commentary on the Book of Habakkuk' Important Discovery or Hoax?" *Jewish Quarterly Review* 39, no. 3. New Series (1949): 235–247.

———. "The Dead Sea Scrolls: Fantasies and Mistranslations." *Jewish Quarterly Review* 48, no. 1. New Series (1957): 71–85.

———. "The Hebrew Scrolls and the Status of Biblical Scholarship." *Jewish Quarterly Review* 42, no. 2. New Series (1951): 133–192.

———. "The Propaganda of the Hebrew Scrolls and the Falsification of History." *Jewish Quarterly Review* 46, no. 3. New Series (1956): 209–258.

———. "The Word B'Talmud and the Method of Congruity of Words." *Jewish Quarterly Review* 58, no. 1. New Series (1967): 78–80.

Index